Social Entrepreneurship and Citizenship in China

Over the last 30 years, social entrepreneurship has boomed in the People's Republic of China (PRC). Currently, there are hundreds of thousands of legally registered NGOs (nongovernment organizations), and millions more unregistered, working in the areas of the environment, education, women's issues, disability services, community development, LGBTQ rights, and healthcare. The rise of these Chinese NGOs and their implications for civil society merits the focus of significant scholarly attention.

This book draws upon the personal stories of social entrepreneurs in China, as well as their supporters and beneficiaries, in order to examine what the rapid growth of social entrepreneurship reveals about China's complex and dynamic society in the twenty-first century. It discusses the historical, cultural, and political circumstances that allowed and inspired people to become social entrepreneurs and create new forms of democratic engagement. The book examines what social entrepreneurship with Chinese characteristics looks like and explores how it is changing the relationship between Chinese citizens and the state, and goes on to explain the subsequent effects on Chinese society.

Highlighting the importance of citizen activism in the PRC from an interdisciplinary perspective, this book will be of interest to students and scholars of Chinese Studies, Chinese Politics, Civil Society and Sociology.

Carolyn L. Hsu is Associate Professor of Sociology at Colgate University, USA. She is the author of *An Institutional Approach to Chinese NGOs* (2015) and *Creating Market Socialism* (2007).

Routledge Research on the Politics and Sociology of China
Series Editor: Reza Hasmath
University of Oxford, UK

The modern Chinese state has traditionally affected every major aspect of the domestic society. With the growing liberalization of the economy, coupled with an increasing complexity of social issues, there is a belief that the state is retreating from an array of social problems from health to the environment. Yet, as we survey China's social and political landscape today, we not only see that the central state is playing an active role in managing social problems, but also that state actors at the local level are emerging in partnerships with relatively new actors such as social organizations and private enterprises.

The *Routledge Research on the Politics and Sociology of China* series is interested in examining the sociology and politics of this 'new' China. The series will engage with contemporary research that explores the intricacies of institutional interactions, and analysis of micro-level actors, such as migrant workers, ethnic minorities and women, who are shaping China's future. The book series seeks to promote a discourse and analysis that views state and society as contested spaces for power, authority, and legitimacy. As a guiding principle, the series is notably interested in books that use China as a laboratory for confirming, modifying or rejecting existing mainstream theories in sociology and politics.

Social Entrepreneurship and Citizenship in China
The Rise of NGOs in the PRC
Carolyn L. Hsu

Social Entrepreneurship and Citizenship in China
The Rise of NGOs in the PRC

Carolyn L. Hsu

LONDON AND NEW YORK

First published 2017
by Routledge
2 Park Square, Milton Park, Abingdon, Oxon OX14 4RN

and by Routledge
711 Third Avenue, New York, NY 10017

Routledge is an imprint of the Taylor & Francis Group, an informa business

© 2017 Carolyn L. Hsu

The right of Carolyn L. Hsu to be identified as author of this work has been asserted by her in accordance with sections 77 and 78 of the Copyright, Designs and Patents Act 1988.

All rights reserved. No part of this book may be reprinted or reproduced or utilized in any form or by any electronic, mechanical, or other means, now known or hereafter invented, including photocopying and recording, or in any information storage or retrieval system, without permission in writing from the publishers.

Trademark notice: Product or corporate names may be trademarks or registered trademarks, and are used only for identification and explanation without intent to infringe.

British Library Cataloguing in Publication Data
A catalogue record for this book is available from the British Library

Library of Congress Cataloging in Publication Data
Names: Hsu, Carolyn L., 1969– author.
Title: Social entrepreneurship and citizenship in China : the rise of NGOs in the PRC / Carolyn L. Hsu.
Description: Abingdon, Oxon ; New York, NY : Routledge, 2017. | Series: Routledge research on the politics and sociology of China | Includes bibliographical references and index.
Identifiers: LCCN 2016037049| ISBN 9781138684911 (hardback) | ISBN 9781315543598 (ebook)
Subjects: LCSH: Social entrepreneurship–China. | Non-governmental organizations–China.|Civilsociety–China.|China–Socialconditions–2000–
Classification: LCC HD60.5.C5 H68 2017 | DDC 361.7/650951–dc23
LC record available at https://lccn.loc.gov/2016037049

ISBN: 978-1-138-68491-1 (hbk)
ISBN: 978-1-315-54359-8 (ebk)

Typeset in Times New Roman
by Wearset Ltd, Boldon, Tyne and Wear

To my father, J. Carl Hsu (1942–2014), who always believed in me.

Contents

List of figures   viii
Acknowledgments   ix

1. The earthquake   1
2. Was there charity in Imperial China?   23
3. The pioneer: from socialism to social entrepreneurship   43
4. The perfect *suzhi* fairy tale   66
5. Getting in bed with the state   96
6. Environmental NGOs: foreign funding and Chinese connections   122
7. Conclusion: after the earthquake   151

Index   161

Figures

1.1	Map of the People's Republic of China	1
2.1	*Guanxi* network in late Imperial China	27
3.1	"Mutual help in plowing has brought in more food," 1953	46
3.2	Expanding *guanxi* network in post-1949 China	50
4.1	"A rock as a desk," 1993	66
4.2	Su Mingjuan: "I want to study, too," 1991	67
4.3	"Lead the people to victory," 1975	72
4.4	"Studying for the mother country," 1986	73
4.5	"After the guard in charge of the grain has gone (victory)," *c.*1945–1947	75
4.6	"Hold high the great red banner of Mao Zedong thought: thoroughly smash the rotting counterrevolutionary revisionist line in literature and the arts," 1967	77
4.7	"Carry out family planning, implement the basic national policy," 1986	80
5.1	Primary school student population, in millions, from 1995–2013	103
5.2	Mei Hu primary school, Hunan Province, 2008	105
5.3	Shaoshan key school, Hunan Province, 2008	106
6.1	Total global GREEN aid 1971–2008, in fixed 2000 US$	130
6.2	Total GREEN aid to the People's Republic of China 1971–2008, in fixed 2000 US$	136
6.3	The influence of Friends of Nature on Chinese ENGOs, *c.*2004	144

Acknowledgments

Without the contributions of many wonderful people, this book would not exist – or at least it would have even more weaknesses, flaws, and errors than it currently contains.

I must begin by thanking the Chinese activists and social entrepreneurs who were in my study. Sociologists spend most of their lives mired in terribly depressing topics. To spend so much time with such generous, enthusiastic, smart people whose work makes the world a better place was a joy and a blessing. I wish that even more of your amazing stories could have made it into the final version of the book. Special thanks goes to those who went above and beyond the role of simple interviewee and helped me with their insights, introductions, corrections, and even friendship: Peter Xu, Ruth Ji, Yang Xing, Yang Peidan, Xu Yongguang, Caroline Watson, Vance Wagner, Lila Buckley, and Jin Jiaman.

Thanks to all the scholars who shaped my understanding and analysis of the rise of NGOs in China, especially Jennifer Hsu, Reza Hasmath, Jessica Teets, Andrew Kipnis, Karla Simon, and Shawn Shieh. I am grateful beyond words for their incisive criticisms, probing questions, and useful advice, not to mention their brilliant and influential scholarship. Susan Brownell has no idea of this, but she is the reason why I began studying this topic. Sometime in the early 2000s, on a panel at one of the annual meetings of the Association of Asian Studies, she said, "Why isn't anyone studying Project Hope? What is going on here?" I was an anonymous young scholar in the audience, and I thought, "She's right!" This sent me down a rabbit hole from which I have not yet escaped.

Funding for this project came from the Spencer Foundation and the Colgate University Research Council. I am grateful to Yuzhou Jiang, my research assistant, for all of the work in the summer of 2009. All my friends know that I can barely write an email without typos, so many thanks to everyone who helped me with the tedious work of making sure this manuscript was readable, clear, consistent, and presentable, especially Mary Charest, Chelly Crouch, and Karen Austin.

To turn closer to home, I am grateful to Lara Scott, not just for the excellent illustrations and map, but also for being my best friend. Thank you for the analytical discussions about everything, and the constant reminder that God is good.

I am thankful to my brilliant and beautiful daughter, Lin, both for helping me format the bibliography and for putting up with my whining about this book. I'm sorry I'm not a better example. To my husband, Christopher Henke, thank you for letting me exploit your sociological, research, and writing expertise at home. You love me far more than I deserve. My father, J. Carl Hsu, always believed that I could become a scholar. I'm sorry you didn't get to see the book, Daddy, but this one is dedicated to you.

1 The earthquake

On the afternoon of May 12, 2008, I was sitting in my apartment in central Beijing when the building began to sway. I was not sure what was happening until the news reports began trickling in over the internet a half hour later – an earthquake had struck Wenchuan, Sichuan Province, just northwest of Chengdu. Chengdu? Chengdu is over 900 miles (1500 kilometers) away from Beijing. How could an earthquake near Chengdu shake buildings in Beijing?

We know the answer to that question now. It was a huge earthquake, 8.0 on the Richter scale – one that caused a devastating amount of damage in a densely

Figure 1.1 Map of the People's Republic of China.
Source: map by Lara Scott.

populated region. The numbers were horrific to the point of mind-numbing: almost 70,000 people dead, 375,000 injured, and five million homeless. This enormous tragedy, broadcast all over the globe via television and internet, inspired an enormous response. Governments, NGOs (nongovernment organizations), and businesses from around the world donated over US$450 million dollars of cash donations to China, accompanied by material aid and volunteers.

However, there was another source of funding and volunteers: China itself. Yao Ming, Jackie Chan, Jet Li and other glamorous celebrities organized high-profile fund-raising events, and contributed well-publicized donations.[1] Almost half of the companies listed on the Chinese stock exchange gave money to relief efforts. Yet a huge amount of the funding came not from the wealthy and powerful, but instead from ordinary Chinese citizens. A man named Yang Zhengsheng donated ¥10,000 (US$1500), his entire annual salary. He had been born in a relief tent during the 1976 Tangshan Earthquake, the deadliest quake of the twentieth century. "As a survivor of an earthquake, I must do something," he explained.[2] Many of his fellow citizens agreed, whether they were earthquake survivors or not. Every person I knew in China, young or old, rich or poor, contributed. Schoolchildren donated the change from their pockets. China Unicom and China Mobile offered citizens a way to give money by texting on their cell phones. Netizens organized donation drives on online forums.[3] Within two weeks, domestic donations had topped ¥30 billion (US$4.5 billion), ten times the amount of international funding.

The Chinese government explicitly welcomed foreign aid. International NGOs such as Médecins Sans Frontières, UNICEF, and AmeriCares did send in workers, but the numbers were relatively small. There are several reasons for this: first, relative to other developing nations, fewer international NGOs operated in China prior to the earthquake, both because of its authoritarian government and because its economic boom made it seem less needy. As a result, few international organizations had prior connections to the affected region, and the mountainous geography and earthquake damage made it difficult for newcomers to access disaster areas. Second, many international organizations were busy responding to the devastation of Cyclone Nargis which had struck neighboring Myanmar only ten days before the earthquake.[4]

The lack of international workers was more than offset by a huge surge of Chinese volunteers who headed into the disaster zone. Hao Lin, a psychologist, hopped on a plane to Chengdu and then borrowed a bike to ride into the earthquake zone, seeking victims in need of counseling. To do so, he lied to his wife, who would have been appalled at his headlong plunge into danger. "I haven't done this before," he admitted. "Ordinary people now understand how to take action on their own."[5] Acquaintances from my church in Beijing, who happened to own a truck, collected funds from everyone they knew, filled their vehicle with bottles of water, canned food, and blankets, and drove out to an earthquake-affected village where a friend had a distant relative. A shopkeeper from Guizhou and his friends drove for four hours in four cars filled with medical supplies, cucumbers, and cabbages. He told reporters that he had never volunteered for anything before.[6] The members of an automobile club in the city of Mianyang, Sichuan, drove 60 km into earthquake-damaged areas to transport injured people to Mianyang hospitals – and then turned around to do it again and again.[7] Online forums helped to inspire, mobilize, and organize individual and collective action.[8] On the popular Tianya discussion forum, for example, volunteers in the earthquake area would post lists of the items they needed. Eager readers in cities far away would buy and donate every item on the list and deliver them to individuals willing to travel out to Sichuan.[9]

Although many volunteers were individuals working on their own, some came to Sichuan as members of organizations. Others joined or formed organizations after arrival. These included government-controlled organizations, such as the Chinese Red Cross and the Communist Youth League. But they also included indigenous Chinese NGOs, ranging from celebrity foundations (such as martial arts movie star Jet Li's One Foundation) to small grassroots groups. Members came from organizations based in Beijing and Shanghai, but also from provinces all over China. A survey team from Beijing Normal University counted at least 260 NGOs working in one area.[10] At the same time, the earthquake relief efforts created a critical mass of social entrepreneurs and volunteers in one geographical space, a set of ideal conditions that led to the birth of many new NGOs.

For some Western news outlets and scholars, all this spontaneous action and organization was a sign that China was finally developing a civil society. The *Washington Post* quoted Guo Hong, a sociology professor in Chengdu: "From this disaster, the government has come to realize the power of the grassroots. This power will be helpful in establishing and managing a real civil society."[11] Some dubbed 2008 the "Year of Civil Society" for the People's Republic of China (PRC).[12] The *New York Times* described the volunteering as "defiant" and quoted Bao Shuming of the University of Michigan: "This is a significant turning point for China.... People are becoming more educated and organized, and society is becoming more open."[13] The article also helpfully explained why the prospect of civil society in China is so significant: "Developing a robust civil society is considered a major step if China is to become more democratic."

Was the 2008 Sichuan earthquake a major turning point for Chinese citizens? Was it the moment in which they seized independence and discovered the power of organizing and activism? And if so, do these behaviors really signal the rise of Western-style civil society in China – the kind of civil society that leads to democracy?

In fact, all of these trends – donations, volunteering, non-governmental organizations – predated the earthquake. That is why I was in that swaying Beijing apartment on the afternoon of May 12, 2008: I was in China to study the rise of social entrepreneurship, a project that I had begun in 2004. What I found was that social entrepreneurship was transforming China, but not necessarily in the ways that Westerners would predict. I also discovered that the most important term we need to know to understand China today is not "political oppression" or "civil society," but "quality" (*suzhi*).

Traditional donations, revolutionary social entrepreneurship

What was really new in the Chinese reaction to the earthquake, and what was not? Although the sheer scale of the domestic donations that poured in after the earthquake was impressive and moving, the Chinese citizens who gave money were engaging in behavior that was quite traditional. The vast majority of earthquake donations were channeled through the Chinese government, for example through the state-controlled Chinese Red Cross. This type of giving has a long history in China, stretching back at least 1000 years to the Song Dynasty (960–1279).[14] These charitable practices assume that the government holds the primary responsibility for dealing with social problems. However, in times of disaster, the state can call upon its people to donate resources to help it carry out its duties. In imperial China, usually only state officials and wealthy elites were expected to contribute.[15] However, this changed after the 1949 Communist Revolution with its ideology of egalitarianism and mass action. Now everyone was expected to reach into their pockets when catastrophe struck. By 2008, patriotic citizens were accustomed to donating money when earthquakes, floods, famines, or typhoons harmed any part of China.

The most obvious precursor to the 2008 Sichuan earthquake was the Tangshan earthquake, which struck on July 28, 1976, just a few weeks before the death of Mao Zedong. China has the unfortunate distinction of being the site of many of the deadliest earthquakes in recorded history. Tangshan is usually ranked number two on this list, with a death toll that probably exceeded 650,000 (although the Chinese state reported an official death toll of only 240,000).[16] The Chinese government rejected all offers of international aid and insisted on self-reliance. It deployed the People's Liberation Army and called on citizens for donations. Almost every province and autonomous region in China sent rescue and medical teams to Tangshan. Chinese people all across the country responded with cash contributions. Afterward, these patriotic efforts were celebrated by the state-controlled media, for example with the not-so-subtly titled book: *After the Tangshan Earthquake: How the Chinese People Overcame a Major Natural Disaster*.[17] Hua Guofeng, Mao's hand-picked successor, insisted that "socialist principles had been the key to handling the disaster."[18]

Therefore, when Chinese citizens gave money to earthquake relief efforts in 2008, they were following a familiar tradition – even if some of them were texting contributions over mobile phones rather than dropping cash into collection boxes. The biggest difference between 1976 and 2008 was the scale of the response, both emotionally and financially. In 1976, people read about the earthquake in newspapers or heard about it over state radio. They donated the equivalent of pennies and dimes because that was all they had to spare. In 2008, the nation sat riveted in front of televisions and computer screens for weeks, experiencing by video all the tragedy, heartbreak, and heroism in real time, 24/7. Office workers snuck online at work to stream videos of the latest rescue efforts. At banks, restaurants, and shops, TVs broadcast live coverage on touching human interest stories to customers. Online forums were constantly updated with news and commentary about the earthquake relief efforts. A good friend from Harbin said ruefully to me, "It's getting ridiculous. For two weeks, all I've done is sit in front of a television or a computer and cry." (This statement also accurately described my own life at the time.) When people wanted to channel these powerful emotions into donations, they had a lot more money available to give than they did in 1976. By 2008, China had been experiencing an economic boom for three decades, and it had one of the highest savings rates in the world.[19] The members of China's new middle class could contribute hundreds and even thousands of dollars and the wealthy could donate much, much more.

Yet, by 2008, China was experiencing something that had not existed in 1976: *social entrepreneurship*. Like business entrepreneurs, social entrepreneurs are leaders who seek out opportunities to unleash potential through innovative action.[20] In 1976, Tangshan's "volunteers" were soldiers and workers deployed by the state. But by 2008, there were many Chinese citizens who no longer believed that the state should be responsible for everything. Instead, they designed their own strategies of action. Among these self-directed citizens, some rose to leadership and took charge of organizing volunteers, coordinating donations, setting up online directories for those seeking survivors, and many other tasks. In contrast to the obedient volunteers of the Tangshan era, they were self-motivated, independent, and creative. In Sichuan, social entrepreneurs found ways to release the potential trapped in the national surge of goodwill and sympathy, converting it into action to the benefit of suffering victims. They worked with overwhelmed local governments and helped to develop networks to coordinate the efforts of domestic and foreign NGOs with state organizations, businesses, and informal volunteer groups.[21]

Chinese social entrepreneurship was not born in the rubble of the Sichuan earthquake – it had been on the rise for over a decade. Even so, it was still a relatively new phenomenon. In the early 1990s, there were barely any Chinese nongovernmental organizations working on social problems.[22] After 2000, the number of social entrepreneurs starting NGOs rose precipitously.[23] By 2016 there were over 660,000 organizations registered with the government,[24] and researchers have estimated that there were two to eight million additional unregistered organizations.[25] Although the higher estimates no doubt included organizations such as student clubs or village committees, many NGOs were focused on alleviating social problems. For Chinese social entrepreneurs starting NGOs, the most popular areas have been the environment, education, the disabled, women's issues, community development, and healthcare.[26]

The 2008 Sichuan earthquake had simply revealed to the rest of the world a social movement that had been growing at a rapid pace in China since the turn of the millennium. Instead of passively assuming that social problems were the responsibility of the state, a significant number of Chinese citizens were rising up and taking action. These social entrepreneurs insisted that it was their role to lead rather than to follow. They believed that their country required their ingenuity in order to come up with viable solutions to transform society for the better. Where did they come from? What does the rise of social entrepreneurship mean for China?

The birth of civil society or pawns of the state?

I am not the only China scholar who has noticed the rise of social entrepreneurship in the PRC. Indeed, the growing numbers of Chinese NGOs has drawn the attention of researchers in sociology, political science, and anthropology. For many of them, the central research question has been "Will the rise of Chinese NGOs lead to *civil society* in the People's Republic of China?"[27]

The answer to this question depends on the definition of "civil society." The concept of civil society emerged in seventeenth- and eighteenth-century Europe in the writings of Hobbes, Locke, and Rousseau. However, when scholars first started analyzing the rise of Chinese NGOs, the version of "civil society" they used was based on the theories of Alexis de Tocqueville, which were rooted in his studies comparing the United States' robust democracy with France's descent into Napoleonic dictatorship.[28] Tocqueville assumed that "state" and "society" operate in opposition to each other. States, even in so-called democracies, naturally tend to increase their power at the expense of individuals, evolving toward tyranny. The only way that individual citizens can prevent this from happening is to organize collectively with people outside of their families. "Civil society" is the aggregate of this collective organization. The more robust the civil society is, the more successful the citizenry will be at maintaining a truly participatory democracy and resisting the potential tyranny of the state. For Tocqueville, the sign of a healthy civil society was a critical mass of voluntary associations. These voluntary organizations could be anything from bird-watching clubs to religious organizations to charities, as long as they were independent of the state and included voluntary participation.

How do voluntary organizations contribute to civil society and serve as the foundation for democracy? First, in voluntary associations, people learn the practical skills of democratic citizenship by governing themselves outside the interference of the state. They learn how to be active political participants, rather than passive political subjects. Second, voluntary associations help develop social networks that can be mobilized for citizen political action. While watching birds or volunteering for an NGO, people can meet others who share their complaints about social issues or their desires for social change, and then work together to coordinate a political response. Third, voluntary organizations help citizens protect themselves against potential state tyranny. If the state attempts to take away people's rights or go against their will, these associations make it easier for them to organize action to challenge state behavior and conform it to their desires.[29]

Some scholars argued that if civil society and voluntary associations are a precondition for a robust democracy, then the opposite must also be true. In societies (such as China) where democracy never developed, it must be due to a dearth of voluntary associations and a lack of civil society, leaving people vulnerable to state tyranny.[30] For these civil society proponents, the rise of NGOs is so exciting because the Chinese might finally be developing voluntary associations and learning how to organize independently of the state. At long last, a civil society may be emerging in the PRC, one that can resist the authoritarian Communist Party-controlled government. According to this argument, as Chinese citizens organize in autonomous voluntary organizations, they will surely develop democratic skills and views and begin demanding democratic reforms from the state.

Premodern Chinese conceptions of politics never assumed a division between state and society, so the concept of civil society did not emerge in indigenous Chinese political theories. The very term "civil society" is difficult to translate into Chinese.[31] Even so, after 1989, civil society became a popular topic for Chinese intellectuals as well as for Western researchers of China, for two reasons. First, the collapse of socialist regimes and emergence of democracy in Eastern Europe and the Soviet Union was attributed to civil society. Second, there were signs of voluntary associations and political organization in the 1980s in China. These culminated in the 1989 Tiananmen Protests, which raised hopes among Westerners and Chinese dissidents that the Chinese Communist Party would be overthrown.[32] If civil society could destroy communist regimes and engender democracy in the former Soviet bloc, why couldn't it do the same in China?

Unfortunately, most of the scholars who attempted to apply the civil society framework to China in the 1990s ended up frustrated.[33] The Tiananmen Protests were violently crushed and the movement dissipated. The Chinese state not only punished protestors and dissidents, but also suppressed any signs of civil society, including independent voluntary associations. Upon deeper analysis, researchers discovered that civil society was not the key to democratization in the former Soviet bloc after all.[34] Moreover, it turns out that Western democratic societies may never have followed a Tocquevillian civil society model themselves. Tocqueville may have found American society rife with voluntary associations in the early nineteenth century, but by the late twentieth century researchers seeking civil society in the US found only fragmented individualism.[35]

Despite this, Western scholars and journalists resurrected the hope of finding voluntary organizations/Tocquevillian civil society in China in 2008, inspired in part by the recent eruption of the so-called "color revolutions" in Ukraine, Georgia, and elsewhere. Reporting on the post-earthquake surge of volunteerism, Western journalists declared 2008 the Chinese "Year of Civil Society" and speculated that democracy was finally arising in the PRC.[36] Similarly, the precipitous growth of Chinese NGOs prompted researchers to scramble to see if these organizations fulfilled the prerequisites to be Tocquevillian voluntary associations. Initially, many scholars focused on the following question: Are Chinese social entrepreneurs and NGOs truly autonomous from the state, and therefore the vanguard of an emerging civil society which will lead to democracy?

Unfortunately, after many empirical studies, it appears that the answer was, "no," at least for the first wave of NGOs founded in the market socialist era. Chinese social entrepreneurs and NGOs did not operate independently from the Chinese government/Communist Party and were unlikely to serve as a source of resistance to the authoritarian state. Instead, they often had close ties with Party-state offices and officials. Amazingly, this was even true when the NGOs were technically illegal.[37] There were some organizations that were truly autonomous, but they tended to be smaller, located further from cities, and have a more narrow range of activity than NGOs with state entanglements.[38] In addition, when such organizations increased in size and scope, they often developed state connections.[39] Because so many Chinese NGOs were in bed with the state, so to speak, most of them deliberately avoided any actions that could appear antagonistic or oppositional to the Chinese Communist Party (CCP). In the years following 2008, with the rise of President Xi Jinping and the increase in state authoritarianism, those early hopes of a Tocquevillian civil society/democracy arising in China looked increasingly misguided.

As the connections between Chinese NGOs and state actors became clear, a number of scholars wondered if Chinese NGOs could be a manifestation of state-led corporatism. State-led corporatism is a strategy of government domination. Instead of direct control, the government outsources a portion of its work to an outside organization. The outside organization gains state patronage and the benefits of a monopoly in its sector, but must remain obedient to state directives. (Examples in the United States would be the Amtrak passenger rail system or the US Postal Service.) To the outside eye, these chosen organizations may appear to be independent businesses or charities, but in reality they are the disguised tentacles of an octopus-like state.[40] The Chinese Communist Party has a history of using corporatist surrogates. Mao Zedong's regime (1949–1976) designated a number of sanctioned organizations to handle social welfare issues, including the Chinese Red Cross, Chinese Women's Federation, and Communist Youth League. Scholars give these organizations the deliciously oxymoronic label of "government-organized nongovernmental organization" (GONGO).

However, when researchers examined the rise of Chinese NGOs over the last 20 years in light of the state corporatist model, it did not fit for a number of reasons. First, the corporatist conceptualization of the state is too simplistic. Yes, many Chinese social entrepreneurs have close relationships with the government – except that there is no such thing as "*the* government" in China. The Chinese state is run by a single political party (the Chinese Communist Party), and we often speak of "the party-state" as though it were a monolithic actor, an octopus-like entity with myriad tentacles. But in actual operation, this "party-state" is a conglomeration of many departments, offices, bureaus, and officials, who interact with each other with competing agendas and, in some cases, outright conflicts.[41] A Chinese social entrepreneur never has a relationship with "the government," but instead has a relationship with a specific department or bureaucrat – or with several of them.[42]

Second, in state corporatism, the state designates only one organization and gives it a monopoly over the sector. But in China, multiple, competing NGOs with state ties often worked on the same social issue in the same region.[43] Third, the theory of state corporatism assumes that the state gives directives and the organization obeys. However, researchers found that the relationships between the party-state departments and first wave Chinese NGOs were multidirectional, fluid, and complex.[44] Social entrepreneurs with connections to powerful party-state departments or officials enjoyed leverage over state actors further down the hierarchy.[45] Some social entrepreneurs had the power to design government policies in partnership with state officials.[46] Others influenced state action more indirectly by shaping popular opinion through mass and social media.[47]

In other words, Chinese NGOs were sites where Chinese citizens organized in order to actively shape their society and to influence state behavior. To return to de Tocqueville's theory of civil society, these were voluntary associations where members learn how to be active political participants rather than passive political subjects. Western (and Western-trained) scholars may assume that civil society requires autonomy from the state, and resistance to the state, but this may not be true. Social entrepreneurs, regardless of where they are in the world, respond not to academic theories, but instead to actual, on-the-ground conditions. What were those conditions in China, and what did Chinese social entrepreneurs create in reaction to them?

Social entrepreneurship with Chinese characteristics

Chinese social organizations were not created by scholarly theories, but by ordinary citizens who chose to engage in social entrepreneurship. The term *social entrepreneur* entered widespread usage in the United States in the 1980s. It took the idea of entrepreneurship from the world of business, where it refers to the ability to see opportunities that others fail to notice, combined with the willingness to take risks to use those opportunities. Instead of using entrepreneurial innovation and risk-taking for the purpose of making profit, social entrepreneurs use the same techniques to find novel solutions to solve social problems and meet social needs. Social entrepreneurship is "the pursuit of social objectives with innovative methods, through the creation of products, organizations, and practices that yield and sustain social benefits."[48] Social entrepreneurs engage in an iterative process, continuously learning from their experiences and using those lessons to fuel yet more innovation.

According to this definition, the Chinese citizens who gave donations to state organizations in response to the 2008 Wenchuan Earthquake were not social entrepreneurs, despite their generosity, because the behavior was not innovative. The Mianyang automobile club that organized rides to the hospital for the wounded were applying a novel solution to help people, but their actions did not result in a sustained social benefit so they were not social entrepreneurs either. However, some of the other initiatives that moved after the 2008 earthquake do fall under the definition of social entrepreneurship. Some of the web-based platforms designed to allow individual donors in Shanghai to meet the specific needs of individual victims in Sichuan continued to live on long after the emergency was over because they were useful in other situations. These innovative solutions met an ongoing social need by providing a solution to an ongoing problem: how can contributors reach recipients without incurring too many extra costs?

The focus of this book is social entrepreneurs: men and women who were able to see an innovative way to help society and willing to take the risk to implement their ideas. Their ideas and strategies did not involve working for the party-state, but outside of it, even if they were not as autonomous as Western journalists and researchers wanted them to be. As we shall see, this type of behavior had been effectively suppressed in China for decades. So why did it arise? And why did it take the shape that it took, especially given that scholars of civil society expected it to look differently? And what effect did it have on the relationship between citizens and the government in China?

To understand this phenomenon, we need to understand these people. This is why this book focuses on their personal stories, their inspirations, and their agendas. In order to understand their choices, we need to see the opportunities and constraints they encountered through their eyes. We need to understand the structural and cultural environments that shaped their views, armed them with skills and experiences, and channeled their actions into certain paths.

To collect the stories, my research assistant, Yuzhou Jiang, and I researched 21 Chinese NGOs working in the sectors of environmental protection, educational access, rural development, AIDS awareness, LGBTQ issues, and NGO capacity-building. We gathered our data through interviews, participant observation, and archival research from 2004–2009. The organizations worked in Beijing and the provinces of Yunnan, Hunan, Gansu, Sichuan, Inner Mongolia, and Heilongjiang.

This book draws upon the personal stories of real social entrepreneurs, their supporters, and their beneficiaries in order to answer the following questions.

- As a window into China's complex and dynamic society at the beginning of the twenty-first century, what does the explosion of social entrepreneurship and NGOs reveal? What were the historical, cultural, and political circumstances that allowed and inspired these people to become social entrepreneurs?
- What does social entrepreneurship with Chinese characteristics look like? What kinds of strategies do Chinese social entrepreneurs use to accomplish their missions? How are they changing Chinese society?
- How is social entrepreneurship with Chinese characteristics changing the relationship between Chinese citizens and the state? How is it offering new models of active citizenship?

Democracy, citizenship, and quality (*suzhi*)

When we look at the actual stories of real Chinese social entrepreneurs, we discover that scholars and journalists seeking evidence of civil society and democracy in the rise of Chinese NGOs may be missing the heart of the story because of overly narrow definitions. It turns out that Chinese social entrepreneurs may be developing a model of active and organized citizenship that promotes a certain type of democracy, but not one that they expect.

Elizabeth Perry points out that although Westerners view China as an undemocratic society that is becoming increasingly undemocratic under President Xi Jinping, the Chinese ruling regime actually insists that "democracy" (*minzhu*) is one of its core values. Rather than view this as a sign of hypocrisy, she argues that the Chinese hold a populist conception of democracy, rooted in Rousseau, rather than a "Schumpeterian stress on competitive election."[49] A "democratic" government, according to the populist view, is one that benefits the populace and reflects its will. As President Xi Jinping's father pungently declared in the early days of the Chinese Communist Party, democratic leaders are those who "plant their asses on the side of the masses" (*ba pigu duanduandi zuo zai laobaixing de zheyimian*).[50] Nor was this just the opinion of the political leadership. A 2011 poll revealed that the majority of Chinese citizens, even those with advanced degrees, defined democracy as "a system in which government leaders reflect people's interests, serve the people, and submit to supervision by the people," rather than "a system of periodic elections in which national leaders are chosen through competition between political parties."[51]

In this conception of democracy, a good citizen is not one who organizes to limit the state's power or advocate for multiparty elections, but instead one who informs the state of the needs and concerns of the people and who helps the state address those needs and concerns effectively. In this populist view, Perry explains, "the goal is not to restrain government, but to empower it through the active political anticipation of the citizenry."[52] As we shall see, from 1949 through to the end of the century, most Chinese assumed that the place to practice this kind of good citizenship was within the party-state bureaucracy as a government employee. Chinese social entrepreneurs, by contrast, argued for a role of active citizenship that was positioned outside of the state.

What made this new type of citizenship possible was the rise of a new ideology in China, one that redefined both what a good life looks like for China's populace, and what the role of government was to provide this good life. As this book will describe, under Mao Zedong, in the 1950s to 1970s, the good society was characterized by mass movements and economic equality, and portrayed as populated with robust workers and peasants. The role of the state was to instill revolutionary zeal and administer a paternalistic redistributive economy that took care of its citizens from the cradle to grave. This conception had no room for social entrepreneurs or NGOs.

By contrast, in the 1990s, the image of the good society in the PRC had begun to change to one centered on the idea of *suzhi*, or "quality."[53] The term *suzhi*/quality was used everywhere and by everyone in China. Political officials declared that new policies would raise the *suzhi* of the population.[54] Political dissidents criticized the "low quality" of government officials in order to justify demands for reforms or revolution.[55] Advertisements promised that their products will raise the *suzhi* of their consumers. Factory workers and farmers modestly insisted that I shouldn't bother interviewing them because they have "no *suzhi*." Urban residents complained about the "low quality" of the rural migrants flooding their cities – and constructing their buildings, manning their factories, cleaning their homes, and raising their children. The discourse of *suzhi* was the universal language of snobbery and class stratification in the People's Republic of China. "Low quality" essentially means "low class," and *suzhi* ideology enables "high quality" people to discriminate against and exploit the rural and poorly educated.[56] It was also the language used by Chinese social entrepreneurs to explain their motivations, aspirations, and strategies.

The central ideology underlying *suzhi* is that individuals are shaped by their environment. A person's character is not determined by genetics or a manifestation of their God-given soul, but instead is molded by external circumstances, especially at a young age. High-quality environments create high-quality people. Therefore, if you can improve the quality of external circumstances, you can improve the quality of human beings. At the same time, a critical mass of high-quality people leads to a high-quality community and (on a larger scale) a high-quality nation, creating a virtuous cycle of *suzhi*. The converse is also true: low quality conditions create low-quality people who in turn bring down the quality of their communities and nations in a downward spiral.

Ironically, when pressed by a foreigner to provide a clear definition of *suzhi*, Chinese people struggled to answer. I would ask, "How do you know how much *suzhi* someone has?" The answer was often some variation of "You just know." Others tried to give me examples: high-quality people were courteous, self-controlled, and had straight posture. They wore suits and lived in cities. They could read classical Chinese and understand complex technology. Scientists had *suzhi*, peasants did not. People in cities have more quality than those in the countryside. People from wealthy countries (Japan, the UK, Australia) have more *suzhi* than the Chinese.

In sum, *suzhi* was associated with education, science and technology, economic wealth, urban cosmopolitanism, and high culture.[57] According to this ideology, high-quality people are well-educated, well-off, sophisticated, ethical, and polite. High-quality communities are clean, modern, rich, and orderly. High-quality nations are wealthy, well-run, and powerful. The job of the government, in this view, is to deliver a continually increasing "quality" of life, so that every new generation will have a higher level of *suzhi* than the last. As a result, China will become increasingly strong, rich, and respected among the nations of the world.

Social Entrepreneurship and Citizenship in China tells the story of how the ideology of *suzhi* gave birth to Chinese social entrepreneurship and how Chinese social entrepreneurship began transforming China. For those citizens who were both ambitious and socially concerned, *suzhi* ideology was a call to action. It is a belief system that claims that by improving educational, environmental, and economic conditions, one can transform the lives of people and communities – and make China wealthy and powerful. In addition, this worldview provided some Chinese social entrepreneurs the leverage to change state behavior and encourage collective action. By bringing to public attention areas where the state failed to improve the quality of conditions, they could compel the party-state to increase investment in social welfare – or else risk popular criticism and the loss of political legitimacy. Social entrepreneurs could also use *suzhi* ideology to inspire collective action by providing their fellow citizens with accessible, low-cost ways to improve the quality of the less fortunate.

However, it is important to note that although *suzhi* ideology facilitated the rise of social entrepreneurship in China, it also put limits on who could become a social entrepreneur. It is, after all, an ideology of class stratification that accrues benefits to those at the top at a cost to those at the bottom. As this book reveals, those who started the most successful NGOs in China have been people of high "quality." A disproportionate number of social entrepreneurs have college degrees and live in China's wealthiest cities. They often worked in white collar professions before founding their NGOs. Many are former party-state cadres, while others have relatives or close friends who are government officials. It is important to note that in turn-of-the-century China, these people did not usually have very much personal wealth, so the advantages did not come from money. Instead, a high level of *suzhi* gave these social entrepreneurs a certain level of authority and self-confidence. But even more important, in China high-quality people have high-quality connections. As we shall see, networks (known as *guanxi*) were vitally important for successful social entrepreneurship in China. People with lower levels of *suzhi* did start NGOs in China, but their rates of success and level of impact was significantly lower than those with greater advantages.

Book overview

To understand Chinese social entrepreneurship and the *suzhi* worldview, we need to explore their historical roots. The first half of the twentieth century saw the disintegration of the Confucian imperial system and the rise of Mao Zedong's Communist Party, which took control of the country in 1949. Thirty years later, Mao's radical ideals and institutions were replaced by "market reforms" in a revolution much less violent but just as transformative. *Suzhi* and social entrepreneurship are both the progeny of their imperial and socialist ancestry and products of the revolutions against those systems.

Chapter 2 delves into the historical roots of social entrepreneurship in China. Western missionaries, journalists, and even some scholars have claimed that China has no history of charity, but had to learn it from the West. By exploring the stories of influential Chinese social entrepreneurs in the Song and Ming Dynasties, I reveal China's rich philosophy and history of philanthropy. I also demonstrate that the ways that Chinese people both thought about and acted out charity were very different from what modern Westerners expected charity to look like. This chapter introduces the important concept of *guanxi*, the social connections and networks that were the key to social entrepreneurship both in Imperial China, and in more recent times.

In Chapter 3, I use the life of Peter Xu, the founder of Golden Key, to examine the effect of China's socialist past on the present. Peter was born midway between the fall of the last Emperor in 1911 and the victory of Mao

Zedong's Chinese Communist Party in 1949. Like many others in China's first generation of social entrepreneurs, Peter was raised with Mao Zedong's ideology that social welfare is the responsibility of the state. Yet the post-Mao market reforms taught him that the government could be corrupt and incompetent, while business entrepreneurs could be innovative and admirable. Peter and other early Chinese social entrepreneurs combined these two seemingly contradictory concepts by using entrepreneurial methods and exploiting personal connections (*guanxi*) to help the state to meet its social welfare obligations. As such, they were acting as good citizens of a populist democracy, enabling the government to do its job more effectively.

Chapter 4 illuminates the *suzhi* worldview through the lives of two individuals: a social entrepreneur named Xu Yongguang, and one of his beneficiaries, a young girl named Su Mingjuan. Xu Yongguang founded China's most successful charitable campaign, Project Hope, designed to improve rural education. Project Hope's success came in part from its brilliant marketing campaign, which featured black-and-white images of adorable but grubby children struggling to study in decrepit rural schools. Su Mingjuan was his star poster girl. In the 1990s, Su Mingjuan's pleading eyes over Project Hope's tagline, "I also want to study," moved millions of Chinese citizens to donate money. It also turned her into a minor celebrity.

To unpack the elements that made this campaign so effective, this chapter explores how Project Hope deftly drew upon the visual imagery of socialist propaganda posters to tell a post-socialist story about *suzhi* (quality) and the power of education to transform individuals, communities, and the nation. Project Hope's campaigns not only generated a lot of donations, but also changed state behavior. Before Project Hope, urban citizens knew nothing about rural education, and it was a low priority for the government. But the Project Hope campaign, starring Su Mingjuan's imploring face, created a national moral panic about rural dropouts and dilapidated schools. Seen as a major social problem, the state had to respond with significant policy changes and major investments in rural education.

Chapter 5 begins with a surprising and surprisingly typical story: Gu Wei, a cadre in a Communist Party department, decides that the best way to solve his organization's political problems is to essentially purchase the franchise of a popular NGO. Chapter 5 explores another aspect of Chinese social entrepreneurship: the often deeply entangling *guanxi* relationships between Chinese NGOs and government agencies and officials. The Chinese party-state's official position on social entrepreneurship has been suspicious and even hostile, forcing NGOs to operate in a legal gray area vulnerable to state suppression. Yet individual government bureaucrats and offices often develop very close partnerships with Chinese NGOs.

To understand why, we need to stop seeing the Chinese government as a monolithic entity and instead realize that it is a loose collection of organizations in the form of ministries, bureaus, and departments – each with its own agendas and concerns, but most sharing fears of downsizing. Chinese social entrepreneurs, many of whom were former party-state bureaucrats themselves, understood these vulnerabilities. They could offer state agencies solutions to their problems, solutions that coincidentally furthered the missions of the social entrepreneurs by giving their NGOs access to government resources and protection. This chapter explores state-NGO partnerships through two case studies: the first is declining rural schools and the second is the Communist Youth League. These alliances allowed social entrepreneurs to ramp up the effects of their organization by outsourcing their work to the government. It also put them in a good position to shape state policy. However, in order to maintain state alliances, social entrepreneurs had to abide by certain unspoken rules: avoid politically controversial topics, never criticize the government, and always allow the state to take credit for their work.

Chapter 6 explores the importance of the global nonprofit sector for Chinese social entrepreneurs, both in terms of influence and funding. Nowhere was the impact of foreign money and *guanxi* connections stronger than for environmental NGOs (ENGOs), which made up the largest and most successful arena of social entrepreneurship in early twenty-first century China. This is evident through the life story of Jin Jiaman, a state researcher at the Academy of Environmental Sciences who started her own NGO, the Global Environmental Institute (GEI), in 2004.

Why were Chinese ENGOs so successful? Environmental social entrepreneurs were able to capitalize upon the global environmental movement as a source of both influential ideas and extensive resources. They were able to build international connections with wealthy and powerful partners all over the world. Chinese environmental social entrepreneurs benefited from the fact that the global environmental movement's dominant discourse – the ecological framework – meshed well with *suzhi* ideology, allowing environmental arguments to be easily accepted by both the ruling regime and the Chinese populace. It also helped that the global environmental sector at the turn-of-the-century not only had a lot of money, but was also very interested in investing that money in China's environmental issues.

Yet not all aspiring Chinese social entrepreneurs have access to these opportunities. Those that were able to capitalize on this state of affairs were the ones with *guanxi*, like Jin Jiaman. Indeed, a significant number of China's most influential environmental NGOs can be traced back to a high-status group of friends, classmates, and colleagues in Beijing who enjoyed close ties to important state actors as well as connections to international research institutes and foundations.

Wherever Chinese social entrepreneurs serve, they also spread the ideology of *suzhi*. In doing so, they reinforce the message coming both from the state and from a consumer mass media where the educated, wealthy, and cosmopolitan are glorified. The book's final chapter turns to the stories of the children who grew up in a world defined by *suzhi* ideology, where good middle-class citizenship includes volunteering through NGOs. These include the beneficiaries of the first generation of China's NGOs, peasant children who succeed in gaining *suzhi*'s highest awards: college admission and white-collar job offers in the city. But instead of enjoying their rewards right away, they choose to take a year or two of their lives to volunteer for NGOs, in order to give the gift of *suzhi* to the next generation. We also meet the young people who are not content to work in NGOs but instead decide to become social entrepreneurs themselves. Instead of building partnerships with the government, the new generation has turned to their own arena of expertise: the internet. The Web offers a way to create economies of scale by mobilizing dozens, hundreds, and even thousands of short-term volunteers through social media.

One benefit to this approach is that they could claim that these were not formal organizations at all, but instead just informal social networks, and therefore not under the direct purview of state regulations. Freed from physical reality, these social entrepreneurs did not even have to be in China to serve China, but could be in the US, Europe, or Australia, partnering with former classmates still in China. These social entrepreneurs empowered Chinese citizens by providing a template for publicizing and engaging with social problems in a way that bypassed the state.

Notes

1 See, for example, Associated Press, "Yao to donate money, create foundation to aid earthquake victims." *ESPN*, June 10, 2008. http://espn.go.com/nba/news/story?id=3435735; Xinhua News, "Stars Swing into Action to Help China Quake Victims," *China Daily*, May 20, 2008. http://news.xinhuanet.com/english/2008–05/20/content_8211784.htm.
2 Xinhua News, "Humanitarian emotion glitters in China earthquake relief," May 15, 2008. http://news.xinhuanet.com/english/2008–05/15/content_8177232.htm.
3 Xinhua News, "Virtual community mobilizes, mourns for quake victims," May 17, 2008. http://news.xinhuanet.com/english/200.–05/17/content_8189895.htm; Qu Yan, Philip Wei Wu and Xiaoqing Wang, "Online community response to major disaster: A study of Tianya Forum in the 2008 Sichuan earthquake" (University of Hawaii at Manoa, 2009).
4 Brian Hoyer, "Lessons from the Sichuan earthquake," *Humanitarian Exchange Magazine* (2009): 14–17.
5 Jim Yardley and David Barboza, "Many hands, not held by China, aid in quake," *New York Times*, May 20, 2008. www.nytimes.com/2008/05/20/world/asia/20citizens.html?ref=sichuanprovincechina.
6 Maureen Fan, "Citizens' groups step up in China," *Washington Post*, May 29, 2008. http://articles.washingtonpost.com/2008–05–29/world/36793382_1_supplies-volunteers-yingxiu.
7 Xinhua News, "Humanitarian emotion glitters in China earthquake relief," May 15, 2008. http://news.xinhuanet.com/english/2008–05/15/content_8177232.htm.
8 Guobin Yang, "A civil society emerges from the earthquake rubble," Yale Global Online, June 5, 2008. http://yaleglobal.yale.edu/content/civil-society-emerges-earthquake-rubble.
9 Yan, Wu, and Wang, "Online community response to major disaster."
10 Shawn Shieh and Guosheng Deng, "An emerging civil society: The impact of the 2008 Sichuan earthquake on grassroots associations in China," *The China Journal* no. 65 (2011): 181–194.
11 Fan, "Citizens' Groups Step up in China."
12 Ibid.
13 Yardley and Barboza, "Many hands, not held by China."
14 Smith, *The Art of Doing Good*; J.H. Smith, "Chinese philanthropy as seen through a

case of famine relief in the 1640's," in W. Ilchman, S. Katz, and E. Queen (Eds.), *Philanthropy in the World's Traditions* (Bloomington: Indiana University Press, 1998), 133–168.
15 Vivienne Shue, "State power and the philanthropic impulse in China today," in W. Ilchman, S. Katz, and E. Queen (Eds.), *Philanthropy in the World's Traditions* (Bloomington: Indiana University Press, 1998), 332–354.
16 The 1556 earthquake in Shaanxi, China, ranks as the deadliest in world history, with 830,000 casualties. The 1920 Haiyuan earthquake in Ningxia, China, killed about 200,000. An earthquake in Jili, China in 1290 killed around 100,000. "Earthquakes with 1,000 or more deaths," US Geological Survey. http://earthquake.usgs.gov/earth quakes/world/world_deaths.php.
17 *After the Tangshan Earthquake: How the Chinese People Overcame a Major Natural Disaster* (Beijing: Foreign Language Press, 1976).
18 Jonathan D. Spence, *The Search for Modern China* (New York: W.W. Norton, 1990), 650.
19 In 2007, China's national savings rate was 54 percent of gross national income. For comparison, the savings rate in the United States was under 15 percent. Juann H. Hung and Rong Qian, *Why is China Savings Rate so High? A Comparative Study of Cross-Country Panel Data* (Washington, DC: Congressional Budget Office, 2010).
20 Roger L. Martin and Sally Osberg, "Social entrepreneurship: The case for definition," *Stanford Social Innovation Review* (2007): 28–39.
21 Shieh and Deng, "An emerging civil society," 188; Yang, "A civil society emerges from the earthquake rubble."
22 In 1988, there were 4,446 NGOs registered with the Ministry of Civil Affairs. See Anthony J. Spires, Tao Lin Lin, and Kin-man Chan, "Societal support for China's grassroots NGOs: Evidence from Yunnan, Guangdong, in Beijing," *The China Journal*, no. 71 (2014): 65–90. However, in the political crackdown that followed the 1989 Tiananmen Protests, most organizations were suppressed or failed. Jude Howell, "NGO-state relations in post-Mao China," in D. Hulme and M. Edwards (Eds.), *NGOs, States and Donors* (New York: St. Martin's Press, 1996), 202–215.
23 Shieh and Deng, "An emerging civil society," 185; Spires, Lin and Chan, "Societal support for China's grassroots NGOs," 74.
24 In China, the term "NGO" (*fei zhenfu zuzhi*) does not have a particularly clear or consistent definition, legally or popularly. It is used interchangeably with "social organization" (*shehui zuzhi*), "public benefit organization" (*gongyi zuzhi*), "charitable organization" (*cishan zuzhi*), and "popular organization" (*minjian zuzhi*). In 2016, the Ministry of Civil Affairs reported that there were over 660,000 organizations registered as *shehui zuzhi*, which included foundations (*jijinghui*) and non-profit service providers called "public non-enterprise institutions" (*minban fei qiye danwei*). See Xinhua News, "Over 660,000 social organizations registered in China," *Asia Pacific Daily*, May 1, 2016. http://en.apdnews.com/xin-hua/393249.html.
25 Depending on the method of calculation, these numbers may or may not include mass organizations and GONGOs (government-organized NGOs), student clubs, community-based organizations, virtual organizations that exist only online, or neighborhood and village committees. Nor is it clear, given the lack of data, how many of these organizations have public interest missions. See Shawn Shieh *et al.*, *Chinese NGO Directory (251 NGO Profiles and Special Report): China's Civil Society in the Making* (Beijing: China Development Brief, 2013), xii; Karla W. Simon, *Civil Society in China: The Legal Framework from Ancient Times to the "New Reform Era"* (Oxford University Press, 2013), xxxiv.
26 Shieh *et al.*, *Chinese NGO Directory*, xvi.
27 See, for example, Anthony Jerome Spires, *China's Un-Official Society: The Development of Grassroots NGOs in an Authoritarian State* (Yale University, 2007); Jessica C. Teets, "Let many civil societies bloom: The rise of consultative authoritarianism in

China," *The China Quarterly* 213 (2013): 19–38; Qiusha Ma, *Non-Governmental Organizations in Contemporary China* (New York: Routledge, 2006); Yongnian Zheng and Joseph Fewsmith, *China's Opening Society: The Non-State Sector and Governance*, Vol. 2 (London, New York: Routledge, 2008), 244; Jude Howell, "New directions in civil society: Organizing around marginalized interests," in J. Howell (Ed.), *Governance in China* (Oxford, UK: Rowman and Littlefield, 2004), 143–171.

28 Alexis De Tocqueville, *Democracy in America*, trans. George Lawrence (New York: Perennial Library, 1988); Richard Madsen, "The public sphere, civil society and moral community: A research agenda for contemporary China studies," *Modern China* 19, no. 2 (1993): 183–198; Carolyn L. Hsu, "Beyond civil society: An organizational perspective on state–NGO relations in the People's Republic of China," *Journal of Civil Society* 6, no. 3 (2010): 259–278.

29 Jennifer Alexander, Renee Nank, and Camilla Stivers, "Implications of welfare reform: Do nonprofit survival strategies threaten civil society?" *Nonprofit and Voluntary Sector Quarterly* 28, no. 4 (December 1, 1999): 452–475.

30 Francis Fukuyama, *Trust: The Social Virtues and the Creation of Prosperity* (New York: The Free Press, 1995); Robert Putnam, *Making Democracy Work* (Princeton: Princeton University Press, 1993).

31 Ma, *Non-Governmental Organizations in Contemporary China*, 18–22.

32 Timothy Brook and B. Michael Frolic (Eds.), *Civil Society in China* (Armonk: M.E. Sharpe, 1997); Xiaoguang Kang and Heng Han, "Graduated controls: The state-society relationship in contemporary China," *Modern China* 34, no. 1 (2008): 36–55.

33 See, for example Brook and Frolic, *Civil Society in China*; Heath B. Chamberlain, "On the search for civil society in China," *Modern China* 19, no. 2 (1993): 199–215; Philip C.C. Huang, "'Public sphere'/'civil society' in China?: The third realm between state and society," *Modern China* 19, no. 2 (1993): 216–240; Madsen, *The Public Sphere, Civil Society and Moral Community*, 183–198; Mary Backus Rankin, "Some observations on a Chinese public sphere," *Modern China* 19, no. 2 (1993): 158–182.

34 For example, post-socialist scholars have debunked the myth that civil society destroyed communist regimes in Eastern Europe and the Soviet Union. See David G. Anderson, "Bringing civil society to an uncivilized place: Citizenship regimes in Russia's arctic frontier," in C. Hann and E. Dunn (Eds.), *Civil Society: Challenging Western Models* (New York: Routledge, 1996), 99–120; Michal Buchowski, "The shifting meanings of civil and civic society in Poland," in C. Hann and E. Dunn (Eds.), *Civil Society: Challenging Western Models* (New York: Routledge, 1996), 79–98; Chris Hann, "Civil society at the grassroots: A reactionary view," in P. G. Lewis (Ed.), *Democracy and Civil Society in Eastern Europe* (London: St. Martin's Press, 1993), 152–165; Susanne Spulbeck, "Anti-Semitism; and the fear of the public sphere in the post-totalitarian society: East Germany," in C. Hann and E. Dunn (Eds.), *Civil Society: Challenging Western Models* (New York: Routledge, 1996), 64–78.

35 See Robert Putnam, *Bowling Alone: The Collapse and Revival of American Community* (New York: Simon & Schuster, 2000); Robert Bellah *et al.*, *The Good Society* (New York: Alfred A. Knopf, 1991).

36 Shieh and Deng, "An emerging civil society," 181–194.

37 Many NGOs in China are in violation of state regulations, for example by failing to register with the state. Spires, Lin, and Chan, "Societal support for China's grassroots NGOs," 80.

38 Qiusha Ma, "The governance of NGOs in China since 1978: How much autonomy?" *Nonprofit and Voluntary Sector Quarterly* 31, no. 3 (2002): 305–328; Anthony Saich, "Negotiating the state: The development of social organizations in China," *China Quarterly*, no. 161 (2000): 124–141; Spires, *China's Un-Official Society: The Development of Grassroots NGOs in an Authoritarian State*; Xin Zhang and Richard Baum, "Civil society and the anatomy of a rural NGO," *The China Journal*, no. 52 (2004): 97–107.

39 See the example of 1KG, described in Chapter 7.

40 Jonathan Unger and Anita Chan, "China, corporatism, and the East Asian model," *The Australian Journal of Chinese Affairs*, no. 33 (1995): 29.
41 For a vivid description of the complicated tensions and conflicts between state agencies in just one area of governance (water issues), see Andrew Mertha, *China's Water Warriors: Citizen Action and Policy Change* (Ithaca: Cornell University Press, 2010).
42 Fengshi Wu and Kin-man Chan, "Graduated control and beyond," *China Perspectives* 2012, no. 3 (2012): 9–17; Jude Howell, "Reflections on the Chinese state," *Development & Change* 37, no. 2 (2006): 273–297; Jennifer Y.J. Hsu and Reza Hasmath (Eds.), *The Chinese Corporatist State* (New York: Routledge, 2013).
43 Patricia M. Thornton, "The advance of the party: Transformation or takeover of urban grassroots society?" *The China Quarterly* 213 (2013): 1–18; Timothy Hildebrandt, *Social Organizations and the Authoritarian State in China* (Cambridge; New York: Cambridge University Press, 2013).
44 Shawn Shieh, "Beyond corporatism and civil society: Three modes of state-NGO interaction in China," in J. Schwartz and S. Shieh (Eds.), *State and Society Responses to Social Welfare Needs in China* (New York: Routledge, 2009), 22–42; Anthony Jerome Spires, "Contingent symbiosis and civil society in an authoritarian state: Understanding the survival of China's grassroots NGOs," *American Journal of Sociology* 17, no. 1 (2011): 1–45; Teets, *Let Many Civil Societies Bloom: The Rise of Consultative Authoritarianism in China*, 19–38. Kang and Han, *Graduated Controls: The State-Society Relationship in Contemporary China*, 36–55.
45 Carolyn L. Hsu, "China youth development foundation: GONGO (Government-Organized NGO) or GENGO (Government-Exploiting NGO)?" (University of Alberta, Edmonton, Canada, 2015).
46 Mingyuan Wang and Jin Feng, "Some thoughts on the amendments to the environmental protection law of China," *Asia Pacific Journal of Environmental Law* 17 (2014): 191.
47 Andrew Mertha, *China's Water Warriors: Citizen Action and Policy Change* (paperback ed.) (Ithaca: Cornell University Press, 2010); Joy Yueyue Zhang and Michael Barr, *Green Politics in China: Environmental Governance and State-Society Relations* (London: Pluto Press, 2013), 159.
48 Chao Guo and Wolfgang Bielefeld, *Social Entrepreneurship: An Evidence-Based Approach to Creating Social Value* (San Francisco; CA: Jossey-Bass & Pfeiffer Imprints, Wiley, 2014) 3–7.
49 Elizabeth J. Perry, "The populist dream of Chinese democracy," *Journal of Asian Studies* 74, no. 4 (2015): 903–915, 907.
50 Ibid.
51 Ibid., 908.
52 Ibid., 907.
53 Ann Anagnost, "The corporeal politics of quality (*Suzhi*)," *Public Culture* 16, no. 2 (2004): 189–208; Carolyn L. Hsu, *Creating Market Socialism: How Ordinary People are Shaping Class and Status in China* (Durham, North Carolina: Duke University Press, 2007); Andrew Kipnis, "*Suzhi*: A keyword approach," *The China Quarterly* 186 (2006): 295–313; Andrew Kipnis, "Homo Hierarchicus or Homo Neo-Liberalis? *Suzhi* discourse in the PRC" (Berkeley, CA, 2004).
54 One prime example would be China's infamous Birth Planning Policy (often erroneously called the One-Child Policy), which promotes "quality" over "quantity." See Susan Greenhalgh and Edwin A. Winckler, *Governing China's Population* (Stanford: Stanford University Press, 2005).
55 In the Tiananmen Protests of 1989, this was a common critique of the Communist Party. See, for example, Minzhu Han (Ed.), *Cries for Democracy; Writing and Speeches from the 1989 Chinese Democracy Movement* (Princeton: Princeton University Press, 1990), 38.
56 Hairong Yan, "Neoliberal governmentality and neohumanism: Organizing suzhi/value

flow through labor recruitment networks," *Cultural Anthropology* 18, no. 4 (2003): 493–523.
57 Kipnis, "*Suzhi:* A keyword approach," 295–313.

Bibliography

After the Tangshan Earthquake: How the Chinese People Overcame a Major Natural Disaster. 1976. Beijing: Foreign Language Press.
Alexander, J., Nank, R., and Stivers, C. 1999. Implications of welfare reform: Do non-profit survival strategies threaten civil society? *Nonprofit and Voluntary Sector Quarterly*, 28(4), pp. 452–475.
Anagnost, A. 2004. The corporeal politics of quality (*suzhi*). *Public Culture*, 16(2), pp. 189–208.
Anderson, D.G. 1996. Bringing civil society to an uncivilized place: Citizenship regimes in Russia's arctic frontier. In: C. Hann and E. Dunn (Eds.), *Civil Society: Challenging Western Models.* New York: Routledge, pp. 99–120.
Associated Press. 2008. *Yao to Donate Money, Create Foundation to Aid Earthquake Victims.*
Brook, T. and Frolic, B.M. (Eds.). 1997. *Civil Society in China.* Armonk: M.E. Sharpe.
Buchowski, M. 1996. The shifting meanings of civil and civic society in Poland. In: C. Hann and E. Dunn (Eds.), *Civil Society: Challenging Western Models.* New York: Routledge, pp. 79–98.
Chamberlain, H.B. 1993. On the search for civil society in China. *Modern China*, 19(2), pp. 199–215.
De Tocqueville, A. 1988. *Democracy in America.* New York: Perennial Library.
Fan, M. 2008. Citizens' groups step up in China. *Washington Post*, May 29, 2008.
Fukuyama, F. 1995. *Trust: The Social Virtues and the Creation of Prosperity.* New York: The Free Press.
Greenhalgh, S. and Winckler, E.A. 2005. *Governing China's Population.* Stanford: Stanford University Press.
Guo, C. and Bielefeld, W. 2014. *Social Entrepreneurship: An Evidence-based Approach to Creating Social Value.* San Francisco; CA: Jossey-Bass & Pfeiffer Imprints, Wiley.
Han, M. (Ed.). 1990. *Cries for Democracy; Writing and Speeches from the 1989 Chinese Democracy Movement.* Princeton: Princeton University Press.
Hann, C. 1993. Civil society at the grassroots: A reactionary view. In: P.G. Lewis (Ed.), *Democracy and Civil Society in Eastern Europe.* London: St. Martin's Press, pp. 152–165.
Hildebrandt, T. 2013. *Social Organizations and the Authoritarian State in China.* Cambridge, UK; New York: Cambridge University Press.
Howell, J. 1996. NGO-state relations in post-Mao China. In: D. Hulme and M. Edwards (Eds.), *NGOs, States and Donors.* New York: St. Martin's Press, pp. 202–215.
Howell, J. 2004. New directions in civil society: Organizing around marginalized interests. In: J. Howell (Ed.), *Governance in China.* Oxford, UK: Rowman and Littlefield, pp. 143–171
Howell, J. 2006. Reflections on the Chinese state. *Development & Change*, 37(2), pp. 273–297.
Hoyer, B. 2009. Lessons from the Sichuan earthquake. *Humanitarian Exchange Magazine*, (43), pp. 14–17.

Hsu, C.L. 2007. *Creating Market Socialism: How Ordinary People are Shaping Class and Status in China.* Durham, North Carolina: Duke University Press.

Hsu, C.L. 2010. Beyond civil society: An organizational perspective on state–NGO relations in the People's Republic of China. *Journal of Civil Society*, 6(3), pp. 259–278.

Hsu, C.L. 2015. China Youth Development Foundation: GONGO (Government-Organized NGO) or GENGO (Government-Exploiting NGO)? In: R. Hasmath and J.Y.J. Hsu (Eds.), *NGO Governance and Management in China.* Oxford: Routledge.

Hsu, J.Y.J. and Hasmath, R. (Eds.). 2013. *The Chinese Corporatist State.* New York: Routledge.

Huang, P.C.C. 1993. "Public sphere"/"civil society" in China?: The third realm between state and society. *Modern China*, 19(2), pp. 216–240.

Hung, J.H. and Qian, R. 2010. *Why Is China Savings Rate so High? A Comparative Study of Cross-Country Panel Data.* 2010–07. Washington, DC: Congressional Budget Office.

Kang, X. and Han, H. 2008. Graduated controls: The state-society relationship in contemporary China. *Modern China*, 34(1), pp. 36–55.

Kipnis, A. 2004. Homo Hierarchicus or Homo Neo-Liberalis? *Suzhi* discourse in the PRC. *Society for East Asian Anthropology*, Berkeley, CA, 2004.

Kipnis, A. 2006. *Suzhi*: A keyword approach. *The China Quarterly*, 186, pp. 295–313.

Ma, Q. 2002. The governance of NGOs in China since 1978: How much autonomy? *Nonprofit and Voluntary Sector Quarterly*, 31(3), pp. 305–328.

Ma, Q. 2006. *Non-Governmental Organizations in Contemporary China.* New York: Routledge.

Madsen, R. 1993. The public sphere, civil society and moral community: A research agenda for contemporary China studies. *Modern China*, 19(2), pp. 183–198.

Martin, R.L. and Osberg, S. 2007. Social entrepreneurship: The case for definition. *Stanford Social Innovation Review*, Spring.

Mertha, A. 2010. *China's Water Warriors: Citizen Action and Policy Change* (paperback ed.). Ithaca: Cornell University Press.

Perry, E.J. 2015. The populist dream of Chinese democracy. *Journal of Asian Studies*, 74(4), pp. 903–915.

Putnam, R. 1993. *Making Democracy Work.* Princeton: Princeton University Press.

Putnam, R. 2000. *Bowling Alone: The Collapse and Revival of American Community.* New York: Simon & Schuster.

Rankin, M.B. 1993. Some observations on a Chinese public sphere. *Modern China*, 19(2), pp. 158–182.

Saich, A. 2000. Negotiating the state: The development of social organizations in China. *China Quarterly*, (161), pp. 124–141.

Shieh, S. 2009. Beyond corporatism and civil society: Three modes of state-NGO interaction in China. In: J. Schwartz and S. Shieh (Eds.), *State and Society Responses to Social Welfare Needs in China.* New York: Routledge, pp. 22–42.

Shieh, S. and Deng, G. 2011. An emerging civil society: The impact of the 2008 Sichuan earthquake on grassroots associations in China. *The China Journal*, (65), pp. 181–194.

Shieh, S., Liu, H., Zhang, G., Brown-Inz, A., and Gong, Y. 2013. *Chinese NGO Directory (251 NGO Profiles and Special Report): China's Civil Society in the Making.* Beijing: China Development Brief.

Shue, V. 1998. State power and the philanthropic impulse in China Today. In: W. Ilchman, S. Katz, and E. Queen (Eds.), *Philanthropy in the World's Traditions.* Bloomington: Indiana University Press, pp. 332–354.

Simon, K.W. 2013. *Civil Society in China: The Legal Framework from Ancient Times to the "New Reform Era".* Oxford: Oxford University Press.

Smith, J.H. 1998. Chinese philanthropy as seen through a case of famine relief in the 1640's. In: W. Ilchman, S. Katz, and E. Queen (Eds.), *Philanthropy in the World's Traditions*. Bloomington: Indiana University Press, pp. 133–168.

Smith, J.H. 2009. *The Art of Doing Good: Charity in Late Ming China*. Berkeley: University of California Press.

Spence, J.D. 1990. *The Search for Modern China*. New York: W.W. Norton.

Spires, A.J. 2007. *China's Un-Official Society: The Development of Grassroots NGOs in an Authoritarian State*. PhD Thesis, Yale University.

Spires, A.J. 2011. Contingent symbiosis and civil society in an authoritarian state: Understanding the survival of China's grassroots NGOs. *American Journal of Sociology*, 17(1), pp. 1–45.

Spires, A.J., Lin, T., and Chan, K. 2014. Societal support for China's grassroots NGOs: Evidence from Yunnan, Guangdong, in Beijing. *The China Journal*, (71), pp. 65–90.

Spulbeck, S. 1996. Anti-Semitism; and the fear of the public sphere in the post-totalitarian society: East Germany. In: C. Hann and E. Dunn (Eds.), *Civil Society: Challenging Western Models*. New York: Routledge, pp. 64–78.

Teets, J.C. 2013. Let many civil societies bloom: The rise of consultative authoritarianism in China. *The China Quarterly*, 213, pp. 19–38.

Thornton, P.M. 2013. The advance of the party: Transformation or takeover of urban grassroots society? *The China Quarterly*, 213, pp. 1–18.

Unger, J. and Chan, A. 1995. China, corporatism, and the East Asian model. *The Australian Journal of Chinese Affairs*, (33), pp. 29.

US Geological Survey. 2014. *Earthquakes with 1,000 or More Deaths 1900–2014*. Reston, VA: US Geological Survey.

Wang, M. and Feng, J. 2014. Some thoughts on the amendments to the environmental protection law of China. *Asia Pacific Journal of Environmental Law*, 17, p. 191.

Wu, F. and Kin-Man Chan. 2012. Graduated control and beyond. *China Perspectives*, 2012(3), pp. 9–17.

Xinhua. 2016. Over 660,000 social organizations registered in China. *Asia Pacific Daily*, May 18, 2016.

Xinhua News. 2008a. Humanitarian emotion glitters in China earthquake relief. *Xinhua*, May 15, 2008.

Xinhua News. 2008b. Stars swing into action to help china Quake victims. *China Daily*, May 20, 2008.

Xinhua News, 2008c. Virtual community mobilizes, mourns for quake victims. May 17, 2008.

Yan, H. 2003. Neoliberal governmentality and neohumanism: Organizing suzhi/value flow through labor recruitment networks. *Cultural Anthropology*, 18(4), pp. 493–523.

Yan, Q., Wu, P.W., and Wang, X. 2009. Online community response to major disaster: A study of Tianya Forum in the 2008 Sichuan earthquake. *Hawaii International Conference on Systems Sciences*, January 5–8, 2009.

Yang, G. 2008. A civil society emerges from the earthquake rubble. *Yale Global Online*.

Yardley, J. and Barboza, D. 2008. Many hands, not held by China, aid in quake. *New York Times*, May 20, 2008.

Zhang, J.Y. and Barr, M. 2013. *Green Politics in China: Environmental Governance and State-Society Relations*. London: Pluto Press, p. 159.

Zhang, X. and Baum, R. 2004. Civil society and the anatomy of a rural NGO. *The China Journal*, (52), pp. 97–107.

Zheng, Y. and Fewsmith, J. 2008. *China's Opening Society: The Non-state Sector and Governance*. London; New York: Routledge.

2 Was there charity in Imperial China?

The Fan clan's charitable estate

What are the historical roots of social entrepreneurship in China? Did the Chinese practice charity back in the time of the emperors? Or was philanthropy something that they had to learn from the West? This chapter offers a whirlwind tour of Chinese history, including the rise and fall of traditional Chinese charitable practices. As we shall see, the ways that Chinese people thought about and acted out philanthropy were very different from what modern Westerners expected. In dynastic China, the two central institutions of society were the patriarchal clan and the imperial state, and they were the key players when it came to charity.[1]

Let's begin with the story of a famously generous man from the Song Dynasty (960–1279). A boy named Zhu Yue grew up in Shandong in northeastern China.[2] He was studious and brilliant, two useful traits to have during the Song Dynasty. By this time in Chinese history, hereditary aristocrats had been replaced with a new upper class: mandarins.[3] These were scholar-officials, whose status was determined by passing the civil service examinations and achieving positions in the meritocratic government bureaucracy. The civil service exams were a series of standardized examinations open to any adult male in China.[4] Zhu Yue passed test after test until he reached the highest one of all: the *jinshi* examination taken before the emperor himself.[5] His success there led to an official appointment in the government, the ultimate path to status and wealth in Song China.

As an adult, Zhu Yue made a shocking discovery – he was not really a member of the Zhu family. His biological father was a man named Fan Yong, who had died when he was still a toddler. His mother had remarried into the Zhu clan and changed her son's name from Fan Zhongyan to Zhu Yue. Chinese families were patriarchal, tracing descendants through the male line. Since his father was not a Zhu, neither was Zhu Yue. Upset at these revelations, the young man traveled to the city of Suzhou to find his father's family. The Fan clan was not particularly welcoming, and they only grudgingly agreed to receive him when he promised not to make any claim upon them except to restore his name. In 1017, he successfully petitioned the court to change his name back to Fan Zhongyan.[6]

In retrospect, the Fan clan should have been more eager to reclaim him. Fan Zhongyan had a long and successful career in the government and became very wealthy. Personally frugal, he was generous to both his adoptive and biological family during his lifetime and gave them many charitable gifts. However, Fan Zhongyan was not content with serving the Fan clan during his lifetime. After his retirement, he sought a way to make certain his wealth would take care of his kin even after his death. In 1050, Fan Zhongyan decided to create something new. He invested in a parcel of land and designated it as an inalienable trust property held in the name of the Fan lineage. This property would provide income for charitable gifts for clan members in perpetuity.[7] Each member of the Fan clan would receive gifts of rice and silk, as well as gifts of cash at weddings and funerals.[8] Although it evolved over time, the Fan Clan's charitable trust lasted for 500 years. Fan Zhongyan's innovative estate became famous and was widely imitated in China for centuries.[9]

"China has no tradition of helping the misfortunates"

Although Fan Zhongyan was obviously generous, was this really charity? For many Western observers in the nineteenth and twentieth centuries, the answer was no. Charity should be selfless, yet these types of trusts were designed to enhance the status of the family name.[10] Why was Fan Zhongyan only concerned with the needs of his relatives, but not the suffering of those who were not his kin? (This is especially curious since he did not even know he was a member of the Fan family until he was an adult.) Why was Fan only generous with those who would laud him during his lifetime and worship him after he died?

Does China lack a tradition of philanthropy? Did the Chinese have to learn charity from the West? This certainly was the perception among some Westerners, including nineteenth-century missionaries eager to demonstrate the moral paucity of the heathen Chinese. In the 1890s, missionary Arthur Smith noted that there were Chinese who distributed alms to beggars, but he insisted these donors were not giving out of the goodness of their hearts, but instead "essentially buying insurance against the possibility that marauders might raid their homes and warehouses."[11] A century later, journalist Harrison Salisbury wrote a 1989 *New York Times* op-ed that claimed:

> ...the restraining philosophy of humanitarianism is absent or nearly absent in Chinese tradition.... China has no tradition of helping the misfortunates. Too often, lepers or cripples were simply clubbed to death as a burden on society. China developed no great philosophy of charity, aid to the downtrodden or an obligation to help the less fortunate.[12]

We may not be surprised that Christian missionaries and jaundiced journalists cast a suspicious eye on Chinese charity. After all, they had a vested interest in focusing on China's flaws. But until the 1980s, even scholars argued that the Chinese did not engage in "real" charity.

As Joanna Handlin Smith points out, when researchers encountered acts of generous philanthropy in the historical record, they explained them away as strategic actions designed to serve the self-interest of the giver.[13] If elites like Fan Zhongyan set up charitable trusts for their clans, they were doing so to increase the status of their families, and therefore themselves. If wealthy families provided famine relief in times of drought, they were not acting out of concern for the hungry. Instead, they were employing the mechanisms of social control to avoid rice riots. If rich men provided coffins and funeral services for the poor, they were doing so to remove unhygienic and unsightly corpses from their presence.[14]

In fact, there is ample historic evidence that philanthropic activities flourished in Imperial China. Despite the claims of the *New York Times*' Harrison Salisbury, China has a very rich philosophy of humanitarianism and generosity. However, that philosophy was very different from modern Western views of charity, and it often inspired philanthropic behavior that looked different from what Westerners expected.

There is a new a caveat: Imperial Chinese history spans several thousand years. It is obviously impossible to talk about *the* "Imperial Chinese system" in the singular, since Chinese society changed considerably over that long historical stretch. Similarly, everything I write about "Confucianism" is by definition an oversimplification.[15] In this book, I will only touch upon the nuances and complexities of China's great philosophical traditions and the charitable practices they inspired.

The Confucian philosophy of charity

Western concepts of charity are rooted in the Judeo-Christian ideology of unconditional, universal love.[16] Ideally, philanthropic activity is voluntary and self-sacrificing. Jesus tells his disciples that real charity expects no earthly reward:

> When you give to the poor, do not sound a trumpet before you as the hypocrites do in the synagogues in the streets, so that you may be honored by men.... But when you give to the poor, do not let your left hand know what your right hand is doing, so that your giving will be secret; and your Father who sees what is done in secret will reward you.[17]

According to St Paul, charity "does not brag and is not arrogant, does not act unbecomingly; it does not seek its own..."[18] In this tradition, the heroes of charity – Jesus, St. Francis, Mother Teresa – leave their families and pour out their lives for strangers in need. Charity should be personal and private, disconnected from state interference.

In practice, the charitable actions of Westerners often fail to comply with these ideals. People engage in philanthropic behavior in order to gain status, enhance social networks, or receive tax deductions. Western people have been coerced into giving donations because of social pressures or institutional obligations. Nor have Western charities always been independent of the state. In many

Western countries, including the United States, the government is the major source of financial support for the nonprofit sector, and the state relies on these organizations to carry out a substantial amount of its work.[19] One can easily find mixed motives, even in those nineteenth century Christian missionaries, who were so critical of Chinese morality. In the US, foreign missionary work conveniently became popular when industrialization undermined the rural economy. For many young men and women who had no future on the farm, Christian missions sounded more appealing than factory work.[20]

Yet, despite these contradictions, these ideals (self-sacrifice, volunteerism, serving strangers, and autonomy from the state) were the lens through which many Westerners judged the behavior of non-Western philanthropic behavior – and found it lacking.[21] However, the central tenets of traditional Chinese charity are almost exactly the opposite of Western expectations: charitable giving was obligatory and rooted in social networks. It was considered more virtuous to give to those close to you than to strangers, and beneficiaries were expected to reciprocate to donors. The dividing line between government philanthropy and personal charity was blurred to the point of nonexistence.

Particularized love versus universal love

The philosophy of charity in Imperial China focused on the concept of *ren*, a word that can be translated as "love," "humaneness," or "benevolence." In all four key Confucian texts (the *Analects*, the *Mencius*, the *Mean*, and the *Great Learning*), benevolence/*ren* is considered one of the most important virtues for a moral life. Like the word "charity" in English, Confucian benevolence is associated with both sympathetic emotions and generous action.[22]

In contrast to Christian views, Confucian philosophers insisted that particularized love (loving certain people more than others) is more virtuous than universal love (loving everyone equally). In the fourth century, Mencius argued explicitly against universal love. He insisted that the foundation for love and virtue was the family. Therefore, denigrating the family to the level of strangers would destroy a person's moral compass.[23] Mencius also insisted that universal love went against human nature. In a rebuttal to a proponent of universal love, he exclaimed, "Does I Chih really think that a man's affection for the child of his own brother is just like his affection for the child of his neighbor?"[24] If people attempted to love everyone equally, they would fail to carry out their particular obligations and responsibilities to the people who needed them. Mencius declared that "universal love ... entails the denial of one's parents. To deny one's parents or to deny one's sovereign is to be an animal."[25] Far from finding Jesus or St. Francis admirable, Mencius believed that those who were willing to deny their families to serve strangers had lost their humanity.

Modern Western beliefs about charity are not just shaped by Judeo-Christian religious traditions, but also by Enlightenment philosophies. Rousseau and Locke taught Westerners to see themselves as free and equal individuals with rights.[26] By contrast, Confucian philosophy teaches that people are embedded in social networks and are defined by their responsibilities and obligations to the other members of their network. The people in your network are divided into two groups: kin and "familiar people." Kin (*jiaren*) include not only the nuclear family, but also everyone in your family lineage, defined through the male line. "Familiar people" (*shuren*) included friends, teachers, classmates, neighbors, and business partners. These people are considered a kind of faux-kin; children are taught to refer to an elderly neighbor as "Grandma," while employees call their boss "Uncle." The people outside of your network are strangers (*shengren*). People are morally obligated to feel love and act with generosity toward kin and "familiar people." But toward strangers, generosity is not only unnecessary, but possibly immoral, since it wastes resources that relatives and friends deserve (see Figure 2.1).

Therefore, when Fan Zhongyan wanted to use his wealth for good, of course he felt obligated to serve his family first rather than strangers, regardless of need. This is true even though he had grown up outside of the Fan clan. To do

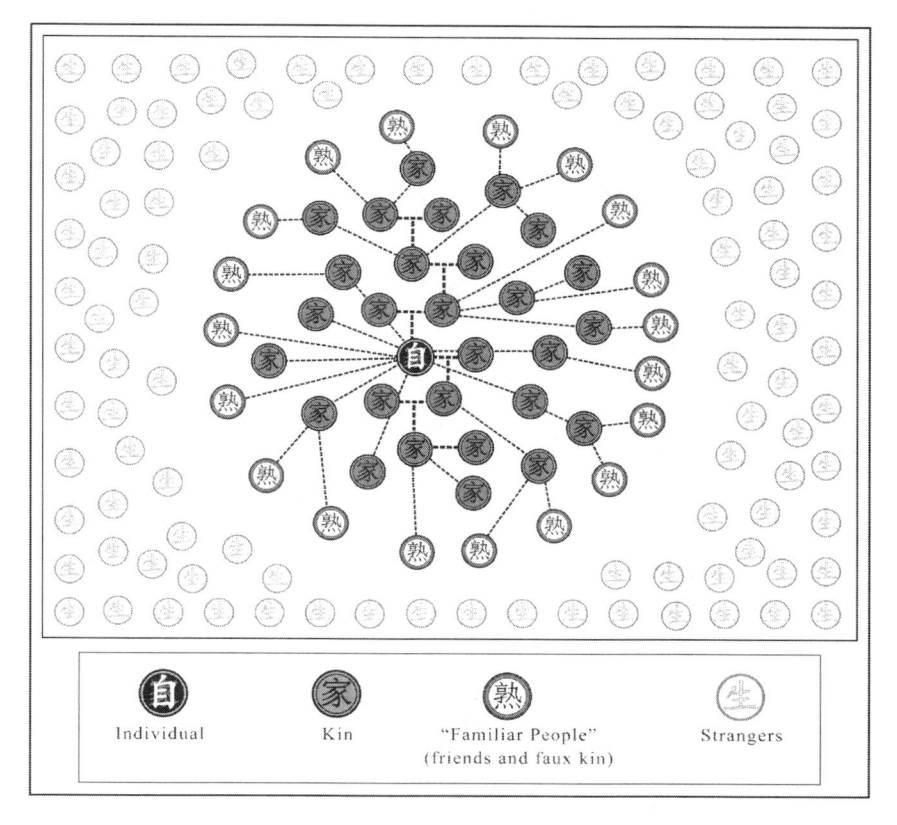

Figure 2.1 Guanxi network in late Imperial China.
Source: illustration created by Lara Scott.

otherwise would have been to act inhumanely and shirk his responsibility. Fan Zhongyan would have grown up reading biographies of virtuous men who were praised for living in frugal simplicity in order to give their salaries to their poorer relatives.[27] His innovative trust simply made it possible for him to continue giving to clan members even after death. As Fan Zhongyan explained:

> Our clan in [Suzhou] is very numerous; some among them are close, and others distant, relatives. Yet, if we regard them from the viewpoint of our ancestors, all are equally descendants without distinction of the degree of relationship. How could I not feel shame over their suffering from cold and hunger?[28]

Reciprocity versus altruism

In the modern Western view, true charity is voluntary rather than obligatory, and the genuinely charitable person gives without expecting anything in return. To return to St. Paul in 1 Corinthians, charity "does not seek its own." Real love should have no strings attached. Expectations of reciprocity or payback would taint true generosity, denigrating it from a virtue to an act of manipulation. This is why it is ideal to give to strangers.

From this Western perspective, relationships of charity (between giver and beneficiary) are inherently different from relationships of the market (between buyer and seller) and relationships of affection (between family members or friends). Relationships of the market are supposed to be perfectly reciprocal: the amount of money I give you should be perfectly equal to the value of the product you sell to me. In a market relationship, each person is supposed to have self-serving motivations: I am participating in this interaction not out of obligation or an emotional connection with you, but instead because I expect to benefit financially or materially from this transaction. Market relationships are also temporary in that they only last for the duration of the interaction.

By contrast, relationships of affection between friends and family are the opposite of market relationships. They are supposed to be unconditional rather than reciprocal, motivated by emotional connection rather than material benefit, and they are supposed to be long lasting rather than temporary. In the Western view, relationships of affection should ideally be protected from the taint of the market.[29] This is why, in the US, people split the check after dining together in a restaurant so no one is ever in debt to a friend. This is why Americans such as myself would feel terribly embarrassed to offer a friend a loan even when we know she needs the money. In the US, parents try to save money for their retirement so that they will never "be a burden" on their children. A person who "uses someone" to gain material benefits is not a true friend.

In the Western perspective, relationships of charity are different from either relationships of the market or relationships of affection. First, the relationship between the donor and the beneficiary is inherently unequal, unlike the relationship between buyers and sellers or between friends. The transaction elevates the giver while emphasizing the low position of the beneficiary. Second, the donor should be motivated by an emotional connection to give unconditionally, but the recipient benefits materially. Third, the duration of the relationship lasts only as long as the donor desires to donate, so it can be as brief as a market transaction or as long lasting as a relationship of affection. In real Western societies, of course, these three different types do not stay pure in practice, but they do influence Western views of what charity (or friendships or business relationships) should look like.

By contrast, Confucian concepts mix together characteristics that Westerners assume need to stay separate. In the Chinese view of relationships of affection, people should be motivated by emotional connection *and* a desire for material benefits because emotional connections are strengthened by the exchange of gifts and favors. Reciprocity and obligation are the foundation of relationships of affection, rather than signs of the market taint. In addition, relationships of charity are a type of relationship of affection, rather than something inherently different.

Confucian teaching offers the Five Cardinal Relationships as the foundation of social life; i.e., the relationship between *ruler and subject*, between *parent and child*, between *husband and wife*, between *older and younger siblings*, and between *friends*.[30] In every case, the emotional connection of the relationship is expressed through obligations of reciprocity (*bao*). These reciprocal obligations involve not just emotional responsibilities but also material ones. If you care about someone, you give him or her gifts of meals, of loans, of cash, of jobs, of social connections, and (of course) of useful and desirable consumer goods. Or, if you have material needs or wants, you demonstrate the closeness of your relationship by asking your friend or relative for a loan, a job, a discount, and so on.

Genuine relationships of affection are cemented by indebtedness, obligation, and expectations of reciprocity. Emotional relationships are created and sustained through the exchange of gifts and favors.[31] If you give me a costly gift (or money), you are signaling that you want our relationship to deepen. You have put me in your debt, so now our lives are entangled at least until the debt is discharged. According to the rules of reciprocity, I am now obligated to return the favor. Moreover, to demonstrate that I value our relationship, I should give you a gift that is more valuable than the one you gave me. Now in a position of debt to me, and the relationship must continue. In the same way, if you ask me for a costly favor, you are telling me that you want to be in my debt and more closely tied to me. Your message is that you want our relationship to be closer.

From this perspective, to "use" your friend or relative for material benefit will strengthen the relationship, rather than betray it. In anthropology, this is known as gift exchange.[32] Although Western missionaries and journalists may have seen this type of behavior as selfish and immoral, gift exchange is a moral system that is common around the world.[33] In a gift exchange society, a person who avoids obligation and debt is a person who is avoiding personal connection. (This is why Chinese people, to this day, find it appalling when Americans split the check after a restaurant meal.) This view of relationships is instilled in the modern Chinese term *guanxi*. It can be translated as "relationship," and "social connection," the "benefits and obligations attached to personal relationships" or the "exchange of favors based on social connections." Many China scholars (and businesspeople) see *guanxi* as the key to understanding Chinese society, even in the twenty-first century.[34]

In the Chinese perspective, acts of charity are based on *guanxi*; they are an exchange of material gifts that build an emotional relationship between two people. As such, they are not inherently different from relationships between friends/family members or even relationships between business partners. They occupy a different place on the same continuum. There is no contradiction in giving philanthropic gifts to kin rather than strangers, and there is no contradiction in expecting reciprocity in return for generosity.

When Fan Zhongyan set up the trust for the Fan Clan, he described it as an act of reciprocity. His good fortune, he insisted, had come from the clan.

> ..."virtue" has been accumulating from our ancestors for more than a century, but has for the first time brought forth its fruits in myself. Now that I have achieved high office, if I should alone enjoy my riches and honorable position without thought for my fellow clansmen, how shall I in future days be able to face our ancestors in the next life, and how should I be able to enter the ancestral temple?[35]

By his generosity, Fan Zhongyan signaled his willingness to invest in his relationship with his relatives. Of course he knew that the clan members would be obliged to reciprocate with praise and obedience during his lifetime, and dutiful ancestor worship afterward. This did not mean that Fan's motives were tainted by a desire for selfish gain. Instead, he meant that he wanted his relationship with them to be closer than ever during the remaining years of his life, and to continue beyond his death.

The judge and the food crisis

According to Confucian teaching, if every person is embedded in a clan, there should be little need for charity to strangers – as long as society is peaceful and prosperous. It is the responsibility of the Imperial state to provide that peace and prosperity. It is also the responsibility of the state to provide special care for its people in times of special difficulty, violence, or natural disasters, when clan charity is insufficient.

In the last years of the Ming Dynasty (1368–1644), various regions of China suffered from terrible food shortages. One of the areas to suffer was Shaoxing Prefecture in Zhejiang Province. In 1641, as Prefectural Judge Chen Zilong returned to his post there from a visit to the capital, he reported seeing "thousands of starving people forming mobs; with knives outstretched and sacks on their backs, they crowded around, obstructing the carts."[36] Hungry people were breaking into wealthy households to loot grain.[37]

Fortunately, in the previous year, Chen Zilong had all the local residents register their grain holdings, so he knew who had excess. In the face of the new crisis, Chen wrote,

> I walked through the snow to ask the wealthy households to issue grain, and they were all motivated. Some reduced prices by 30% out of kindness to the villagers; others contributed 20% for the formation of soup kitchens to save the poorest households.[38]

The response to the crisis was quite complicated and required significant manpower. According to reports, the shortage lasted three months, 276 soup kitchens were set up, and tens of thousands of lives were saved. To manage the relief, Chen called upon other local government bureaucrats, but also former officials living in the area and "the graduates of the provincial and prefectural examinations" – these were men who aspired to pass the *jinshi* civil service exam to hold a government position, but who had not yet succeeded. According to Chen, many of these "had also been very worthy and helpful in managing the relief."[39]

Rulers and subjects: the paternalistic state

A modern Western perspective draws a clear line between state-sponsored welfare and private charity. This division was much less clear in late Imperial China. The relationship between ruler and subject is just one of the Five Cardinal Relationships. As with the relationships between parents and children, husbands and wives, and older siblings and younger siblings, the relationship between the government and its people is based on reciprocity. Just as parents provide for their children and children reciprocate with obedience, the government takes care of its people and the people reciprocate with loyalty.

The role of the state was to provide good conditions so that, at the local level, extended families could take care of their own by carrying out their relational obligations. According to Mencius,

> An enlightened ruler will regulate the people's livelihood so as to ensure that, above, they have enough to serve their parents and, below, they have enough to support their wives and children. In years of prosperity they will always have enough to eat; in years of dearth they are able to escape starvation. Only then does he urge the people toward goodness; accordingly, they find it easy to comply.[40]

Good rulers accomplish this by serving as moral role models for their people. But they are also required to have leadership skills in agricultural management, flood control, and disaster response.[41] Therefore, the Confucian state held ultimate responsibility for providing charity to those in need.

Providing social welfare for the people was not just the responsibility of the emperor and his government – it was the foundation for their legitimacy. Chinese rulers did not claim the right to rule because of divine descent like Japanese emperors, or by divine right like European kings. Instead, Confucianism taught that emperors were just ordinary men who were given the mandate to rule because of their virtue and ability to provide for the people. If an emperor were corrupt or incompetent, his people would suffer from poverty, bandits, and natural disasters. Under these circumstances, the people were no longer obligated to reciprocate with loyalty because the emperor no longer held the mandate given by Heaven to true rulers.[42] According to Mencius, a ruler who behaved badly was no longer a ruler at all, but merely a thief and a robber.[43] The people not only had the right to overthrow his regime, but the responsibility to replace him and his court with virtuous men.

To return to the story of the food shortage in Shaoxing, it was Chen Zilong's duty as a prefectural-level official to respond to the disaster. He wrote his rather dramatic report to ensure that his supervisors realized how well he carried out his responsibilities.[44] However, the food shortage itself was a sign that all was not well with the Ming Dynasty. The region had been suffering from economic and social problems for years. Local silver mines had been shut down, and bandits had moved into the abandoned hills. Irrigation and flood control infrastructure was deteriorating.[45] The Ming rulers were distracted by wars on the borders and could spare few resources for these local problems. For many people in China, the regime's incompetence revealed that it had lost its mandate to rule. Despite the efforts of Chen Zilong and his partners in responding to the local disaster, the Ming dynasty was overthrown a mere three years later, in 1644.

The gentry and the state

In the story of the 1641 Shaoxing food shortage, Chen Zilong was clearly acting in his official capacity as a government bureaucrat. To carry out relief efforts, he called on other officials in the regional government hierarchy. Yet, many of the people who worked with him did not hold official state positions. These included former officials (currently retired) and midcareer officials who were at home between postings. (In order to avoid local entanglements, Imperial Chinese bureaucrats were never appointed to serve in their home regions, so these men would never have held an official position in Shaoxing.) Chen also noted the contributions of aspiring officials – educated men who had passed the local level civil service tests, but had not yet conquered the imperial *jinshi* examination that would lead to a mandarin post in the government.

All of the men involved in Shaoxing's disaster relief came from the gentry class, late Imperial China's elite. These were the families fortunate enough to produce successful candidates for the civil service examinations, men who could amass wealth and power through their mandarin positions. Given the high failure rate of the civil service exams, it was a rare accomplishment. During the almost three centuries of Ming rule, fewer than 25,000 men passed.[46] (The population of Ming China was well over 100 million people.) These families invested the wealth from their mandarins into land, building an economic foundation that would provide the resources to educate the next generation of sons to pass the civil service tests. Although the examinations were open to all men, in reality the high cost of the necessary education combined with the high failure rate gave a considerable advantage to wealthy families.[47] Candidates often had to take the examination multiple times, and those who passed were often well into middle age. Some of the unsuccessful candidates became tutors and teachers for the next generation.

Chen Zilong called on gentry families to help with the disaster relief not just because they were wealthy, but because they saw themselves as an extension of the state. This is a confusing concept to an American like me, who was brought up to believe that there is a clear separation between public and private, between the government and the people. In Confucian teaching, the relevant division is not between public and private, but between the learned and the uneducated. Because learning (which, of course, means Confucian learning) leads to virtue; the literati are noble, moral, and wise, while the uneducated are petty, undisciplined, and foolish.[48] Therefore, the most educated ought to be given the most authority, since they had the wisdom to rule over others. This is the basis of the meritocratic bureaucracy and the civil service examination.

The authority of the state did not reside in the emperor's bloodline, but in the collective knowledge and wisdom of China's Confucian scholars. The state was a manifestation of Confucian philosophy and morality. Unless Confucian scholars agreed that the government was following that philosophy and morality correctly, it had no legitimacy. These educated men had a responsibility to steer the state in the right direction, even if that meant criticizing the emperor himself. Indeed, these educated men were the state, arguably more so than the emperor himself (since the emperor was replaceable). According to Mencius, "If the ruler has great faults, [his high ministers] should remonstrate with him. If, after they have done so repeatedly, he does not listen, they should depose him."[49] This was the duty of Confucian scholars even if they were not currently holding an official post. After all, both Confucius and Mencius spent their lives traveling from state to state, advising and criticizing rulers even though they usually had no official appointment.

To revisit the example of Shaoxing, Chen Zilong called on the gentry to participate in the government's relief efforts because both he and they saw the gentry class as an extension of the government. Whether they were retired officials, between official postings, or aspiring to government position, they were all Confucian scholars trained in the philosophy of government, benevolence, and virtue.

Gentry charity: Yang Dongming's benevolent society

The Chinese gentry did develop some philanthropic traditions that, in practice, resembled Western concepts of charity. Until the sixteenth century, the gentry would respond with generous actions when the state called upon them, but were more hesitant to act out on their own. They were concerned that public displays of independent philanthropy could be associated with political rebellion.[50] Historically, when a dynasty was in decline, ambitious men would position themselves to take over the throne by broadcasting their virtue through generous acts of charity – stepping in to serve the people where the current regime had failed.

This changed in the late Ming Dynasty, when it became fashionable for the gentry to engage in independent acts of philanthropy and to make sure that those acts were well publicized. Local governments began publishing lists of notable charitable deeds, complete with brief biographies of the virtuous men who did them.[51] The beneficiaries were the poor and the needy in the local region. The charitable gentry were not abandoning the Confucian concept of particularized love by embracing universal love, but instead they were extending the reach of their care one more circle outward, from kin to friends to neighbors. They set up soup kitchens, repaired crumbling infrastructure, built schools and hospitals, collected and buried corpses, and forgave debts. One of the most charming acts, inspired by the Buddhist belief in reincarnation, was to liberate animals. Hearing of a goose destined for the pot or a pig about to be slaughtered, the gentlemen would swoop in, purchase the animal victim and set it free.[52]

Most of these acts of gentry charity were ad hoc, rather than organized. However, in the late sixteenth century, a social entrepreneur named Yang Dongming created a new type of charitable organization: the benevolent society. Yang Dongming was born in Henan Province into a wealthy gentry family.[53] He passed the *jinshi* examination and launched into a successful career in the government. In 1590, Yang took temporary leave of his official position and returned home. Yang Dongming was very interested in the philosophy of *ren/* humaneness and sought ways to turn this theory into action. Upon his return, he immediately joined other local elites to organize a community granary to prevent food shortages.[54] In the following years, he established a school for the poor, organized a soup kitchen during severe snowstorms, and sponsored a program to distribute warm winter clothing to the indigent.[55]

Yang also tried to follow the example of his forebears in another way: he joined a poetry club. This was a well-known tradition at the time: when scholar-officials found themselves out of office (whether they were between postings, out of favor at court, or retired), they were supposed to meet together in beautiful settings, imbibe wine, and compose poetry. However, Yang found the poetry club meetings disappointingly dull, involving more inebriation than literary transcendence. He suggested that the club change its focus from poetry to good deeds.[56] The members would contribute money, which could be used to aid the poor and sick, repair roads, fix bridges, and help the needy with marriage and funeral expenses. His friends agreed and created the first recorded example of a Chinese benevolent society. The concept spread, and benevolent societies flourished all over China until the early twentieth century.[57]

The late Imperial benevolent society appears to be a logical precursor to today's Chinese NGOs. In both cases, ambitious social entrepreneurs set up organizations to mobilize the resources of well-off citizens to benefit the less fortunate. Yet, when social entrepreneurship re-emerged in China in the late twentieth century, no one mentioned the benevolent society as a precedent. Instead, nonprofit social welfare organizations were seen either as the descendants of nineteenth-century foreign Christian charities, or as a totally new type of organization for China. In order to understand how late Imperial benevolent societies were erased from China's collective memory, we need to examine how social welfare changed drastically with the decline and fall of the Qing Dynasty and the rise of the Chinese Communist Party.

The decline of the Confucian system: the story of Ning Taitai

When Fan Zhoneyan set up his charitable trust in 1050, China was more prosperous, more peaceful, and more powerful than any state in Europe. This was arguably still true seven centuries later, in the eighteenth century. When the English began accumulating wealth from the Industrial Revolution, they wanted to spend their money on products from China. British silver poured into China in exchange for silk, porcelain, and (above all) tea – the caffeinated fuel of capitalism. Unfortunately for the British, the Chinese did not find English products worth buying. This resulted in a trade imbalance. In the 1760s, trade resulted in the transfer of 3 million taels of silver from England to China.[58] In the 1780s, 16 million taels of British silver moved to China.[59] The British government tried to reduce the trade imbalance, but could not reduce the population's insatiable desire for Chinese goods.

Yet, in the course of little more than a century, the Chinese empire had disintegrated. By the early twentieth century, the Imperial court and civil service no longer existed. In the 1930s, Japan invaded China's northernmost territories, Manchuria, while a civil war raged through the rest of the country. The economy was in shambles, and tens of millions of people lived in dire poverty.[60] What happened? And what did it mean for charity in China?

To answer these questions, let us look at the story of one woman, Ning Taitai.[61] (*Taitai* means "wife," so Ning Taitai could be translated "wife of Ning" or "Mrs. Ning."[62]) She was born in 1867, the youngest child of the Hsu family of Penglai, Shandong Province.[63] Her family had once been prosperous. Her father had grown up with property and servants, and he had studied the classics in the hope of passing the civil service exam, albeit without success. But by the time she was born, the family land and houses had been sold. Her father had been reduced to odd jobs, such as peddling snacks in the street. "Each year there was less than the year before," Ning Taitai recalls.[64]

The family's downward mobility reflected the declining fortunes of China's last dynasty, the Qing. In the late eighteenth century, the British finally found a product to sell to the Chinese to reverse the trade imbalance: opium from India. It was phenomenally successful; by the 1820s enough opium was imported into China to sustain one million addicts.[65] The trade imbalance reversed; so much Chinese silver was going to England that it caused serious inflation and other economic problems.[66] In 1838, the Qing emperor banned opium. Under the banner of "free trade," the British and their allies (including the United States) declared war on China. The Qing was defeated in the Opium Wars (1839–1860), and China was forced to accept humiliating treaties with the Western powers and to pay expensive war indemnities. Sensing that the Qing Dynasty had lost its mandate to rule, some ambitious Chinese began fomenting rebellions against the regime. The most destructive was the Taiping Rebellion of 1850, which affected a large swath of southeastern China and led to the deaths of 20 million people. All of these difficulties sent the Chinese economy into a downward spiral, affecting ordinary families such as Ning Taitai's.

At the age of 13, Ning Taitai was married to a man twice her age. He was an opium addict. Initially, opium was smoked by the well off, but in the late nineteenth century the habit spread to laborers and even peasants. Ning Taitai's husband's addiction not only rendered him unable to earn money, but drove him to steal:

> He took everything and sold it for opium. He could not help it. He took everything. I dared not wash a garment and put it out to dry without staying to watch it. If I had a copper coin under the matting of the [bed] he found it.[67]

To avoid starving to death, Ning Taitai and her two young daughters depended on her mother and brother for food. But her mother died and her brother left to fight the Japanese, so Ning Taitai was reduced to begging in the streets.

> One year after my mother died I got a stick and a bowl and started out begging. It was the spring of the year and I was 22. It is no light thing for a woman to go out of her home. That is why I put up with my old opium sot so long. But now I could not live in my house and had to come out. When I begged I begged in the parts of the city where I was not known, for I was ashamed.[68]

Ning Taitai's husband helped her beg, but still longed for his drug. He tried to sell their younger daughter to a brothel, but was thwarted by his wife and neighbors.[69] Several years later, he succeeded in selling the little girl to a wealthy family. Ning Taitai was devastated:

> When he came home without her I knew what he had done. I said I would hang myself and that I would hang [their other daughter], and that we, mother and child, should die together. I rolled on the ground in my agony, in my anger, and in my pain.[70]

Although her husband managed to convince her not to kill herself, Ning Taitai decided to leave him, taking her remaining daughter with her. She went to work as a servant.

The story of Ning Taitai reveals the way that political and economic crises led to the breakdown of Confucian norms and values in the late nineteenth century. People failed to live up to their responsibilities in the Five Cardinal

Relationships. Instead of providing for his wife, her husband stole from her. Instead of raising and protecting his children, the father sold his daughter. There was no clan charitable estate to help her out. (The Fan clan's charitable estate ended in 1760.[71]) Both Ning Taitai's birth clan and the family she married into were once prosperous. But in her lifetime, each person struggled to earn enough money to eat. No one had any extra for charity. After she left her husband, Ning Taitai depended on a social network of reciprocal *guanxi* relations with faux kin, made up of employers, co-workers, and friends.[72] She does not report encountering a benevolent society, although she did occasionally eat at soup kitchens that the wealthy set up to feed the poor. We should not be surprised that so many nineteenth-century Western missionaries and journalists in China concluded that it had no culture of charity.

Perhaps the most significant failure of a Confucian relationship was the one between ruler and subject. Instead of peace and prosperity, Ning Taitai lived in a world of random violence, unenforced laws, corruption, rampant inflation, and widespread poverty. The Imperial institutions of social welfare and security were weak or nonexistent. Although it was illegal for her husband to sell their daughter, neither Ning Taitai nor anyone else went to the police or courts for redress. They had no evidence that any state power would ever help them. In their experience, receiving the attention of authorities was dangerous. At one point, several soldiers entered Ning Taitai's neighbor's house to try to rape a 15-year-old girl, and had to be fought off by the neighbors. The soldiers returned later to assault the girl's parents and an innocent bystander.[73] The Qing Dynasty had been fatally weakened by foreign wars, internal rebellions, and the social costs of widespread opium addiction. In 1911, the last Chinese emperor abdicated the throne.

Abandoned by the state and her clan, Ning Taitai's family received philanthropy from a completely different source: Western Christian missionaries who had set up Western-style charities, churches, and schools in China. Ning Taitai worked as a maidservant for a foreign missionary family named Burns. Through her connections with foreigners, Ning Taitai's granddaughters were educated at mission schools. One, Su Teh, even studied abroad in America and returned to teach at a college in Beijing.[74] However, in 1937, the Japanese invaded Beijing. Refusing to live under Japanese rule, Su Teh left her teaching position to flee to unoccupied China and fight for her country.[75]

During the 1930s and 1940s, it seemed highly likely that China would cease to exist and fragment, like so many other empires had in the twentieth century. (Both the Ottoman and Habsburg Empires had already disintegrated, and the British Empire would soon be only a shadow of its former glory.) After the fall of the Qing Dynasty in 1911, no government managed to control more than a fraction of China's territory for almost three decades. But in 1949, the Chinese Communist Party managed to conquer most of mainland China. On October 1, its leader Mao Zedong declared the birth of the People's Republic of China. It was the beginning of a whole new vision of social welfare, one that did not include extended families, gentry, or private charity at all.

Notes

1 Other institutions, such as Buddhist temples, also provided for the needy at times, but they had a smaller impact on society.
2 Denis Twitchett, "The Fan Clan's charitable estate, 1050–1760," in D.S. Nivison and A.F. Wright (Eds.), *Confucianism in Action* (Stanford: Stanford University Press, 1959), 99.
3 The English word "mandarin" comes from Portuguese, with roots in either the Latin *mandare* ("to rule") or the Sanskrit *mantrin* ("counselor or minister"). "Mandarin" also became the English term to describe the common language of administration used by the mandarins in response to the fact that different dialects of Chinese are often unintelligible to each other. Today, it is the English word used to describe the official dialect of Chinese (called "common speech" or *putonghua* in China) in contrast to regional dialects, such as Cantonese.
4 Although Chinese history offers many stories of men from low social status who achieve political prominence through the civil service examination, in reality the process of studying for the test was both time-consuming and expensive. Most candidates came from wealthy families. The subjects on the Song Dynasty exam were the "Five Studies": military strategy, civil law, revenue and taxation, agriculture and geography, and the Confucian classics.
5 Twitchett, "The Fan Clan's charitable estate," 99.
6 Ibid., 100.
7 Ibid., 101.
8 Ibid., 106.
9 Ibid., 98.
10 James L. Watson, "Chinese kinship reconsidered: Anthropological perspectives on historical research," *The China Quarterly* 92 (1982): 589–622.
11 Joanna Handlin Smith, *The Art of Doing Good: Charity in Late Ming China* (Berkeley: University of California Press, 2009).
12 Harrison E. Salisbury, "In China, 'a little blood'," *New York Times*, June 13, 1989. www.nytimes.com/1989/06/13/opinion/in-china-a-little-blood.html.
13 Joanna Handlin Smith, "Chinese philanthropy as seen through a case of famine relief in the 1640's," in W. Ilchman, S. Katz, and E. Queen (Eds.), *Philanthropy in the World's Traditions* (Bloomington: Indiana University Press, 1998), 133–168.
14 Watson, *Chinese Kinship Reconsidered*, 589–622.
15 Confucius lived around 500 BCE. Since that time, his teachings have been the foundation for multiple schools of philosophical analyses, elaborations, and reinterpretations. In China, this body of learning is not even called "Confucianism" but "the teaching of the scholars." Furthermore, Chinese ideas about charity have been influenced by Taoism and Buddhist notions of karma and merit. We also need to be careful not to draw a straight line between cultural beliefs and actual charitable practices. From the time of Confucius onward, Chinese scholars complained that people were not living up to their Confucian responsibilities. Similar cultural beliefs can lead to different outcomes, depending on how they are institutionalized. See Mary Evelyn Tucker, "A view of philanthropy in Japan: Confucian ethics and education," in W. Ilchman, S. Katz, and E. Queen (Eds.), *Philanthropy in the World's Traditions* (Bloomington: Indiana University Press, 1998), 169–196.
16 Demetrios Constantelos, *Byzantine Philanthropy and Social Welfare* (2nd ed.) (New Rochelle: Aristide D. Caratzas, 1991), 3.
17 Matthew 6:2–4 (New American Standard Bible translation).
18 First Corinthians 13:4–7 (New American Standard Bible translation).
19 Lester M. Salamon, "The rise of the nonprofit sector," *Foreign Affairs* 73, no. 4 (1994): 109–122.

20 Amanda Porterfield, "Mount Holyoke missionaries and non-Western women: The motivations and consequences of 19th century American missionary philanthropy," in W.F. Ilchman, S.N. Katz, and E.L. Queen (Eds.), *Philanthropy in the World's Traditions* (Bloomington: Indiana University Press, 1998), 215–235.

21 A cursory examination of philanthropic activities around the globe reveals that many societies do not share Western mores about charity. For example, in pre-modern sub-Saharan Africa, voluntary giving was understood to be modeled on the parent-child relationship. Wealthy people "adopted" the less well off as "descendants," and they expected their beneficiaries to respond according to the rules of reciprocity. See Steven Feierman, "Reciprocity and assistance in precolonial Africa," in W.F. Ilchman, S.N. Katz, and E.L. Queen (Eds.), *Philanthropy in the World's Traditions* (Bloomington: Indiana University Press, 1998), 3–25. In many Muslim societies, charitable giving was understood to be a religious obligation rather than voluntary choice. In some early cases, almsgiving was enforced by the state. See Gregory Kozlowski, "Religious authority, reform, and philanthropy in the contemporary Muslim world," in W.F. Ilchman, S.N. Katz, and E.L. Queen (Eds.), *Philanthropy in the World's Traditions* (Bloomington: Indiana University Press, 1998), 279–308.

22 Confucius: "A young man is to be filial with his family and respectful outside it. He is to be earnest and faithful, overflowing in his love for living beings and intimate with those who are humane." The Analects 1:6. Confucius, "The Analects," in Wm. Theodore de Bary and Irene Bloom, *Sources of Chinese Tradition* (2nd ed., Vol. 1) (New York: Columbia University Press, 1999), 45.

23 Mencius 3A:5. Quoted in Wing-Tsit Chan (Ed.), *A Source Book in Chinese Philosophy* (Princeton: Princeton University Press, 1969), 71.

24 Ibid., 71.

25 Mencius, "Selections from the *Mencius*," in Wm. Theodore de Bary and Irene Bloom, *Sources of Chinese Tradition* (2nd ed., Vol. 1) (New York: Columbia University Press, 1999), 136.

26 See, for example, John Locke, *Second Treatise of Government*, C.B. Macpherson (Ed.) (Indianapolis: Hackett Publishing, 1980), 8.

27 Twitchett, "The Fan Clan's charitable estate," 101.

28 Ibid., 100.

29 Ming-cheng M. Lo and Eileen M. Otis, "Guanxi civility: Processes, potentials, and contingencies," *Politics and Society* 31, no. 1 (2003): 131–162.

30 The *Mean* 20. In De Bary and Bloom, *Sources of Chinese Tradition*, 336–337.

31 Alan Smart, "Guanxi, gifts, and learning from China: A review essay," *Anthropos* 93, no. 4–6 (1998): 559–565; Lo and Otis, *Guanxi Civility: Processes, Potentials, and Contingencies*, 131–162.

32 Marcel Mauss, *The Gift: Forms and Functions of Exchange in Archaic Societies*, I. Cunnison (Trans.) (New York: Norton, 1967).

33 Ibid.

34 Mayfair Meihui Yang, *Gifts, Favors, and Banquets* (Ithaca: Cornell University Press, 1994); Lo and Otis, *Guanxi Civility: Processes, Potentials, and Contingencies*, 131–162; Alan Smart and Carolyn L. Hsu, "Corruption or social capital? Tact and the performance of *guanxi* in market socialist China," in M. Nujiten and G. Anders (Eds.), *Corruption and the Secret of Law: A Legal Anthropological Perspective* (Burlington: Ashgate, 2007), 167–190.

35 Twitchett, The Fan Clan's charitable estate, 100.

36 Smith, *The Art of Doing Good: Charity in Late Ming China*, 157.

37 Ibid., 160.

38 Ibid., 158.

39 Ibid., 158.

40 Mencius, "Selections from the *Mencius*," in Wm. Theodore de Bary and Irene Bloom, *Sources of Chinese Tradition* (2nd ed., Vol. 1) (New York: Columbia University Press, 1999), 123.
41 Ibid., 130–134.
42 "The Great Learning." Ibid., 130–134.
43 When a nervous ruler asked Mencius if the slaying of the notorious King Zhou was justified, the sage responded,

> One who despoiled humaneness is called a thief; one who despoiled rightness is called a robber. Someone who is a robber and a thief is called a mere fellow. I have heard of the punishment of the fellow Zhou but never of the slaying of a ruler.
> (Mencius, "Selections from the *Mencius*," 125)

44 Smith, The Art of Doing Good: Charity in Late Ming China, 158.
45 Ibid., 156–157.
46 Benjamin A. Elman, *A Cultural History of Civil Examinations in Late Imperial China* (Berkeley: University of California Press, 2000), 696.
47 Hilary J. Beattie, *Land and Lineage in China: A Study of T'ung-Ch'eng County, Anhwei, in the Ming and Ch'ing Dynasties* (Cambridge, UK; New York: Cambridge University Press, 1979), 208.
48 "The Great Learning," in Wm. Theodore de Bary and Irene Bloom, *Sources of Chinese Tradition* (2nd ed., Vol. 1) (New York: Columbia University Press, 1999), 130–134.
49 Mencius. "Selections from the *Mencius*," 147.
50 Smith, *The Art of Doing Good: Charity in Late Ming China*, 5.
51 Ibid., 5.
52 Even at the time, critics of the practice pointed out that the "liberated" animals would most likely be recaptured, sold, and eaten soon thereafter. It could be that liberating animals was a way to act generously to poor vendors without the usual patronizing condescension of charity. The vendors received a good payment and were treated as a partner in a charitable act rather than as a needy beneficiary. Smith, *The Art of Doing Good: Charity in Late Ming China*, Chapter 1.
53 Smith, *The Art of Doing Good: Charity in Late Ming China*, 45.
54 Ibid., 53–54.
55 Ibid., 54.
56 Ibid., 46.
57 Ibid., 43–44.
58 One tael is about 40 grams.
59 Jonathan D. Spence, *The Search for Modern China* (New York: W.W. Norton, 1990), 129.
60 Ibid., 424–434.
61 Ida Pruitt, *A Daughter of Han* (Stanford, CA: Stanford University Press, 1967).
62 In imperial time, Chinese people had multiple names, rather than a single one for life, and they were called different names by different people, depending on the nature of the relationship. Ning Taitai was given a "milk name" at birth ("Little Tiger"), used only by her parents. Her older siblings called her Mei Mei ("Little Sister"). The neighbors called her by her family name and the number corresponding to her position among her family's children (Hsu Wuzi – the fifth child of the Hsu family). Once she was married, people would refer to her in relation to her husband, hence Ning Taitai (wife of Ning). When she became elderly, it was courteous to add *lao* (old) to her name to indicate her respected position (Ning Lao Taitai.) If she had gone to school (an option available only for boys through most of China during her childhood), she would have been given an official school name. It was also common for educated males to acquire a courtesy name to use publicly. In most cases in this chapter, I use

school names or courtesy names when referring to people. However, as an uneducated woman, Ning Taitai had neither.
63 Since my own family also comes from Shandong province (although from a different city) and shares her birth family's surname, I have often wondered if Ning Taitai and I are distantly related. There are many people named Hsu in Shandong Province, so it is unlikely. Nonetheless, I have a soft spot for Ning Taitai.
64 Pruitt, *A Daughter of Han* (Stanford, CA: Stanford University Press, 1967), 12.
65 Spence, *The Search for Modern China*, 129.
66 Ibid., 149. In late Imperial China, ordinary people used copper points for daily currency, but had to pay for important purchases – most notably their taxes – in silver. As more and more Chinese silver flowed to Britain, the price of silver went up in China with respect to copper. As a result, people had to pay more and more copper to buy the same amount of silver to pay their taxes.
67 Pruitt, *A Daughter of Han*, 46.
68 Ibid., 62–63.
69 Ibid., Chapter 7.
70 Ibid., 71.
71 Twitchett, "The Fan Clan's charitable estate," 97–133.
72 Pruitt, *A Daughter of Han*, 110. See the example of her "sworn mother," a peddler woman who helps Ning find work.
73 Ibid., 25–27.
74 At the time, the Chinese Nationalist regime had moved the capital to Nanjing, so Beijing was renamed Beiping. ("Jing" means capital.)
75 Ida Pruitt, Ning Taitai's American biographer, left China after the Japanese invasion. As a result, we do not know what happened in the rest of her life.

Bibliography

Beattie, H.J. 1979. *Land and Lineage in China: A Study of T'ung-ch'eng County, Anhwei, in the Ming and Ch'ing Dynasties.* Cambridge, UK: New York: Cambridge University Press.
Chan, W. (Ed.). 1969. *A Source Book in Chinese Philosophy.* Princeton: Princeton University Press.
Confucius. 1999. The Analects. In: W.T. De Bary and I. Bloom (Eds.), *Sources of Chinese Tradition* (2nd ed.). New York: Columbia University Press, pp. 44–63.
Constantelos, D. 1991. *Byzantine Philanthropy and Social Welfare* (2nd ed.). New Rochelle: Aristide D. Caratzas.
De Bary, W.T. and Bloom, I. (Eds.). 1999. *Sources of Chinese Tradition* (2nd ed.). New York: Columbia University Press.
Elman, B.A. 2000. *A Cultural History of Civil Examinations in Late Imperial China.* Berkeley: University of California Press.
Feierman, S. 1998. Reciprocity and assistance in precolonial Africa. In: W.F. Ilchman, S.N. Katz, and E.L. Queen (Eds.), *Philanthropy in the World's Traditions.* Bloomington: Indiana University Press, pp. 3–25.
Holy Bible: New American Standard Bible. 1995. LaHabre, CA: The Lockman Foundation.
Kozlowski, G. 1998. Religious authority, reform, and philanthropy in the contemporary Muslim world. In: W. Ilchman, S. Katz, and E. Queen (Eds.), *Philanthropy in the World's Traditions.* Bloomington: Indiana University Press, pp. 279–308.
Lo, M.M. and Otis, E.M. (2003). Guanxi civility: Processes, potentials, and contingencies. *Politics and Society*, 31(1), pp. 131–162.

Locke, J. 1980. *Second Treatise of Government*. Indianapolis: Hackett Publishing.

Mauss, M. 1967. *The Gift: Forms and Functions of Exchange in Archaic Societies*. New York: Norton.

Mencius. 1999. Selections from the *Mencius*. In: W.T. De Bary and I. Bloom (Eds.), *Sources of Chinese Tradition* (2nd ed.). New York: Columbia University Press, pp. 116–158.

Porterfield, A. 1998. Mount Holyoke missionaries and non-western women: The motivations and consequences of 19th century American missionary philanthropy. In: W.F. Ilchman, S.N. Katz, and E.L. Queen (Eds.), *Philanthropy in the World's Traditions*. Bloomington: Indiana University Press, pp. 215–235.

Pruitt, I. 1967. *A Daughter of Han*. Stanford, CA: Stanford University Press.

Salamon, L.M. 1994. The rise of the nonprofit sector. *Foreign Affairs*, 73(4), pp. 109–122.

Salisbury, H.E. 1989. 06/13; 2014/2. In China, "a little blood". *New York Times*. ISSN 03624331.

Smart, A. 1998. Guanxi, gifts, and learning from China: A review essay. *ANTHROPOS*, 93(4–6), pp. 559–565.

Smart, A. and Hsu, C.L. 2007. Corruption or social capital? Tact and the performance of *guanxi* in market socialist China. In: M. Nujiten and G. Anders (Eds.), *Corruption and the Secret of Law: A Legal Anthropological Perspective*. Burlington: Ashgate, pp. 167–190.

Smith, J.H. 1998. Chinese philanthropy as seen through a case of famine relief in the 1640's. In: W. Ilchman, S. Katz, and E. Queen (Eds.), *Philanthropy in the World's Traditions*. Bloomington: Indiana University Press, pp. 133–168.

Smith, J.H. 2009. *The Art of Doing Good: Charity in Late Ming China*. Berkeley: University of California Press.

Spence, J.D. 1990. *The Search for Modern China*. New York: W.W. Norton.

The Great Learning. 1999. In: W.T. De Bary and I. Bloom (Eds.), *Sources of Chinese Traditions* (2nd ed.). New York: Columbia University Press, pp. 330–333.

Tucker, M.E. 1998. A view of philanthropy in Japan: Confucian ethics and education. In: W. Ilchman, S. Katz, and E. Queen (Eds.), *Philanthropy in the World's Traditions*. Bloomington: Indiana University Press, pp. 169–196.

Twitchett, D. 1959. The Fan Clan's charitable estate, 1050–1760. In: D.S. Nivison and A.F. Wright (Eds.), *Confucianism in Action*. Stanford: Stanford University Press, pp. 97–133.

Watson, J.L. (1982). Chinese kinship reconsidered: Anthropological perspectives on historical research. *The China Quarterly*, (92), pp. 589–622.

Yang, M.M. 1994. *Gifts, Favors, and Banquets*. Ithaca: Cornell University Press.

3 The pioneer
From socialism to social entrepreneurship

Peter Xu and Golden Key

Peter Xu (Xu Bailun) was an architect in Beijing. In 1971, his life was derailed when he contracted a rare illness and lost his sight at the age of 40. He struggled with depression for years. But then Peter, who had become a Christian, felt a "call from God." He realized that, as an educated man with access to good health care and a pension, he was really quite fortunate. In China, most of the blind and visually impaired were poor peasants. As if their disability were not enough of a burden, the vast majority were illiterate. Their impoverished local schools were unable to serve children with disabilities, and their families had no money to send them to special schools for the blind.

In 1986, Peter decided to start an organization to serve these people. Golden Key would develop resources so that blind and visually-impaired children could receive an education in local schools. Peter believed that education was the "golden key" for these people to raise their "human quality" (*renkou suzhi*) and have a better life. Golden Key developed teacher training modules so that even poorly-educated rural teachers could educate blind children. It also designed and produced low-cost tools to make learning accessible, such as reading lights, magnifying glasses, and braille writers. Peter visited provincial and local political officials, offering his products and prototypes for their school systems. Twenty-five years later, Golden Key materials were used in a number of Chinese provinces. Most of the funding for the organization came from foreign sources, including European foundations.

It is hard to overstate how radical Peter Xu's actions were at the time. When he started Golden Key in 1986, private charities and social welfare NGOs were all but unknown in China. For that matter, they would remain rare in PRC for another decade. Even in the 1990s, Chinese newspapers felt the need to define the term "charity" (*cishan*) for their readers. In 1998, an article in the *China Society News* noted, "'charity,' this long unheard-of notion, has come up again and is being relearned by the public."[1] Part of the problem with "charity" (*cishan*) was that it was associated with the Christian missionaries, those imperialist bad guys who had been ousted from China in the socialist revolution of 1949. According to a *People's Daily* article published in 1994, for charity to be accepted as part of Chinese society, it would need to be "rehabilitated" and cleansed of its taint of political incorrectness.[2]

What made a blind man in his fifties decide to become a social entrepreneur in the People's Republic of China? How did he succeed, given that he had almost no experience with NGOs or private charities? Peter had spent his adult life working for a state institution, the Beijing Institute of Architectural Design. His wife and all their friends and relatives also worked for state organizations. What made Peter Xu decide that the right way to serve a vulnerable population was to personally start an independent, private organization, rather than to work through the Chinese government? On the other hand, why did Golden Key try to change the government-run public school system rather than to serve people directly?

To make sense of Peter's story, we need to understand how his life was embedded in a particular historical moment. When he was born, in 1931, China was in chaos, wracked by civil war and threatened by Japanese invasion. Twenty years earlier, the last Chinese emperor had abdicated, ending centuries of imperial rule. Twenty years after Peter's birth, China was controlled by the Chinese Communist Party under Mao Zedong, who implemented his own version of Marxist socialism. The imperial and the socialist political systems had very different ideologies and structures for serving the poor and needy. Peter Xu's charity would have been unimaginable in either. Yet Peter incorporated elements of imperial and socialist culture when he developed Golden Key.

Socialist paternalism under the Chinese Communist Party (1949–1976)

Peter Xu came from an educated, well-off, urban family, the kind of family that would be considered "high quality" 50 years later. Since this was well before the ideology of *suzhi* arose in China, however, Peter used different language when talking about his childhood. He described his father as "a man of culture," highly educated and well connected. In a previous generation, a man like this would have aspired to become a mandarin in the Imperial bureaucracy. But it was the twentieth century, so Peter's father was part of an intellectual elite that believed that state Confucianism had failed and needed to be replaced by a new, better political philosophy, one that could help China find its path to wealth and power. Young scholars devoured Western texts, seeking answers in books about liberalism, social Darwinism, fascism and Marxism. The arguments were not just academic. From 1927 to 1949, Mao Zedong's Communist Party and Chang Kai-shek's Nationalist Party fought a bitter civil war to determine whose philosophical vision would shape China's future. (The two sides united briefly after the Japanese invaded, but resumed battling against each other in 1945.)

In 1949, when Peter Xu was 18 years old, the Chinese Communist Party succeeded in taking over the Chinese mainland, driving the Nationalists to the island of Taiwan. In victory, Mao Zedong and his followers had gained a country of over 500 million people spread over a huge landmass. (In comparison, the 2015 population of the United States, which is about the same size, was about 320 million.) Decades of war and invasion had destroyed much of the country's infrastructure and devastated the economy, driving a substantial portion of the population into dire poverty. There was an urgent need for effective social welfare institutions.

Breaking with the past

Mao Zedong, the Communist leader, saw himself as a follower of Marx and Lenin, although he worked hard to revise their theories to fit "Chinese conditions." Regardless, it was a self-consciously revolutionary movement that explicitly rejected the past. Mao himself was a master storyteller. Through his speeches and his writings, as well as through his state propaganda system, he told the story of how the Chinese Communist Party (CCP) was leading the way to a New China and leaving behind an Old China, which had been miserable, weak, and impoverished by Western imperialism and Confucian "feudalism."[3]

The new leaders attacked and disempowered all the traditional sources of social welfare from the Imperial era: the meritocratic state, the gentry upper class, and the patriarchal clan. The Imperial government bureaucracy was overthrown, and the Confucian educational system condemned. The gentry were denounced as "exploiting landlords," and their property was confiscated and redistributed among the poor. Social clubs, religious institutions, and charitable organizations (including benevolent societies) were either destroyed or absorbed into the state sector.[4] Even the multigenerational clan was undermined as ancestor associations and family trusts were denounced as elitist and "feudal." Mao and his followers taught the Chinese to see themselves as members of nuclear families, rather than embedded in a complex network of extended kin. Beyond the nuclear family, everyone was part of a mass citizenry, relating to each other as comrades. In addition to attacking Chinese "feudalism," the new regime also attacked Western influence as "imperialism," expelling all foreign charities.

After overthrowing all the competing sources of charity, the party-state now had a monopoly on social welfare in China. Indeed, providing social welfare was the basis of the Communist Party's political legitimacy. According to Mao Zedong, the CCP deserved to rule China because it delivered an ever-rising standard of living to its citizens. Unlike Old China, he explained, New China was characterized by abundance and equality. In his speeches, Mao measured the success of the CCP against the old regime in terms of economic productivity.[5] State propaganda departments plastered the country with eye-catching posters depicting the prosperity of New China: lavish harvests, plump children, vigorous adults, sound houses, and wonderful consumer goods (see Figure 3.1). The reality of Chinese society never lived up to these glowing images, but they offered an aspirational view of what the future would be as long as Chinese citizens remained loyal to the Maoist regime.

46 The pioneer

Figure 3.1 "Mutual help in plowing has brought in more food," 1953.

Source: Li Qun, 1958, "Mutual Help in Plowing Has Brought in More Food, the Livelihood of the Army Dependents Has Grown Stronger" (互助代耕多打粮军属生活过得强). Publisher: People's Liberation Army Pictorial Publishing House. International Institute of Social History, Amsterdam/Stefan R. Landsberger Collections. Call number: BG E13/917. http://chineseposters.net/posters/e13-917.php.

Ironically, despite the revolutionary rhetoric of Mao Zedong, his ideology echoed the Confucian mandate where the Emperor had the right to rule because he could deliver prosperity and peace to his subjects. Mao's regime was just as paternalistic as the Imperial court, imagining the government as the parent and the citizenry as its children. However, in practice, Mao Zedong's socialist paternalism was quite different from the Imperial paternalism.

Contributing to society in a state-controlled economy

Without the aid of private charities or clan-based philanthropy, how could the state provide social welfare for the entire citizenry of China? The CCP set up a *redistributive economy*. Capitalist societies have *market economies*, where everyone sells and buys from each other. (Farmers grow apples, and then they sell apples to whoever wants to buy them. Rich people can buy more apples, while the poor may not be able to buy any at all.) In a redistributive economy, the state collects all the products and then redistributes them to the population according to its own rules of fairness. (All the apple farmers sell their apples to the government. The government then redistributes the apples to the population so that each person gets one apple.)

In reality, societies exist on a continuum between the two poles. Even in capitalist societies there is some government redistribution (schools, for example, or food ration books during war time), and markets never completely died out in China. Moreover, there were always local variations in state control in the PRC, even at the peak of government power. However, under Mao, the Chinese party-state controlled a significant proportion of the economy, especially in cities. It doled out rice, wheat flour, cotton cloth, bicycles, medical care, apartments, and farmland according to its own ideology-driven rationale. To its credit, in its first 15 years, the CCP did manage to raise the standard of living for the majority of its citizens (although the political miscalculations of the Great Leap Forward in 1958 caused three years of devastating famine in rural areas). The state was quite successful in providing urban residents with jobs, adequate food and shelter, and access to basic healthcare. Crime rates were low, and almost all children could go to school. Peasants in the countryside, who were the majority of the population, did not benefit as much as their counterparts in the cities, but most of them still lived much better than they did under the traumatic and unstable conditions of the first half of the twentieth century.[6]

Maoist China had no space for social entrepreneurs. Private charities or NGOs would have been seen as an affront to the CCP, a usurpation of its central mission. Instead, the government, operating through state corporatism, designated its own welfare organizations to take care of any citizens who fell through the cracks of the redistributive economy.[7] These included the China Welfare League, the Red Cross Society of China, the Women's Federation, and the Communist Youth League. Some of these organizations were former private charities absorbed by the state. Others were created by the government. Regardless, they were part of the party-state bureaucracy and controlled by the government. Social scientists refer to them with the amusingly oxymoronic name of GONGOs – government-organized NGOs.

In Maoist China, intelligent and ambitious young men such as Peter did not become entrepreneurs, social or otherwise. Instead, they sought positions in the state bureaucracy. In Maoist China's redistributive economy, the state had significant control over the supply of goods and services, but also over the distribution of jobs – at least the high-status jobs. Under Maoist socialism, the government managed all of the schools, universities, hospitals, sizable factories, railways, movie studios, research institutes, and museums, to offer just a partial list. As a result, it served as the gatekeeper to almost every white-collar or managerial position available in the PRC. There was no open job market for positions in these workplaces. Instead, young people were assigned state positions upon graduation from college or high school, but only if they were deemed worthy.

Despite the CCP's ideology of equality, in reality the Chinese party-state used its control over resources to create a new system of class stratification. Class was, of course, an enormously important concept in Mao Zedong's political philosophy. The purpose of the CCP revolution was to wrest power away from people in the bad classes (capitalists and landlords) and give it to people in the good classes (industrial workers and peasants).[8] Every citizen was assigned a class label, determined not only by their own occupation, but by their parents' position in society, in order to break the cycle of the unearned benefits exploitation passed down through the generations.[9] However, the government's new economic policies also created a new class hierarchy, one that favored urban industrial workers over agricultural peasants.

Those workplaces that were considered most important by the government (such as steel factories) received the most resources. The people who worked there received the best compensation packages available in the PRC, described by the Chinese as "iron rice bowls": lifetime employment, good wages, nice apartments, daycare centers, high-quality healthcare, generous pensions, and access to scarce consumer products. Other state workplaces only received "wooden rice bowl" compensation, with lower wages and fewer benefits. Urban citizens outside of the state economy had to fend for themselves in a society where few goods and services were available for sale. Within state workplaces, employees higher up on the hierarchy received better compensation than those in the lower reaches. Moreover, these desirable jobs were generally only available to urban residents. There was no rice bowl of any kind available to the majority of China's population, who were agricultural peasants residing in rural villages. The government organized rural residents into collectives or communes to increase productivity through economies of scale, and then expected them to contribute agricultural goods to the redistributive economy. (Even with all of these built-in inequalities, though, the gap between rich and poor was very small. The elite in Mao Zedong's China lived quite modestly, especially compared with the wealthy in a capitalist country – or in China today.)

The CCP justified this engineered inequality by promoting a moral system based on service to the "people" through the state.[10] According to this logic, those who contributed more to society deserved more compensation. Of course it was the Communist Party that decided what counted as a greater or lesser contribution, and insisted that the only contributions that mattered were the ones made as part of the party-state bureaucracy. The idea that entrepreneurship outside of the state could be a form of contribution was unimaginable. Business entrepreneurs were either labeled as "petty bourgeois," who were considered relatively harmless but useless, or as "capitalists," who were considered a danger to Chinese society. (Social entrepreneurship was not a concept that existed at all.) If the regime believed that heavy industry was the key to China's development, rather than light industry, then it would give steelworkers better compensation than the factory workers who made socks or candy. Because the Maoist regime wanted to industrialize China, it viewed manufacturing as more important than agriculture. Of course officials in the party-state bureaucracy, known as *cadres*, were the most important of all. Cadres not only ran the government, but they served as managers in all of the state-run factories, institutes, schools, hospitals, and welfare organizations.

To obtain a high-status, well-compensated position in the state bureaucracy, a young person had to develop the characteristics that the CCP found most valuable. These included skills and knowledge, of course, but also the correct political background and views. The system rewarded those who came from "good" class backgrounds. Ideal candidates were also well-versed in Mao's teachings, displayed ideological zeal and leadership skills, and remained loyal and obedient to the ruling regime.[11] Unfortunately, in Maoist China, few people possessed all of these virtues, and many tensions and conflicts arose over the proper weight to give to class background versus academic scores versus political enthusiasm.

As a young man in Mao Zedong's China, Peter Xu wanted to serve the people and make a contribution to society. From his point of view, the best and only way to do so was through a position in the state bureaucracy. Unfortunately, he came from a pre-revolutionary upper class background. Fortunately, he lived in the city, was a good student, a hard worker, and was politically correct. He trained as an architect and was assigned a position in a prestigious state institute in Beijing. He married a woman who worked in veterinary science, also at a high-level state research institute. They had three children. Their life was among the most pleasant that China under Mao had to offer. In a society that had supposedly erased class inequality, they were part of the upper class. Twenty years later, they would have been viewed as the perfect "high-quality" family: educated, urban, cosmopolitan, associated with the sciences, and highly cultured.

Then, in 1979, a shocking medical condition rendered Peter blind at the age of 40. Because of his "iron rice bowl" position, his work unit would take care of him for the rest of his life with a pension. However, Peter told me that he still felt "tortured" and miserable. He was "good for nothing," a worthless person in a society that valued contribution.

Going through the back door: *guanxi* as the key to survival

At this point, Peter's life took a bit of a detour, and so will we. To "prove the value of my life," despite his blindness, Peter decided to write a novel. He was inspired by the Soviet author, Nikolai Ostrovsky, who wrote *How the Steel was Tempered* when he was both blind and suffering from paralysis. The 1936 socialist realist novel and the 1942 Soviet film based upon it were very popular in China during Peter's youth. Young people like Peter idolized the self-sacrificing protagonist, a heroic soldier of the Russian Revolution. After four years of work, Peter showed his manuscript to his father, who introduced him to one of his friends, the well-known playwright and screenwriter Xia Yan. Xia Yan induced his daughter, who worked for a major state publisher, to take the manuscript around. The response was not positive, Peter told me with a rueful smile: "They didn't think it was worthwhile at all." Xia Yan kept in touch with Peter, gave him tips for improving his writing, and even showed him some of his own works in progress. The mentorship helped, and 1983, Peter published a science fiction novel for children. In Peter's words, "From 1971 till 1983, my writing was worth nothing. Finally, twelve years after I first became ill, I finally published a book, and fortune smiled at me."

Peter's foray into a literary career reveals the large role that social connections, or *guanxi*, played in socialist China. Although using *guanxi* seems like the

50 *The pioneer*

antithesis of philanthropic charity, it reveals what Chinese citizens had to do to ensure their own social welfare under Maoist socialism. *Guanxi* practice outlived Mao Zedong's regime, and eventually became a key ingredient for successful social entrepreneurship. Therefore, it is worth examining the ways that *guanxi* practice changed significantly from its premodern incarnation into its twentieth century version.

In Imperial times, people had *guanxi* with kin and friends/pseudo-kin (see Chapter 2, Figure 2.1), activating those relationships through the exchange of gifts and favors. Under socialism, however, *guanxi* practice became untethered from the family.[12] Marxist ideology and political campaigns attacked the institution of the Confucian clan. With the extended family network undermined, people had fewer kin with whom to build *guanxi* connections. They made up for this loss by drawing more "familiar people" (faux-kin) into their networks. We can see this by comparing the Imperial-era *guanxi* network in Figure 2.1 with the Maoist-era network in Figure 3.2A.

Under Maoist socialism, the practice of *guanxi* changed so it became much easier for a person to build a network through "familiar people." In the Imperial era, *guanxi* ties could only be activated through the exchange of gifts and favors with a person with whom one had a pre-existing basis for a relationship, such as a relative or a teacher. Instead, under the new post-1949 rules of *guanxi*, a person could build a *guanxi* relationship with anyone, just by offering or asking for a

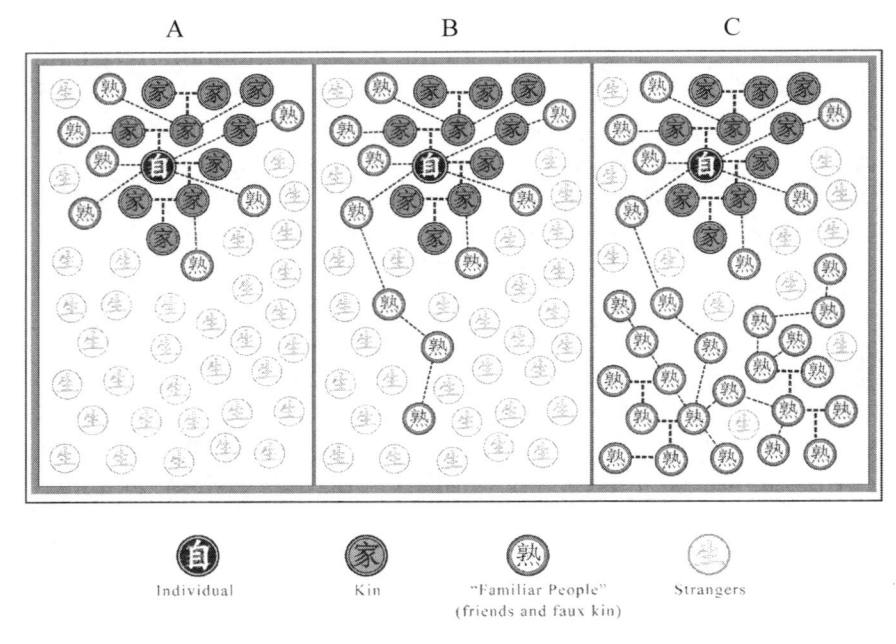

Figure 3.2 Expanding *guanxi* network in post-1949 China.
Source: illustration created by Lara Scott.

favor.¹³ It became possible to convert a stranger into a "familiar person" or "friend" simply by beginning an exchange of gifts or favors. For example, you could chat with a stranger on a bus, discovering during the course of conversation that he was a doctor and in the throes of planning his son's wedding. You could offer to introduce him to your cousin who worked at a liquor factory and could get him some bottles at a good price. The rules of reciprocity still applied; if someone gave you a gift or did you a service, you were obligated to respond with greater generosity. Two weeks after the wedding, assuming the alcohol had come through, you could approach your new "friend" for medical advice or access to a scarce drug. To fail to reciprocate was to lose "face" (*mianzi*), or standing in the community, so he must do his best to oblige you.

Under Maoist socialism (and long afterward) Chinese people insisted that a good *guanxi* network was more valuable than money and joked that studying "*guanxi*-ology" was more useful than any school subject.¹⁴ Chinese people needed to utilize *guanxi* because of the inherent flaws of Marxist socialism. By their very nature, redistributive economies are slow and ponderous.¹⁵ Because everything is managed from the top down, there is little room for flexibility or innovation. Under Mao, if a Chinese factory needed more supplies, it was impossible to buy them directly. Instead, its leaders had to go through layers of government bureaucracy to procure what they needed. Nor, with the iron rice bowl of permanent job security, was there any easy way to hire or fire employees. In response to these issues, firms and organizations hoarded resources and skilled workers so that they would be available in times of need, causing shortages elsewhere in the system. The fact that the party-state prioritized heavy industry over the production of consumer goods exacerbated the problems of scarcity for ordinary people.

All of this made life sufficiently frustrating for citizens in China (and the USSR, Poland, Romania, and every other Marxist-Leninist state) that they sought ways to work around the system.¹⁶ In China, people revived and adapted the *guanxi* practices of reciprocity and gift exchange that had once been anchored in the Confucian Five Cardinal Relationships (as described in Chapter 2). By exchanging goods and services among "familiar people" as "favors," *guanxi* allow people to access goods and services more efficiently than the ponderous bureaucracy would officially allow. The Chinese term for this was "going through the back door" (*zou houmen*). If bicycles were scarce, but you had a "familiar person" at the bicycle factory, she could find a way to get one for your family – in exchange for a much-coveted radio from your factory. A nice gift to a well-placed official allowed you to bypass obstructionist formal regulations and get the permit or paperwork you needed. If you had an established relationship with someone (even if the "relationship" had been established two weeks earlier on the bus), that person would work very hard to help you out.

However, in encounters with strangers, life was difficult. If you had no *guanxi* relationship with someone, they would do as little as possible for you, as anyone who had to deal with a Chinese bureaucrat or salesclerk during those years could attest. When Peter Xu wanted to publish his first manuscript, he did not approach a publisher directly. As a stranger approaching a stranger, he knew he would get nowhere. Instead, Peter worked through his father's friend, Xia Yan. When Xia Yan was unable to get the book published, he made up for his failure by becoming Peter's writing mentor.

Guanxi was especially useful because of what I call the "chain of favors" rule. (If Person X asked Person Y for a favor which Person Y could not provide, rather than refuse a friend, Person Y would turn to another member of her network (Person Z) to secure the favor.) Illustration B, Figure 3.2 demonstrates this. The "self" represented by the black circle could receive help from the "familiar person" at the end of the chain down in the bottom right-hand corner, even though the two have never met. This is what happened in Peter Xu's case. Peter asked his father for help with the novel. His father asked Xia Yan for a favor. Xia Yan asked his daughter, who worked for a publisher, to advocate for Peter's book. Under the "chain of favors" rule, each person is only obligated to the next person in the chain, rather than the stranger who may actually accomplish the favor. Peter would not have ended up in debt to Xia Yan's daughter, even if the book had been published. Instead, Peter owed his father for the favor, his father owed Xia Yan, and Xia Yan owed his daughter. The "chain of favors" rule meant that if Person X asked Person Z for a favor, he was not only accessing all of her resources, but the resources of her entire social network.[17] As illustration C in Figure 3.2 reveals, Chinese *guanxi* networks did not just have the potential to expand, but to expand exponentially.

Although "going through the back door" allowed families skilled at building *guanxi* to improve their conditions, it was generally not a good way for the poor and needy to access social welfare. Instead, *guanxi* was a system that favored the haves over the have-nots, and exacerbated class inequality. Those who had the most to gain through the game of *guanxi* were the ones who had the most to offer. Cadres in powerful positions were besieged by gift givers. People from well-positioned families were more likely to go to school with the children of important people. Unlike Peter Xu, most people would not have a father who was friends with a famous playwright. As we shall see, in the post-Mao era, *guanxi* continued to be important, and those with high levels of *suzhi*/quality had better networks than those with lower levels.

Guanxi also created conditions that easily devolved into corruption. Traditional norms of reciprocity and "face" made it difficult for political officials to turn down gifts and favors – and it can be a small step between grudgingly accepting gifts and actively soliciting bribes. Despite this, most people in China believed that *guanxi* could be practiced benignly, and indeed was necessary for survival. As Peter would soon discover, *guanxi* was also a key component of successful social entrepreneurship.

The fall of Maoist socialism and the rise of market socialism

In the 1970s, as Peter Xu suffered from depression and tried to reconstruct his life, Maoist socialism was also encountering its own difficulties. In the first half of the twentieth century, many nations experimented with socialism, from Eastern Europe and the Soviet Union to China and Vietnam. In most, the system imploded within a few decades for the same three reasons.[18]

First, redistributive economies are inherently inefficient, and they inadvertently encourage a destructive cycle of hoarding and scarcity. With decision-making tied up in bureaucratic red tape, flexibility and innovation are almost impossible. After an initial burst of economic productivity, growth stalls.

Second, the Communist Party's ideology insists that revolutionary fervor and lower class background are the most important virtues to be rewarded. Unfortunately, in most twentieth century socialist countries, the people who possessed these characteristics were usually poorly educated, and many lacked the necessary skills for running a modern, industrial economy. The people who had the education and expertise were often those, like Peter Xu, from "bad" class backgrounds (i.e. the old upper class), and they sometimes lacked the fervor of true believers. The regime vacillated between insisting on the one hand, that political criteria should be used for hiring and promotion, and on the other hand, admitting that expertise was more important than class background. As a result, many cadres in the state bureaucracy were long on enthusiasm, but short on competence.

Third, there is an inherent contradiction between the Communist Party's explicit ideology of equality and its actual practice of using economic perks to reward certain people over others. The party-state's propaganda machine taught people to be suspicious of the wealthy, but the system gave China's cadres all kinds of perks that were denied to ordinary citizens. Mao Zedong was appalled when the bureaucracy he established led to the rise of a new upper class, one that sometimes displayed the same kind of corruption and greed as the elites overthrown by the revolution. He responded by periodically launching political campaigns against corruption, nepotism and elitism. Seeking to return to the fervor and simplicity of the revolution, he whipped up mob sentiment to denounce the guilty.[19] The most destructive of these campaigns was the 1966 Cultural Revolution, which was so catastrophic that China descended into chaos for several years. The country did not fully recover its stability until 1976, the year that Mao Zedong died.

How Peter Xu became a social entrepreneur

Peter Xu was 45 years old in 1976, the year of Mao Zedong's death. Over the next couple of decades, Peter's life changed drastically, often in ways that would have been unimaginable under Maoist socialism. In 1983, he published his science fiction novel for children. He explained to me, "At the time, science fiction was very popular." In any case, he felt that as a published author, "I gained the acceptance of society and could continue my life." Where he had once sought self-validation through contribution to the state, he now found it through successfully entertaining paying customers.

Unfortunately, Peter's happiness was short-lived. His beloved wife became ill and died. Although the official diagnosis was lung cancer, Peter was convinced that the real cause was exhaustion:

> My wife was a scientist. She had worked day and night. She also had to help my children with their studies, help me find references for my writing, and manage our family. She had to do all of her work and all of the work that should been done by me. She couldn't keep up with it all and was diagnosed with lung cancer in the advanced stages. She cared for my minor ailment like it was a serious disease, but she treated her own serious disease like a minor ailment. And she finally passed away.

Distraught and heartbroken, Peter sought "some meaning from this painful experience." He found his answers in a place that would have been unthinkable a decade earlier: Christianity. The religion, which had been seriously suppressed under Mao and effectively banned during the Cultural Revolution, experienced a rise in popularity under market socialism.[20] In 2011, according to the Pew Research Center, there were 67 million Christians in China.[21]

Peter believed that God had a message for him. "I felt a call," he explained.

> I realize that my life was not the worst. I had experienced a good marriage and career, and I still had relatives, friends, and children. I had a pension for the rest of my life. But for those who are born blind, their life is so much harder. I was the proper person to help them.

His calling was confirmed in 1987, when he traveled to Hong Kong and met a Christian nun: "She told me the reason for my suffering is because God had chosen me." Although he did not know the term at the time, he was taking his first step on his journey to becoming a social entrepreneur.

Since there was a shortage of reading materials for blind children, in 1985 Peter decided to start a magazine for them. At first, he sought a state institute or office to sponsor his project. After all, as someone who had grown up under Maoist socialism, he assumed that this kind of service should come from the state. And as someone who had worked in the party-state bureaucracy, he had personal and family connections (*guanxi*) to make contacts. Even so, trying to start something new, without the help of his wife, was terrifying for Peter:

> Before that, I was always living in a very small circle with the help of my wife, so I had very little contact with the rest of society. I didn't even know the bus routes well, or much about the organizations I was trying to visit. It is very difficult for someone blind to go out in society, and sometimes society is not very welcoming to the blind. There were times I would arrive at an office, and they wouldn't even let me go in the door. Other times, they would talk to me briefly and politely show me out. There was little success but so much difficulty. Falling down in the street, not being able to find the toilet, missing meals.

Despite his hard work, Peter never found a sponsor. Thanks to his *guanxi* connections, many of his contacts have felt obliged to give him something, so he ended up with ¥12,000 (US$4000) in donations, but no one was interested in publishing the magazine. The funding was enough for him to start his magazine, but he would have to do it by himself. So Peter Xu, at the age of 54, found himself as the head of a start-up nonprofit. His only assistant was his wife's former carer, another Christian convert named Ruth Ji. (Eventually, Ruth would become Peter's second wife.)

The next year, two things happened that changed the direction of Peter's nascent organization. First, he discovered to his chagrin that only 3 percent of blind and visually impaired Chinese children were enrolled in school. In 1980s' China, most cases of blindness and visual impairment were caused by diseases related to poverty. Those who were stricken usually lived in rural areas served by under-resourced schools. Since these schools were not equipped to deal with disabled children, and since the families had no money to send the children to schools for the blind, these young people remained uneducated and illiterate. For Peter, it was a blow:

> I thought I had done so much for these children by publishing [the magazine]. And then I found out that only 3 percent of the blind children in China could get any benefit from it. What the children needed the most was not literature – because they can't read. What they need is to go to school. So I took helping them to go to school to be my responsibility.

Peter tried to use his connections to lobby political officials on behalf of education for the blind and visually impaired, but this had limited results. So he transformed his magazine into a charitable organization, an NGO. Although it continued to publish the magazine, its new focus would be to give blind and visually impaired children the key to improving their future: education. That is why he named it Golden Key, because he believed that schooling was the key to a better quality of life for these blind and visually impaired children. As we shall see, *suzhi* ideology was just emerging in China. Peter subscribed wholeheartedly to its central argument that the key to improving people was through improving their external conditions so that they could develop their level of quality.

Second, Golden Key found a new source of funding. Through Peter's Christian contacts – his *guanxi* connections – he built a relationship with two German charities for the blind: Christoffel Blinden Mission and Hildesheimer Blidenmission. He also developed a connection with UNESCO. These foreign sources ended up being the main donors for Golden Key, mainly because Peter never figured out how to access funding except through *guanxi*. With these resources, Golden Key attacked the obstacles preventing poor, rural blind and visually-impaired children from going to school. It developed teacher training modules so that even poorly educated rural teachers could serve these children. It designed and produced inexpensive lamps, magnifying glasses, braille writers and other tools that facilitated learning. Peter traveled to see provincial and county governments, lobbying officials to adopt Golden Key's materials for their schools. He had become a social entrepreneur, seeking opportunities where a little innovation could unleash a great deal of potential. His little organization, which never had more than four paid employees, transformed poor rural schools into valuable resources that served blind and visually-impaired children.

In later years, Peter became concerned about the blind and visually-impaired students that Golden Key helped to educate. What happened to them when they grew up? In China, one traditional area of employment for blind and visually-impaired people is acupressure massage therapy, a subdiscipline of traditional Chinese medicine (TCM). Golden Key began to offer scholarships for its best students to come to Beijing to receive training in acupressure massage. In 2007, it even opened a small TCM massage therapy center in order to offer some of its graduates employment, although most ended up working elsewhere in the city. (By this time, TCM acupressure massage parlors were common in Chinese cities.)

In 1986, a mere ten years had passed since the death of Mao Zedong, who had led a revolution to ensure that the Communist-Party-led state would be the sole source of social welfare for China's citizens. Yet in 1986, a middle-aged blind man started a foreign-funded private charity. Although Peter Xu could not realize it at the time, he was in the vanguard of a new social movement that would eventually lead to an explosion of social entrepreneurship 15 years later. What happened in China to make this possible?

Deng Xiaoping and market socialism

The changes in Peter's life reflected great changes in Chinese society. After Mao Zedong's death, a new generation of leaders rose up in China who were exhausted by ideological excesses and wanted pragmatic results. Under Deng Xiaoping, the CCP launched a new policy of "Reform and Opening Up" in 1978. Instead of a grand philosophical vision, these reforms sought practical solutions. Under Deng's leadership, the party-state implemented several significant policy changes.

First, the new regime was no longer interested in launching dramatic political campaigns. Many of the new leaders, including Deng Xiaoping, had experienced traumatic attacks during the Cultural Revolution and were justifiably wary of large groups of people being whipped up into an emotional frenzy. (In 1989, when crowds of students protested in Tiananmen Square, these leaders ordered the violent crackdown, which was televised around the world.) In contrast to Mao, Deng Xiaoping cared very little about ideological purity. He famously quipped, "It doesn't matter if a cat is white or black, as long it catches mice."[22]

Second, the new regime prioritized economic growth above all else, and was willing to compromise the redistributive economy in order to achieve it. Deng announced that his regime's "political objective" was to achieve an annual gross national product of US$1 trillion and a per capita gross national income of US$800 by the year 2000.[23] (He succeeded on both counts, posthumously.) To counteract the ponderous inefficiency of the government-controlled economy, he gave state firms more autonomy and flexibility. He wanted factory heads to act less like Communist Party cadres and more like capitalist managers.[24] Government officials should be judged by their ability to deliver economic growth, not political obedience. He also made it legal to start small private businesses in those economic sectors that the state deemed less important. Deng Xiaoping was a true believer in socialism, and he assumed that these small private businesses would remain marginal while the state economy would remain central. This assumption was wrong, but Deng's decision to unleash Chinese entrepreneurship resulted in over three decades of unprecedented economic growth in China.

After decades of denouncing capitalists, the Chinese started to see making money as a legitimate way to measure self-worth, at least under some circumstances. By 1983, Peter Xu could feel better about himself just because of book sales, regardless of the lack of socialist contribution involved. Twenty years later, when Golden Key opened up its TCM acupressure massage parlor, the shop was one drop in an ocean of Chinese small businesses.[25] Its clientele were the members of China's new middle class, stressed out by the fast pace and anxieties of competing in a market-driven society.

Third, Deng Xiaoping opened China up to international relations and international investment. For most of Mao Zedong's rule, China had been relatively isolated from the rest of the world, especially from capitalist countries.[26] While Mao taught Chinese citizens to contrast the glories of New China with the miseries of Old China, Deng Xiaoping explicitly compared China's economic conditions with those of Western capitalist nations.[27] Deng's goal was for China to become a major player on the global market. To that end, he was willing for the Chinese to learn from foreigners, even capitalists. For the first time in decades, some Chinese were permitted to travel abroad, and foreigners were allowed to come into China. Although the situation in China in the 1980s was still highly constrained compared with that of a capitalist country, foreign companies could start doing business in the PRC, and even set up joint venture companies. Some international books, magazines, TV shows, and movies became available for Chinese consumers.

With new opportunities to interact with the wider world, some Chinese people came in contact with foreign NGOs and charities. Many of the Chinese social entrepreneurs I interviewed had never heard of an NGO until they read about one in a magazine or encountered one while attending a conference abroad. In 1995, Beijing hosted the Fourth World Conference on Women. Many of the foreign women who attended worked for nongovernmental organizations. For Chinese participants, it was mind blowing to learn of all the different ways that people could address women's issues outside of the state. Before Deng's reforms, Peter Xu would have never been able to build a relationship with Christoffel Blinden Mission or with UNESCO. Indeed, it is unlikely that he would have become a Christian, or traveled to Hong Kong to meet the nun who explained his calling.

Fourth, Deng Xiaoping wanted to both shrink the size of the government bureaucracy and change the criteria for recruitment and promotion. He complained that during 30 years of Maoist policies, too many people had been hired and promoted through political criteria, rather than educational credentials and skills. As a result, intoned an article in a top state newspaper, too many cadres were of "a low cultural standard." The piece went on to explain that only people with at least a vocational college degree[28] were capable of "leading the masses and achieving the Four Modernizations [in agriculture, industry, national defense, and science and technology]."[29] The new regime made a concerted effort to recruit educated candidates. In 1984, only 4 percent of Communist Party members had a college degree, while 82 percent only had a junior high school education or less. By 1998, 43 percent of Communist Party cadres had some college education.[30]

Deng Xiaoping's focus on educational credentials, reinforced by the party-state's new recruiting policies, influenced popular views in several ways. On one hand, the message that educational credentials were the most valid measure of a person's worth was absorbed by ordinary Chinese citizens. As we will see in the next chapter, this message did not just come from the state, but from other sources as well. Eventually it coalesced into the ideology of *suzhi*: the belief that the quality of a person was the result of the quality of the conditions in which he/she grew up, especially in terms of schooling. So it is not surprising that when Peter Xu received his call from God and decided to help blind and visually-impaired children, his first strategy was to produce quality literature, and his second strategy was to improve access to education.

On the other hand, Deng Xiaoping's campaign to improve the educational qualifications of the cadre corps also had an unintended result: it made many Chinese citizens lose respect for cadres and begin to doubt the entire justification for the Maoist class hierarchy.[31] After all, the Chinese populace was being told over and over again by the highest authorities that the party-state bureaucracy was staffed with too many poorly-educated and poorly-qualified people. Yes, the regime was changing its policies, but it obviously was not going to be able to replace the entire mass of bureaucrats overnight. Plenty of cadres were still dead wood. At the same time that the state media was reinforcing the value of educational credentials, it was also devaluing the worth of class background and political devotion. The Maoist ideology of socialist contribution was being undermined, setting up the conditions for the rise of a new ideology of class stratification based on *suzhi*, which privileged the middle class over the working class.[32]

The declining status of cadres was exacerbated by other factors. As the market economy took off, China began experiencing inflation for the first time in decades.[33] Those who had been brave enough to start their own businesses made more money, but those with iron rice bowl salaries found themselves pinched. Positions in the state bureaucracy began to lose their appeal. At the same time, certain cadres were suddenly able to make a lot of money, under suspicious circumstances. After decades of socialism, China's market conditions were very underdeveloped. Cadres were some of the few people who had access to products to sell on the market. They could buy goods at state prices and sell them on the market for much more, making a killing. Thanks to a weak system of law, no one knew whether this was legal or not. Then again, since the new regime was no longer issuing political campaigns, cadres were also able to engage in overtly corrupt behaviors, such as soliciting bribes, with less fear of punishment. In 1989, anger over political corruption inspired hundreds of thousands of people to march into Tiananmen Square and other city centers in protest.[34]

As a result, the new idols of the age were no longer political heroes, such as the revolutionary soldier in Ostrovsky's *How the Steel Was Tempered*. Instead, they were entrepreneurs (*qiyejia*). In the 1990s, biographies of famous American capitalists were wildly popular in China. Lee Iacocca (Chrysler), Jack Welch (General Electric), Andy Grove (Intel), and Bill Gates (Microsoft) were household names in the northeastern industrial city of Harbin where I was conducting research. (I can only assume that Mao Zedong was rolling in his grave.) These particular capitalists were considered admirable because they combined intellectual "quality" with moneymaking; their business success was rooted in their high-tech knowledge.[35] Unlike cadres, they had high levels of *suzhi*.

For a man like Peter Xu, who wanted a better society, it no longer felt reasonable to uncritically trust the party-state to lead the way. The CCP-led government no longer seemed like an all-knowing father, wisely caring for its children and leading them to a future of prosperity. Instead, it was an inefficient, overstuffed bureaucracy run by fallible people, many of whom appeared to be incompetent and corrupt. With his education and connections, Peter resembled the high-quality capitalist heroes more than most of the cadres in the government did. Although Peter did try to lobby bureaucrats to pay more attention to the needs of blind and visually-impaired children, in the end he could not depend on them to carry out the innovative changes necessary to make a difference. He had to take matters into his own hands to develop the teacher training modules and design (and manufacture) the inexpensive braille writers. Like Bill Gates and the other entrepreneurial heroes, Peter Xu had to apply his own knowledge and experience to solve the problems that he was passionate about, developing new solutions to create the change that he desired in the world.

Social entrepreneur or socialist entrepreneur?

When Peter Xu founded Golden Key, he did not see himself as working in the tradition of the Chinese benevolent society. Even so, we can see some continuities. Like the philanthropic gentry of the late Imperial era described in Chapter 2, Peter was a highly educated, thoughtful man who believed that it was his moral duty as a person of privilege to help those less fortunate than himself. Like Yang Dongming, the inventor of the benevolent society, Peter sought to develop a new, more effective and organized way to channel the resources of the wealthy to help the needy. However, unlike his Imperial-era predecessors, Peter's charity was not embedded in the Confucian social network of family, friends, and neighbors. Whereas Yang Dongming invented a way so that his gentry friends could serve their less privileged neighbors in their own city, Peter Xu used money from strangers (donors in Germany) to serve others. And instead of serving people nearby, he sought out beneficiaries in the poorest, least developed regions of China, thousands of miles away from his urban life in Beijing.

Nor did Peter classify himself as a "social entrepreneur." After all, he started Golden Key in 1986, when the term had just begun to be popular in the West. While "entrepreneur" (*qiyejia*) became an important buzzword in the 1990s in China, "social entrepreneur" did not gain the same kind of traction.[36] Peter did not even know what an NGO or a private charity was before his contacts with Christians in the West. Rather than categorizing himself as something as admirable as an entrepreneur, he modestly described himself as an ordinary Christian who was trying to do good works in response to the blessings that God had given him. He believed that it was God who allowed him to be born into a high-quality family and to gain *suzhi* himself through his education and first career as a government architect. Therefore, it was only right that he tried to provide those afflicted with the same disability as himself with as much *suzhi* as possible.

Even in Golden Key, we can see Peter Xu's roots in Maoist socialism. As a bright and ambitious young man in the Mao Zedong's China, he followed the expected path and worked in the state bureaucracy. He served the people by obediently doing his part in a redistributive economy, and he was rewarded by an iron rice bowl of government benefits. From the ages of 18 to 45, Peter Xu was taught that the state held the ultimate responsibility for providing citizens with social welfare. In many ways, he never relinquished this belief. Golden Key was not designed to serve its beneficiaries directly, but to help the state do its job better. According to Peter:

> Our work is to support the government.... It is the government's responsibility, not mine, to provide nine years of public education [to all children]. But we promote and advance the work of the government by offering it a system. We provide the materials and we proved to the government that the work isn't too difficult to do. We show them through experiments on a small scale so they can do it on a big scale.

Every time Peter persuaded a county or province to adopt Golden Key's training program and materials, the visually-impaired students of an entire region would benefit. The government officials would often take the all the credit, but this did not bother Peter. What mattered to him was that the children were served. Golden Key changed the lives of blind and visually-impaired children by (gently, gradually) reforming the Chinese state.

Although some aspects of Peter Xu's social entrepreneurship can be seen as rooted in China's socialist past, his behavior was still revolutionary. It was radical to assume that a private individual could start a private organization in order to tell the Chinese party-state how to do its job better. It was radical in China to build *guanxi* connections to foreign foundations and use their money to help people you did not even know. It was radical to believe that entrepreneurship was not just about serving yourself and making money, but instead serving the people on your own terms. Peter Xu started Golden Key despite the fact that he had no experience or knowledge about nongovernmental organizations. He did this in a country where there was no legal support or infrastructure for this type of organization, and where local citizens had no tradition of giving donations to private charities. No one at Golden Key knew how to write grant applications or solicit funds from foundations.

Perhaps this is the reason why the organization never grew very large. When I first visited Golden Key in 2008, its offices were an overstuffed apartment in a nondescript neighborhood on the edge of Beijing. Besides Peter, there were only three other employees, one of whom was his wife, Ruth Ji. There were usually several volunteers working for the organization as well, but they turned over so quickly that Ruth complained that they were more trouble than they were worth. For Peter and for Ruth, Golden Key was a labor of love. But it was difficult to find anyone in the next generation willing to make the same sacrifices they did, so they just kept working and working. It was not until 2010, when he was 79, that Peter finally retired. He handed over Golden Key not to another social entrepreneur, but to the Chinese Disabled Persons Federation (CDPF), a government-run organization once headed by Deng Xiaoping's paraplegic son. In the end, Golden Key was absorbed by the state it had worked so hard to change.

When the government took over Golden Key, did a little spark of civil society die? Peter Xu did not see the transition in those terms. He was sad that no one was willing to take over the organization and continue its work after his retirement, but was pleased that the work would go on with the increased resources available from the state. Peter's concern about the takeover by the government was not the loss of autonomy, but instead that the pace of innovation would slow down or even cease. (We will discuss the stultifying effects of state bureaucracy in the next two chapters.) Indeed, from the perspective of populist democracy, the fact that Golden Key became part of the government could be seen as a victory. As discussed in Chapter 1, according to the populist democratic view, a good citizen is not one who successfully limits government power, but one who empowers the state to serve its citizens better.[37] In creating Golden Key, Peter had pioneered a new form of activist citizenship, a method for both bringing citizen concerns to the attention of the state and providing the state with a solution to address those concerns.

Notes

1 "The emergence of charity," *China New Analysis*, 1617 (1998): 1–10.
2 In Chinese Communist political language, "rehabilitation" referred to the transformation from politically incorrect to politically acceptable ("Bourgeois enemies" had to be "rehabilitated" into communist comrades before they could return to society). See Carolyn L. Hsu, "'Rehabilitating charity' in China: The case of Project Hope and the rise of non-profit organizations," *Journal of Civil Society* 4, no. 2 (2008): 81–96.
3 "Feudal" is a term that the Chinese Communists learnt from Marx. They use it even though there are significant differences between European feudalism and the Imperial

Chinese politico-economic system. For more on Mao's storytelling skills, see David Apter and Tony Saich, *Revolutionary Discourse in Mao's Republic* (Cambridge: Harvard University Press, 1994).
4 Nara Dillon, "New democracy and the demise of private charity in Shanghai," in J. Brown and P.G. Pickowicz (Eds.), *Dilemmas of Victory: The Early Years of the People's Republic of China* (Cambridge, MA: Harvard University Press, 2007), 80–102.
5 For example, in a 1957 speech, Mao proclaimed,

> In 1949, National Steel output was only a little over 100,000 tons. Yet now, a mere seven years after the liberation of our country, steel output already exceeds 4,000,000 tons. In old China, there was hardly any machine-building industry, to say nothing of automobiles and aviation industries; now, we have all three.
> (See Mao Zedong (Tse-tung))

"On the correct handling of contradictions among the people," in *Selected Readings from the Works of Mao Tse-Tung 1926–1963* (Honolulu: University Press of the Pacific, 2001 [1957]), 432–479, 444.
6 To learn more about the standard of living in urban China under Mao, see Martin K. Whyte and William L. Parish, *Urban Life in Contemporary China* (Chicago: University of Chicago Press, 1984). For conditions under Mao in rural China, see Anita Chan, Richard Madsen, and Jonathan Unger, *Chen Village: Under Mao and Deng* (2nd ed.) (Berkeley: University of California Press, 1992).
7 For more on state corporatism, see Chapter 1, second section.
8 Mao Zedong (Tse-tung) Mao, "On the people's democratic dictatorship," in *Selected Works of Mao Tse-Tung, Vol 5* (New York: International Publishers, 1954 [1949]). 411–24.
9 David S. G. Goodman, *Class in Contemporary China* (Cambridge, UK: Polity Press, 2014). Chapter 1.
10 For more on the ideology of contribution, see Carolyn L. Hsu, *Creating Market Socialism: How Ordinary People are Shaping Class and Status in China* (Durham, North Carolina: Duke University Press, 2007).
11 Susan L. Shirk, *Competitive Comrades* (Berkeley: University of California Press, 1982).
12 Ming-cheng M. Lo and Eileen M. Otis, "Guanxi civility: Processes, potentials, and contingencies," *Politics and Society* 31, no. 1 (March, 2003): 131–162.
13 Ibid., 138–139.
14 Mayfair Meihui Yang, *Gifts, Favors, and Banquets* (Ithaca: Cornell University Press, 1994).
15 Katherine Verdery, *What was Socialism, and what Comes Next?* (Princeton: Princeton University Press, 1996).
16 For a comparison of practices in China versus the USSR, see Carolyn L. Hsu, "Capitalism without contracts versus capitalists without capitalism: Comparing the influence of Chinese guanxi and Russian blat on marketization," *Communist and Post-Communist Studies* 38 (2005): 309–327. For more on the *guanxi*-like practices in USSR and post-Soviet Russia, see Alena Ledeneva, *Russia's Economy of Favors* (Cambridge, UK: Cambridge University Press, 1998). For Poland, see Janine Wedel (Ed.), *The Unplanned Society: Poland during and After Communism* (New York: Columbia University Press, 1992). For Romania, see Katherine Verdery, *What was Socialism, and what Comes Next?* (Princeton: Princeton University Press, 1996).
17 The "chain of favors" is one of the key ways that Chinese favor practices were different (and more productive) than those in Russia. See Carolyn Hsu, "Capitalism without contracts versus capitalists without capitalism: Comparing the influence of Chinese guanxi and Russian blat on marketization," *Communist and Post-Communist Studies* 38 (2005): 309–327.

18 Much of this argument about the inherent flaws of socialism comes from Verdery, *What was Socialism, and what Comes Next?*
19 For an excellent description of political campaigns and the toll they took on Chinese society, see Chan, Madsen and Unger, *Chen Village: Under Mao and Deng* (Berkeley: University of California Press, 1992).
20 For more on the dramatic rise of Christianity in China since the 1980s, as well as its culturally unique practices and theology, see Daniel H. Bays, *A New History of Christianity in China* (Chichester, West Sussex; Malden, MA: Wiley-Blackwell, 2012), 241; Nanlai Cao, *Constructing China's Jerusalem* (Stanford, CA: Stanford University Press, 2011).
21 Pew Research Center's Forum on Religion & Public Life, *Global Christianity*, December 2011, Appendix C. www.pewforum.org/files/2011/12/ChristianityAppendixC.pdf.
22 Li Hong, *China's Political Situation and the Power Struggle in Peking* (Lung Men Press, 1977). 107.
23 Deng Xiaoping, "Our magnificent goal and basic principles," in *Selected Works of Deng Xiaoping*, Vol. 2 (Beijing: Foreign Language Press, 1994 [1984]), 85–87.
24 Deng Xiaoping, "Carry out the policy of opening to the outside world and learn advanced science and technology from other countries," in *Selected Works of Deng Xiaoping*, Vol. 2 (Beijing: Foreign Languages Press, 1984 [1978]), 143–144.
25 For more on entrepreneurship in China, see Carolyn Hsu, "Cadres, Getihu, and good businesspeople: Making sense of entrepreneurs in early post-socialist China," *Urban Anthropology and Studies of Cultural Systems and World Economic Development* 35, no. 1 (Spring, 2006): 1–38, www.jstor.org/stable/40553488.
26 The Chinese Communist Party was initially strongly supported by the Soviet Union. But beginning in 1956, ideological differences began to split the two countries apart. In 1961, the CCP denounced the Communist Party of the Soviet Union under Khrushchev as "revisionist traitors."
27 For example, in a 1977 speech, Deng Xiaoping complained:

> Now it appears that China is fully 20 years behind the developed countries in science, technology, and education. So far as scientific research personnel are concerned, the United States has 1,200,000 and the Soviet Union has 900,000, while we only have 200,000.
>
> (Deng Xiaoping, "Respect knowledge, respect trained personnel," in *Selected Works of Deng Xiaoping*, Vol. 1 (Beijing: Foreign Languages Press, 1984 [1977]), 53–54, 53)

A year later, he snapped, "If the rate of growth of the productive forces in a socialist country lags behind that in capitalist countries, how can we talk about the superiority of the socialist system?" See Deng Xiaoping, "Hold high the banner of Mao Zedong thought and adhere to the principle of seeking truth from facts," in *Selected Works of Deng Xiaoping*, Vol. 2 (Beijing: Foreign Language Press, 1984 [1978]), 137–139, 139.

28 Unlike a college that offers bachelor's degrees, vocational colleges offer two- or three-year degree programs that focus on a technical skill. Although they are considered significantly less prestigious than bachelor's degree colleges, even in the 1980s only a tiny percentage of the Chinese population had any post-secondary schooling at all.
29 Carolyn L. Hsu, *Creating Market Socialism: How Ordinary People are Shaping Class and Status in China* (Durham, North Carolina: Duke University Press, 2007), 87.
30 Ibid., 87–88.
31 Ibid., Chapter 4.
32 D.S.G. Goodman, *Class in Contemporary China* (Cambridge, UK: Polity Press, 2014).
33 The rate of inflation in 1978 was less than 1 percent. In 1988, it was over 18 percent.

34 In the Western media, the Tiananmen protests were framed as a pro-democracy movement. Although democracy was an important issue, both the student protesters and the urban citizens who joined them listed corruption as their most important concern. See Craig J. Calhoun, *Neither Gods nor Emperors: Students and the Struggle for Democracy in China* (Berkeley, CA: University of California Press, 1994), 246–248.
35 Carolyn L. Hsu, *Creating Market Socialism: How Ordinary People are Shaping Class and Status in China* (Durham, North Carolina: Duke University Press, 2007), 139–140.
36 Carolyn Hsu, "Cadres, Getihu, and good businesspeople: Making sense of entrepreneurs in early post-socialist China," *Urban Anthropology and Studies of Cultural Systems and World Economic Development* 35, no. 1 (Spring, 2006), 1–38.
37 Elizabeth J. Perry, "The populist dream of Chinese democracy," *Journal of Asian Studies* 74, no. 4 (2015), 903–915.

Bibliography

Apter, D. and Saich, T. 1994. *Revolutionary Discourse in Mao's Republic*. Cambridge: Harvard University Press.
Bays, D.H. 2012. *A New History of Christianity in China*. Chichester, West Sussex; Malden, MA: Wiley-Blackwell.
Calhoun, C.J. 1994. *Neither Gods nor Emperors: Students and the Struggle for Democracy in China*. Berkeley, CA: University of California Press.
Cao, N. 2011. *Constructing China's Jerusalem*. Stanford, CA: Stanford University Press.
Chan, A., Madsen, R., and Unger, J. 1992. *Chen Village: Under Mao and Deng* (2nd ed.). Berkeley: University of California Press.
Deng, X. 1994 [1984]. Our magnificent goal and basic principles. *Selected Works of Deng Xiaoping*. Beijing: Foreign Language Press, pp. 85–87.
Deng, X. 1984 [1977]. Respect knowledge, respect trained personnel. *Selected Works of Deng Xiaoping*. Beijing: Foreign Languages Press, pp. 53–54.
Deng, X. 1984 [1978]. Carry out the policy of opening to the outside world and learn advanced science and technology from other countries. *Selected Works of Deng Xiaoping*. Beijing: Foreign Languages Press, pp. 143–144.
Deng, X. 1984 [1978]. Hold high the banner of Mao Zedong thought and adhere to the principle of seeking truth from facts. *Selected Works of Deng Xiaoping*. Beijing: Foreign Language Press, pp. 137–139.
Dillon, N. 2007. New democracy and the demise of private charity in Shanghai. In: J. Brown and P.G. Pickowicz (eds.), *Dilemmas of Victory: the Early Years of the People's Republic Of China*. Cambridge, MA: Harvard University Press, pp. 80–80–102.
The Emergence of Charity. 1998. *China New Analysis*, 1617, pp. 1–10.
Global Christianity. 2011. Washington, DC: Pew Research Center.
Goodman, D.S.G. 2014. *Class in Contemporary China*. Cambridge, UK: Polity Press.
Hong, L. 1977. *China's Political Situation and the Power Struggle in Peking*. Hong Kong: Lung Men Press.
Hsu, C.L. 2005. Capitalism without contracts versus capitalists without capitalism: Comparing the influence of Chinese guanxi and Russian blat on marketization. *Communist and Post-Communist Studies*, 38, pp. 309–327.
Hsu, C.L. 2006. Cadres, Getihu, and good businesspeople: Making sense of entrepreneurs in early post-socialist China. *Urban Anthropology and Studies of Cultural Systems and World Economic Development*, 35(1), pp. 1–38.

Hsu, C.L. 2007. *Creating Market Socialism: How Ordinary People are Shaping Class and Status in China.* Durham, NC: Duke University Press.

Hsu, C.L. 2008. "Rehabilitating charity" in China: The case of Project Hope and the rise of non-profit organizations. *Journal of Civil Society*, 4(2), pp. 81–96.

Ledeneva, A. 1998. *Russia's Economy of Favors.* Cambridge, UK: Cambridge University Press.

Lo, M.M. and Otis, E.M. 2003. Guanxi civility: Processes, potentials, and contingencies. *Politics and Society*, 31(1), pp. 131–162.

Mao, Z. 1954 [1949]. On the people's democratic dictatorship. *Selected Works of Mao Tse-tung, Vol 5.* New York: International Publishers.

Mao, Z. 2001 [1957]. On the correct handling of contradictions among the people. *Selected Readings from the Works of Mao Tse-Tung 1926–1963.* Honolulu: University Press of the Pacific, pp. 432–479.

Perry, E.J. 2015. The populist dream of Chinese democracy. *Journal of Asian Studies*, 74(4), pp. 903–915.

Shirk, S.L. 1982. *Competitive Comrades.* Berkeley: University of California Press.

Verdery, K. 1996. *What Was Socialism, and What Comes Next?* Princeton: Princeton University Press.

Wedel, J. (Ed.), 1992. *The Unplanned Society: Poland During and After Communism.* New York: Columbia University Press.

Whyte, M.K. and Parish, W.L. 1984. *Urban Life in Contemporary China.* Chicago: University of Chicago Press.

Yang, M.M. 1994. *Gifts, Favors, and Banquets.* Ithaca: Cornell University Press.

4 The perfect *suzhi* fairy tale

Project Hope's poster girl

From peasant to professional

Figure 4.1 "A rock as a desk," 1993.

Source: Project Hope marketing image, taken in Yunnan Province, 1993. Permission for use given by the China Youth Development Foundation.

The children did not understand why the people from the city wanted to take pictures of them with expensive cameras. They were not used to people like this coming to their schools and paying attention to them. They certainly did not know that their photos would be used in posters, billboards, newspapers and magazines in cities all over China in the 1990s. Printed in dramatic black and white, the images were stark and arresting. They depicted the adorable, but grubby children in their decrepit schools, trying to study under miserable conditions (see Figure 4.1). The photos were accompanied by text describing a

The perfect suzhi *fairy tale* 67

crisis in rural education in China: high dropout rates, rising fees, crumbling facilities, insufficient supplies, and overburdened and underprepared teachers. But, the text went on, you could help. You could contribute money to Project Hope and sponsor a child or a school.

Emotional pleas from child-sponsorship charities, featuring the photos of poor children, may have been common in the West for decades, but no one had seen anything like this before in China. Indeed, no one had ever heard of a child sponsorship program. Despite its novelty, the advertising campaign was extremely effective. Millions were moved to donate money to Project Hope and to sponsor children.

The most famous Project Hope advertisement featured a little girl with big, pleading eyes, holding a pencil. The caption read, "I want to study, too" (see Figure 4.2). For people all over China, the weight of her gaze felt like an emotional blow. They gave her a nickname: "Big Eyes." By some estimates, her image was used 100 million times.

The girl in the photo was Su Mingjuan, and the photo was taken when she was eight years old and a beneficiary of Project Hope. She was the daughter of peasants who lived in the mountains of Anhui Province. She had no idea that her face was famous in cities all over China until three years later, when she was "discovered" by doctors in a nearby town when she became so ill she required a trip to the hospital. The farmer's daughter from the little village found herself

Figure 4.2 Su Mingjuan: "I want to study, too," 1991.

Source: Xie Hailong, Project Hope marketing image. Photo taken in Anhui Province, 1991. Permission for use given by the China Youth Development Foundation.

treated like a celebrity, interviewed by reporters and invited to appear on television shows. When Su Mingjuan was accepted into a top university in her province in 2002, it made national news in China.[1] When she was recruited for a position in one of China's biggest banks in 2010, the People's Daily offered photos of a sophisticated, glamorous Su Mingjuan, in a professional outfit and sleek hairdo, posed in front of her iconic Project Hope photo.[2]

It was the perfect fairy tale ending. Yet this particular fairy tale was a very different kind of story than the ones told in Mao Zedong's China. This was not a socialist story of a paternalistic state that took care of its obedient citizens and led them to a bright future. It was a *suzhi* fairy tale, where an individual was given the right conditions to develop herself and raise her quality, thereby raising the quality of her community and of her nation. Instead of being saved by the Communist Party, the heroine was rescued by a charity started by a social entrepreneur. Instead of being transformed from exploited victim to socialist citizen, Su Mingjuan was transformed from a low-quality peasant girl into a high-quality, modern, cosmopolitan professional. The key to her salvation was not communist ideology but education. Where did this fairy tale come from? And why was it that the Chinese found it so compelling that they were willing to open their wallets and give money to a type of organization that they had never encountered before?

The social entrepreneur

Su Mingjuan's life changed because of Project Hope, arguably the most famous charitable campaign in turn-of-the-century China. Project Hope was run by a very successful and rather controversial organization called the China Youth Development Foundation (CYDF). Its founder was a charming and ambitious social entrepreneur named Xu Yongguang.

Like the People's Republic of China, Xu Yongguang was born in 1949. He grew up in Wenzhou, a midsized city in Zhejiang Province. His father, a shopkeeper, died when he was a baby, so the family was very poor. Xu Yongguang told me that Wenzhou is known in China for its entrepreneurs, and he was born with "the Wenzhou spirit." However, in the 1950s and 1960s, an entrepreneurial spirit was not valued in China. His four older siblings used education as a means for social mobility, becoming schoolteachers. Unfortunately, Xu's own schooling was disrupted by the Cultural Revolution (1966–1976) so after middle school he first became a soldier and then a factory worker. When the Cultural Revolution was over, the self-motivated and intelligent young man managed to secure a position in the Communist Youth League in Beijing. The Youth League is the junior branch of the Chinese Communist Party, an organization for young people between the ages of 14 and 28 who are being groomed for Communist Party membership.

Xu told me that as he rose through the ranks of the Youth League, he started to wonder whether he really wanted a political career. This was a radical notion in the 1980s. Even though Deng Xiaoping had launched his market socialist reforms in 1978, working for the party-state bureaucracy was still seen by most people as the best career path available in China. But Xu did not want to be a cog in a bureaucratic machine for the rest of his life. He wanted to implement his own ideas and be his own boss. More importantly, Xu had found a cause: rural education. His work for the Youth League had taken him to China's rural areas. In Guangxi Province, he had discovered that poor peasant children were dropping out of school at an alarming rate.

At the time, Chinese law guaranteed every child nine years of state-sponsored education. In the 1970s, one of the crowning achievements of the Chinese socialist state was that 100 percent of the relevant age group was enrolled in primary school.[3] But Deng Xiaoping's market socialist reforms had shrunk the size of the national government. More and more of the responsibility for local education had devolved onto provincial and local governments. Meanwhile, the redistributive economy was declining, slowly being replaced by a more market-based system. This led to an economic boom, but the new wealth was not evenly distributed across China. Cities along the southern and eastern coasts grew wealthy, and the farmers closest to them could grow rich selling their produce in urban markets.[4] However, the rural areas far away from urban centers were left behind. Some regions even suffered economic declines as financial support from the national government weakened. Remote areas found it difficult to retain teachers because the state no longer controlled the job market and educated people could find better career opportunities in cities. Local school districts, struggling to cover costs, began to charge their students fees, and the fees grew higher every year.[5] Poor rural families began pulling their children out of school and putting them to work.

I should point out that it is difficult to find concrete evidence that the number of rural school dropouts actually increased in the 1980s compared with, say, the 1950s and 1960s.[6] It is also difficult to accurately compare the quality of education in rural areas between those two time periods. But even if the condition of rural schools had not worsened, what Xu Yongguang saw still appalled him. What had undoubtedly increased in China was the gap in the standard of education available in rich versus poor communities. In eastern and southern cities, new money poured into schools until they were indistinguishable from their First World counterparts. As a result, middle-class urban schoolchildren worked on state-of-the-art computers while in the countryside, some schools had no heat and could not afford chalk. For a successful cadre like Xu, accustomed to the best schools of Beijing, the conditions at these poor rural schools were shocking.

What made it even more upsetting, Xu explained to me, was that almost no one in China's urban middle class had any idea that conditions were this terrible for children in their own country. It was never mentioned by the government-controlled media, which had no interest in disseminating stories that made the state look bad. Xu was convinced that if middle-class urbanites could learn about the problems facing rural education, they would want to channel some of their wealth to help these children: "People didn't know about the problem. They couldn't see it. And the government didn't publicize it. It didn't make them look good.... But I felt that if people just knew about it, they would definitely want to help."

Interestingly enough, even though Xu Yongguang worked for the Chinese Communist Youth League, he did not expect direct government action to solve the problem. Instead, he was convinced that there was an alternative, better way to deal with the issue. If he could just raise public awareness of the plight of these children, people with means would surely be willing to give money. If he could just channel those resources effectively, rural schools and schoolchildren would benefit. In other words, Xu wanted to engage the issue as a social entrepreneur, rather than as a bureaucrat.

What happened next is a matter of some debate. According to Xu, he and several colleagues left the Communist Youth League in 1989 to start the China Youth Development Foundation (CYDF). Some journalists and scholars dispute this account and argue that the Chinese Youth League actually founded CYDF and ran it. In other words, they insist that CYDF was never an independent NGO, but instead a GONGO (a government-organized NGO).[7] As we shall see in the next chapter, the relationship between the Chinese Youth League and CYDF has always been highly entangled and complicated. Yet under Xu Yongguang, CYDF operated as an independent organization with apparently minimal (if any) state interference at the administrative level.[8] On the other hand, it is important to note that CYDF would never have been as successful as it was without the *guanxi* that Xu Yongguang had with a very powerful Communist Party organization.

In any case, what is not up for debate is CYDF's innovation and success. It began collecting donations in 1989 for an endowed fund. Immediately, however, contributors expressed dissatisfaction with their money going into a general pot of money rather than to a specific beneficiary. Xu explained to me, "Donors were writing in, asking to be able to choose the child they supported. They wanted a relationship, to help the students in other ways." Instead of the distant giving relationship that characterizes much of Western charity, these donors wanted *guanxi*. They sought a more Confucian-style reciprocal relationship with their beneficiaries, where an exchange of gifts and favors reinforced an emotional connection. In 1991, Xu came up with the idea to allow donors to "adopt" a child through a sponsorship program. Although such models have been common for decades for Western charities, Xu said that he had never heard of them. Given that Xu, at that point had almost no experience or contact with Western charities, his claim is plausible. (This was prior to the rise of the internet, after all.)

The response was immediate and overwhelming. By 1992, over 300,000 children were sponsored. By 1994, the number had risen to one million. Project Hope developed a program to allow wealthier donors to sponsor entire schools, funding construction, infrastructure, teacher training, and/or supplies. At its tenth anniversary in 1999, the China Youth Development Foundation could boast of helping over two million students return to school and of building more than 7000 "Hope" schools in impoverished regions. It also spawned a host of imitators.[9]

How did Xu Yongguang and CYDF persuade Chinese citizens to care so much about a social problem that almost nobody noticed before 1989? The answer lies in Project Hope's brilliant marketing campaign, featuring (among other things) Su Mingjuan's big, pleading eyes. First, pictorially, the photos reconfigured familiar elements of Chinese socialist propaganda art to offer a new story about China. Second, this new story resonated so powerfully because it tapped into Chinese people's growing obsession with quality, or *suzhi*.

Art inspires the masses

Socialist propaganda posters: ideal people in an ideal China

In the early 1990s, when Project Hope posters and advertisements first appeared in China, they caused a sensation. CYDF had taken the familiar tropes of socialist propaganda posters and turned them on their head. Socialist propaganda posters were familiar to everyone in China because they were visible everywhere during the Maoist era. From the 1950s to the early 1980s, they were one of the only forms of art and decoration that most people could afford. Cheap and widely available in state-run bookstores, the Chinese put them up not only in their offices and factories, but even in their homes to bring a little color to their drab living spaces.[10]

This, of course, was exactly what the Chinese Communist Party (CCP) intended. Its goal, after all, was to transform the Chinese people into socialist citizens. Because so much of the population in the early years of the PRC was illiterate or semi-literate, the visual arts were a vital weapon in the Communist Party's arsenal. By making brightly colored propaganda posters available and affordable even to peasants, the government ensured that almost every flat surface was conscripted to proclaim the party-state's messages. Propaganda posters promoted new policies, disseminated useful information, and taught good practices (such as hygiene and vaccinations). Above all, these posters sought to change China by giving its citizens models of ideal behavior, ideal values, ideal people, ideal communities, and an ideal society.

Mao Zedong had strong ideas about the role of art in shaping communist society. In 1942, seven years before he became the leader of the PRC, he declared that the purpose of art was to serve the masses by raising their standards. He proclaimed,

> ...life as reflected in works of literature and art can and ought to be on a higher plane, more intense, more concentrated, more typical, near the ideal, and therefore more universal than actual everyday life. Revolutionary literature and art should create a variety of characters out of real life and help the masses to propel history forward.[11]

Chinese socialist propaganda posters offered concrete images of New China, featuring hyper-realistic people in hyper-realistic settings. Most of the posters depicted people. Mao Zedong was the favorite subject, but posters also showed

72 The perfect suzhi *fairy tale*

Figure 4.3 "Lead the people to victory," 1975.
Source: Geng Yuemin. Publisher: Jilin Renmin Chubanshe, second edition, print number 8091.658, International Institute of Social History, Amsterdam/Stefan R. Landsberger Collections. Call number: BG E13/341. http://chineseposters.net/toomanybooks/17–20.php#18.

idealized versions of ordinary citizens. The men, women, and children in these images were bursting with robust health, with stocky bodies, glossy hair, and straight teeth. In Chinese culture, the color red is traditionally associated with celebration, health, and youth, so poster painters made everyone's skin ruddy and dressed them in a lot of red clothing.[12] Propaganda posters also reinforced Maoist theories of class. The perfect citizens depicted in the images almost all came from the "good" lower classes, with workers, peasants, and soldiers most common (see Figure 4.6).

In the propaganda posters, the central human subjects are often surrounded by symbols of abundance and progress. For example, in Figure 4.3, the children are well-fed and healthy and wear colorful, well-maintained clothing. They sit in a clean, bright room full of books. A soccer ball is at their feet, reinforcing the fact that they have plenty of time for leisure. Everything in the picture looks brand new: their clothes, the books, the ball, the furniture, and even the bows in the girls' hair. In Figure 4.4, a well-dressed, pink-cheeked girl sits amidst a bounty of flowers. Behind her is a dreamlike landscape, depicting the content of her thoughts. It is filled with images of China's technological prowess from the past, present, and future. There is the Great Wall, but also a concrete dam, skyscrapers, rockets, and spaceships.

According to these images, Chinese history moves in a single direction, progressing from a worse past to a better future. Moreover, it is the Chinese

The perfect suzhi *fairy tale* 73

Figure 4.4 "Studying for the mother country," 1986.
Source: Li Kong'an. Publisher: Lingnan Meishu Chubanshe, International Institute of Social History, Amsterdam/Stefan R. Landsberger Collections. Call number: BG E13/412. http://chineseposters.net/posters/e13-412.php.

Communist Party that leads the way as the country progresses into modernity. In the 1950s, 1960s, 1970s, and 1980s, these propaganda posters simultaneously offered an image of a desirable future and served as a reminder of how far China had already come under the rule of the Chinese Communist Party. Although reality fell far short of the idyllic images of the propaganda posters, children were healthier, women were less oppressed, and consumer products were more available than before the revolution. New China was better than Old China. In contrast to the pre-revolutionary decades of civil war, invasion, and chaos, life was already more peaceful and prosperous, and it would surely only be better in the future.

Trapped in Old China: Project Hope advertisements

When Xu Yongguang and CYDF designed Project Hope's advertising images, they took the familiar tropes of socialist propaganda posters and manipulated them in ways that made the end results feel both familiar and shocking to viewers. Like the socialist propaganda posters, Project Hope images were hyper-realistic. They also focused on a single individual or a small group of people set

74 *The perfect* suzhi *fairy tale*

against a symbolic background. Like many propaganda posters, Project Hope images portrayed winsome children, full of aspirations. But these Project Hope children were not ruddy, chubby cherubs enjoying the prosperity of New China; they were grubby, gaunt, and sad. Instead of engaging in recreation and growth, they were struggling against terrible obstacles. Instead of clean, beautiful, modern surroundings, they were surrounded by symbols of poverty: dirt, decaying infrastructure, and inadequate resources.

The children in the Project Hope image shown in Figure 4.1 crouch on a dirt floor in bare feet, and they use rocks in lieu of desks. Their lives are nothing like those of the children in Figure 4.3 with their soccer ball, fun books, and pretty clothes. Su Mingjuan, in Figure 4.2, sits at a desk and holds a pencil, just like the little girl in Figure 4.4 – but she has no bow her hair or lace on her collar. Instead of dreaming of a bright future, she gazes imploringly at the viewer and begs for help.

If the socialist propaganda posters declared that New China was better than Old China, CYDF's Project Hope photographs implied that Old China still lived on, tragically. In choosing to publish its photographs in black and white, Project Hope evoked prerevolutionary images associated with misery, exploitation and poverty. The advertisements looked disturbingly similar to the black-and-white photographs from the early twentieth century that the Communist Party used as evidence of how terrible life was before the Revolution. They also looked like an even earlier form of political art: revolutionary woodcuts. In the 1930s and 1940s, Chinese leftist artists adapted Western-style woodcuts to create powerful, accessible images.[13] Like the socialist propaganda, the purpose of this art was to engage the populace and change their thinking and behavior. However, instead of inspiring obedience through idealized pictures, revolutionary woodcuts wanted to rouse the masses to radical political action against the Japanese invaders and Chang Kai-shek's conservative Nationalist Party. They did so by creating stark black-and-white images of exploitation, suffering and poverty (see Figure 4.5).

Like the revolutionary woodcuts, CYDF's Project Hope photographs offered black and white images of innocents suffering from unjust circumstances, mired in grim poverty and dirt. By using elements of both prerevolutionary woodcuts and socialist propaganda, Project Hope created a jarring and painful juxtaposition. At first glance, the photos in the advertisements seemed to be from the grim past of Old China, but they were in fact from the present. The pictures told a story: these poor children were trapped in the past, stuck at some previous level of development. Worse, as long as they were trapped in the past, so was China itself. It was not progressing to modernity in the way that it should, but instead parts of it remained "backward" (*luohou*), falling further and further behind the developed countries of the world.

Who was to blame for this terrible situation? According to CYDF's Project Hope advertisements, it certainly was not the children themselves. They were innocent and precious, not delinquent, lazy, or genetically substandard. Nor did the photos blame their parents or relatives, who were absent from the story depicted. Instead, the culprit was the low-quality conditions that surrounded the

The perfect suzhi *fairy tale* 75

Figure 4.5 "After the guard in charge of the grain has gone (victory)," *c.*1945–1947.
Source: Li Hua. Picker Art Gallery, Colgate University, gift of Professor and Mrs Theodore Herman, 1968.43.

children: the crumbling walls, the dirt floor, the freezing classrooms, the decrepit (or missing) desks, the nonexistent school supplies, and the overburdened, undertrained teachers. It was these external conditions that prevented these children from developing their *suzhi*. As a result, they could not grow into the high-quality modern Chinese citizens that they were supposed to become. By extension, China could not develop into a high-quality, modern nation.

Therefore, the solution to save these children (and to save China) was to improve the *suzhi* of the conditions that surrounded them. What the children needed were better school buildings, desks, books, pencils, and teachers. According to these images, external conditions, rather than internal characteristics, were the key because external conditions would shape the internal person. (There was no hint that the children needed to improve their "self-esteem," which was the buzzword in the United States during this time period.) In contrast to the socialist propaganda posters, these children would not be saved by politically correct beliefs or faith in the Party. Indeed, the state is completely absent from the story. Instead, Project Hope claimed that the solution would come from private donations, which would fund high-quality educational conditions to allow these children to develop into the high-quality adults that China needed them to be.

Project Hope's powerful images also offered a subtle critique of Maoist theories of class. The children in these photos are obviously poor peasants, but their lower-class background is not a source of socialist virtue. They are in a rural setting, but it is nothing like the environment of verdant fields and abundant harvests of the socialist propaganda posters of the 1950s and 1960s (see Figure 3.1). Instead, the viewer is supposed to feel pity for these children because they are not members of the urban middle class. Mao Zedong's hierarchy of classes had been turned on its head.

The rise of *suzhi* ideology

CYDF's Project Hope advertising campaign was so successful not only due to its brilliant use of pictorial imagery, but also because its central story drew upon a worldview centered on *suzhi*. The ideology of quality was already a popular belief system among the urban residents CYDF targeted. They already believed that a person's character is not determined by genetics, but instead is molded by external circumstances, especially during childhood. They already believed that a critical mass of high-quality people leads to a high-quality community and a high-quality nation, and that the converse is also true (low-quality people lead to a low quality nation). They also believed that they knew what high-quality people looked like: they had good educational credentials and earned a lot of money in white-collar jobs. They were cosmopolitan urbanites. They understood science and technology and all the new innovations of modern life. They were also self-controlled and morally upright. And last but not least, they were highly cultured, adept in Tang poetry, traditional calligraphy, and Western classical music.[14] Where did these beliefs come from?

"To read many books is harmful" – Mao Zedong[15]

Suzhi ideology argues that education is the key to creating virtuous people and producing economic development.[16] I have often been told by both Chinese and non-Chinese people, "The Chinese have always valued education." After all, for thousands of years, China was ruled by a meritocratic bureaucracy, where political power was given to educated people on the basis of an academic examination. If this is true, perhaps there is nothing new about *suzhi* ideology. Unfortunately, it is not true, historically speaking. Despite stereotypes, the Chinese have not always valued education, and formal schooling was particularly devalued in the decades directly prior to the rise of *suzhi* ideology. The military debacles and economic crises of the late nineteenth and early twentieth centuries not only took down the last Imperial dynasty, but undermined the legitimacy of the entire Confucian meritocracy. The fact that Western nations could defeat and humiliate China was taken as evidence that the Confucian obsession with learning was not that useful or valuable after all.

When Mao Zedong and his Chinese Communist Party took over China in 1949, they insisted that they, as representatives of the revolutionary working class, possessed the true knowledge for national development. The highly educated, who were known as "intellectuals," were seen as part of the problem rather than the solution.[17] After all, intellectuals almost always came from the oppressor upper classes. As a result, Mao Zedong's regime promoted political education as far more valuable than academic education. In socialist propaganda posters, learning takes place at home, at factories, in villages, and in fields, but almost never in a classroom. Students are taught by workers, peasants, soldiers, children, but almost never by teachers.[18] (In Figure 4.3, the children are not learning from a teacher in a classroom, but from political propaganda books about socialist heroes.) Similarly, the images are ambivalent at best about intellectuals, who are recognizable because they wear eyeglasses. (Among the extravagantly healthy people portrayed in socialist propaganda posters, intellectuals are the only ones consistently depicted with a physical disability.) In propaganda art, intellectuals were far less likely to be portrayed than peasants, workers, or soldiers (see Figure 4.6).[19]

Despite Mao Zedong's ambivalence toward academic education and intellectuals, the new regime required the expertise of educated people, whose

Figure 4.6 "Hold high the great red banner of Mao Zedong thought: thoroughly smash the rotting counterrevolutionary revisionist line in literature and the arts," 1967.

Source: Designer unknown. Publisher: Shanghai Renmin Meishu Chubanshe. International Institute of Social History, Amsterdam/Stefan R. Landsberger Collections. Call number BG E13/719. http://chineseposters.net/posters/e13–719.php.

skills and knowledge were a scarce commodity. In the 1950s and 1960s, the regime vacillated between emphasizing ideological purity at the expense of productivity, or seeking productivity at the risk of losing political control. When the state prioritized productivity, it hired well-educated people for cadre positions, regardless of their problematic class background. When ideology was ascendant, the state would attack intellectuals for being elitist and reactionary and promote cadres who came from lower class backgrounds and exhibited political zeal. The most extreme swing to ideological purity (and ideological fanaticism) was the Cultural Revolution (1966–1976), when the entire educational system was denounced. Mao called on students to attack their teachers and take over their schools, and many responded enthusiastically and violently. All educated people, whether they were doctors, professors, bureaucrats, or writers, were valid targets for abuse. (In Figure 4.6, the intellectuals are the pathetic little gray figures at the bottom, crumpled beside their broken spectacles. The three heroes in the image are, from left to right, a peasant, a soldier, and a worker.)

A Beijing worker recalled how his illiterate father, a Communist Party activist, harangued professors at one of China's top universities:

> The old man can't read a word, but there he was giving all those university people shit. The Cultural Revolution screwed me up from when I was a kid, but that's just how it was: "All power to the proletariat." "Studying to become an official" was criticized, and everyone was talking about studying being useless. You should have seen all us little seven-year-old farts running around criticizing this stuff. We were full of crap! But what use is studying? My teacher only made fifty yuan a month, half of what my dad got, and he was much older than Dad.[20]

Far from viewing education as inherently valuable, many Chinese families during this time debated whether educational credentials were worth the investment.[21] A good school performance might raise a person's chances of being assigned to a desirable iron rice bowl position by the state, but it could also cause a person to be a target in the next political campaign. Perhaps it made more sense to lay off the books and focus more on demonstrating political obedience and zeal.

Quality over quantity: Deng Xiaoping's reforms

How did *suzhi* ideology, which worships almost everything the Cultural Revolution condemned, become the dominant ideology in China a mere two decades after the death of Mao Zedong? It was not the product of government policies and propaganda, although certain policies and types of propaganda certainly contributed to it. Instead, *suzhi* ideology was assembled by ordinary Chinese citizens out of the elements taken from the global environmental movement, Deng Xiaoping's reforms, intellectuals' anti-government protests, and messages from (and about) Western capitalists.

The term *suzhi* was first promulgated by the state, as part of Deng Xiaoping's 1978 market socialist reforms.[22] Prior to that, the term *suzhi* denoted a person or thing's inborn nature before it has been affected by society.[23] This, ironically, is the opposite of its current definition. The roots of the new definition may have come from the West. As we shall see in Chapter 6, in the early 1970s the global environmental movement began having some influence among certain officials in the Chinese party-state. One of the environmental arguments that had a huge effect on the PRC was that unchecked population growth led to poverty and disaster.[24] Before the 1970s, Mao had actually promoted population growth as a strategy to strengthen the nation.[25] The Deng regime, by contrast, was persuaded the key to a higher *quality* population was to decrease the *quantity* of people. This was the central premise of the 1980 Birth Planning Policy, known somewhat erroneously in the West as the "One-Child Policy." (From its inception, the policy allowed certain families to have a second child, and it started adding exceptions to the one-child rule almost immediately.[26])

To promote this new policy, the CCP invented a new term: "human population quality" (*renkou suzhi*).[27] This is the first known use of *suzhi* in the contemporary definition, where it denotes not a person's inborn nature but the result of a carefully managed external environment. Birth control propaganda exhorted families to choose "quality" (*suzhi*) over "quantity," insisting that with fewer children, each child could receive more cultivation and investment. According to the campaign, "quality" was represented by the educated, middle-class, urban, one-child family, surrounded by symbols of science and technology (see Figure 4.7). Propaganda linked the development of the child to the development of the nation. In 1986, when the poster in Figure 4.7 was published, skyscrapers were a rare sight even in the middle of Beijing or Shanghai, and no Chinese city even remotely resembled the scene depicted behind the woman and her child. According to the image, reducing the number of children would help China reach this glorious, modern, urban, and high-tech future. The mother in the image is not dressed in the symbolic garb of a worker, peasant, or soldier, but as a member of the middle class.

The term *suzhi* spread to other areas of state discourse. In 1985, the CCP Central Committee announced a new set of education reforms, whose basic goal was to "raise the *suzhi* of the people of the nation."[28] Starting in the late 1980s, "*suzhi* education" (*suzhi jiaoyu*) became the shorthand term to describe a suite of educational reforms designed to move away from a focus on testing and memorization and toward a more comprehensive, competence-based system. According to these reforms, the purpose of education should be to improve the quality of students, not just prepare them to pass exams. By the mid-1990s, *suzhi jiaoyu* had become a popular phrase in the Chinese media.[29] The reforms and the term cemented the association between education and quality.

Population control was not the only place where Deng Xiaoping wanted to promote quality over quantity, and school reform is not the only place where the

80　*The perfect* suzhi *fairy tale*

Figure 4.7 "Carry out family planning, implement the basic national policy," 1986.
Source: Zhou Yuwei. Publisher: Liaoning "Xin Jiating" Baoshe. International Institute of Social History, Amsterdam/Stefan R. Landsberger Collections. Call number BGE13/415. http://chinese posters.net/posters/e13–415.php.

regime made a connection between education and *suzhi*. Deng and his followers believed that Mao Zedong's ideological policies had burdened China with a government bureaucracy that was too large, and that too many of the cadres working for the party state lacked the knowledge and skills they needed. From Deng Xiaoping's point of view, Mao's periodic attacks on education and intellectuals were a terrible mistake that did nothing but derail China's economic growth. What the PRC needed, he believed, was economic growth propelled by science and technology. He proclaimed:

> Without modern science and technology, it is impossible to build modern agriculture, modern industry or modern national defense. Without the rapid development of science and technology, there could be no rapid development of the economy.... With the same manpower in the same number of man-hours, people can turn out scores or hundreds of times more products than before.[30]

Under Deng Xiaoping's regime, academic and research institutions were revived and even expanded, and intellectuals were allowed to lead these organizations with less government interference.[31] In addition, Deng established that the most important criteria for Communist Party membership and cadre rank should be educational credentials, not class background, ideological enthusiasm, or seniority. In doing so, he upended the Maoist class hierarchy. Those from low class backgrounds with nothing but political enthusiasm and loyalty to offer found themselves passed over. Meanwhile, people with good educational credentials were recruited and promoted to the best positions in the party-state bureaucracy, regardless of their class background.

After the abuses and humiliations of the Cultural Revolution, it is no wonder that Chinese intellectuals were initially enthusiastic supporters of Deng Xiaoping and his reforms. Yet ten years later, in 1989, many of these same intellectuals were protesting vehemently against the government in Beijing's Tiananmen Square. What happened?

In their exuberant embrace of the new regime, many of China's intellectuals made a fundamental error. They assumed that the reforms and new emphasis on *suzhi* meant Deng Xiaoping intended to return intellectuals back to their Confucian position, as the state's moral conscience and political advisers.[32] Rather than focusing on academic and scientific work, narrowly defined, some Chinese intellectuals began to act as though they were responsible for China's fate. They launched an effort to design better guiding principles for the nation, and they offered government officials critiques of political policies.[33] For example, although Fan Lizhi was an astrophysicist rather than a political scientist, this did not stop him from publishing criticisms of Deng Xiaoping, the CCP, and Marxism in general – or from encouraging his students to form political protest movements.[34]

Not surprisingly, Deng Xiaoping and the rest of China's political leaders were displeased with these activities. They had been envisioning China's intellectuals as a tame force for economic progress, not as political advisors, co-rulers, or fomenters of dissent. Once again, the Communist Party had to struggle with the old tension between the state's desire for economic development and its need for political control. Fan Lizhi was ousted from his university and denounced by Deng Xiaoping in the official press. Throughout the 1980s, the state periodically attacked and suppressed intellectuals through vague and confusing political campaigns, which infuriated the educated classes.

Chinese intellectuals had another reason to feel frustrated in the 1980s – a new ailment that they called "money fever." These scholarly people had naïvely assumed that China's citizenry would react to the relative freedom permitted by Deng Xiaoping's reforms by embracing scholarship and putting intellectuals back on the pedestal where they belonged. Instead, they discovered that most Chinese people were more interested in embracing new opportunities to make money and to spend it. People didn't want to study; they wanted to shop. "Professors are not respected," grumbled one scientist. "We were poor [under the Nationalists], but the common people always respected professors. You might still find that respect among older people today. But not the young."[35]

Although intellectuals disparaged "money fever," this did not stop them from complaining about their own perceived poverty. This was a complaint rooted more in perception than reality. Deng Xiaoping's reforms had raised the standard of living of most educated people. However, in contrast to life under Mao, now intellectuals had to watch other people flaunt their wealth, while their lives remained relatively unchanged. In the 1980s, there were three main ways to strike it rich in China, none of which appealed to intellectuals.

First, party-state cadres who had access to goods at state prices could sell them at market prices. It was not clear at all whether this practice was legal or illegal, and many political officials reaped considerable profits. Although the vast majority of intellectuals worked for the state, they were rarely in a position of power over saleable products. Second, ordinary citizens could leave their state sector jobs to start their own small businesses. Because many people distrusted the reforms, fearing a return to more hardline socialism, this was considered very risky. In fact, the slang term for leaving a state position to start a business was "jumping into the sea" (*xia hai*). In addition, since no one had access to much capital, this usually meant peddling homemade goods, opening a small restaurant, or buying products in one city to sell in another. Consequently, this strategy was most appealing to people who never managed to get a good state position to begin with, those with low levels of education and political capital.[36]

Third, it was possible to make a lot of money by working for one of the international companies now moving into the PRC, since salaries were much higher there than at Chinese firms.[37] Eventually, the presence of global corporations in China would increase the value of academic qualifications. After all, foreign capitalists trusted the value of educational degrees, while viewing political credentials, such as Communist Party membership, with suspicion. However, in the early years of the market reforms, the first foreign companies that came to China were in the service sector, such as high-end hotels. Since they were initially staffed by administrators and managers from overseas, these companies had no need to hire intellectuals. Instead, they hired pretty girls and handsome boys as receptionists and wait staff and paid them very well.

None of these three strategies for getting rich required much education. And none of them looked attractive to China's intellectuals, who were strongly invested in the value of their knowledge and their diplomas. Watching crass cadres cruise by in Mercedes-Benzes, noodle shop owners buy new furniture, or hotel girls flaunt their new designer clothes, China's most educated people came down with a bad case of "red-eye disease" (jealousy).[38] To make things worse, in the late 1980s, inflation began rise. Although the PRC never experienced the hyperinflation that plagued other developing countries, rising prices were still a shock to the system for the Chinese who had experienced almost no inflation for decades. For those on fixed state salaries, like most educated professionals, it was upsetting to see their purchasing power erode while vulgar peddlers and immoral cadres profited from rising prices. When Deng Xiaoping's policies to shrink the size of the government began to affect university budgets, scholars and students were incensed enough to launch a public protest. These protests culminated in 1989, in Beijing's Tiananmen Square.

The problem with the government is low-quality cadres

In Tiananmen Square, protesters argued that the Chinese Communist Party was unfit to rule, in part, because its leaders lacked education, and therefore *suzhi*. The Western media coverage of the Tiananmen Protests focused on the students' demand for democracy. However, when surveyed, students claimed that the purpose of the movement was to end political corruption.[39] According to their speeches, posters, and banners, all of China's problems (inflation, inequality, etc.) were due to rapacious political officials, who exploited rather than served the people.

> These "people's public servants" have used the blood and sweat of the people to build palatial retreats all over China ... To buy foreign luxury vehicles, and go abroad on pleasure trips with their children, and even with their children's nannies!... While the country suffers, a tiny handful benefit, and the people end up shouldering the debt.[40]

Why were China's political leaders so corrupt? According to the student protesters, it was because they lacked a sufficient level of education. As one dissident explained:

> We can now see that the proletarian Party in China lacks the promise that Marx had described. For historical reasons, the Chinese proletariat inevitably was congenitally deficient: their number was small, relatively young, and at a low level of cultural development and education.[41]

Ironically, these complaints were not all that different from Deng Xiaoping's own criticisms of China's cadres when he denounced the low education level of party-state bureaucrats. The student protesters, who were soon joined by their professors and other intellectuals, combined Deng's argument with Confucian beliefs about education and morality. They insisted that educated people were better than uneducated people not just because they were more competent, but also because they were more cultured, refined, self-controlled, ethical and wise. Therefore, China's low-quality cadres should be removed and replaced by people of quality. As one protest poster proclaimed, the Chinese Communist Party had failed to "put the strongest men [sic] and the most outstanding minds to work on creating material wealth for society."[42] It was time to right that wrong.

The protesters' argument would not have mattered if only the highly educated had found it persuasive. But China's intellectuals were not the only people who felt stung by rising rates of inflation and upset by the spending habits of the nouveau riche. Urban workers, once touted as the core of the revolution, were

84   *The perfect* suzhi *fairy tale*

also on fixed state salaries with declining purchasing power.[43] They also felt bewildered and offended by the topsy-turvy economic inequality and the displays of conspicuous consumption.[44] For decades, they had been taught to denounce such behavior in political campaigns. Finally, someone was giving them an explanation for all the confusing transformations of the past few years, and providing them with a target for their frustrations: corrupt cadres. Hundreds of thousands of workers flocked into city squares to join the protesters, transforming the student movement into a national crisis. (However, China's peasants, who made up 80 percent of the population at the time, largely ignored the protests.)

The state violently suppressed the protest movement, infamously dispatching soldiers and tanks into Tiananmen Square. Yet although the dissident movement was crushed, its message about corrupt cadres and low quality still maintained its power. The party-state was unable to ignore these accusations, and it spent the next few years devising policies and programs to address the protesters' concerns. It launched a series of major anticorruption campaigns, pageants where scapegoated cadres were publically punished to great media fanfare.[45] (These anticorruption campaigns continue to be an important part of political theater in the PRC. In 2015, President Xi Jinping made waves by arresting Zhou Yongkang, one of the most powerful leaders in the CCP, for bribery, disclosing state secrets, and abusing power.[46])

The party also moved away from claiming that its political legitimacy came from any ideological or moral foundation. Instead, it rebranded itself. It claimed that the Communist Party deserved to rule China not because it was communist, but because it provided economic opportunities and social stability for its people, conditions that allowed people to develop themselves and develop China. It was an economic manager, not an ideological torchbearer.[47] The CCP abandoned Maoist class categories in its language and instead claimed its goal was to expand the middle class.[48] This story successfully undermined the student protesters. Intellectuals might be more moral than cadres, but could China's people really trust idealistic, passionate students to run the country well enough for continuous economic growth? As it embraced its role as economic manager, the party-state shifted even further from politicized criteria and more toward educational credentials for hiring and promoting cadres.

In its endeavor to reclaim its political legitimacy, the CCP was helped by economic growth. The Tiananmen massacre undermined China's economy for a couple of years but, after that, global capitalists found the Chinese market too tempting to resist. Foreign companies and foreign investments poured into the PRC, building not just hotels but factories and technology research labs. These international and joint-venture firms still paid enviable salaries, but now they were searching for people with academic degrees, not just pretty hostesses. The domestic private sector also grew, and more and more Chinese became interested in the stories of world-famous business people, such as Lee Iacocca, Jack Welch, and Bill Gates. The heroes of the new age were no longer cadres and revolutionaries, but well-educated technology entrepreneurs.

The path of glory: ordinary people assemble **suzhi** *ideology*

No doubt the Chinese government, antigovernment protesters, and international business people believed that they all held very different, even oppositional, views about China and its future. Ordinary citizens, however, focused on the areas where the arguments converged. Everyone seemed to agree that educational credentials were a more accurate measure of quality than the political criteria that had mattered so much under Mao Zedong's regime. Everyone also seemed to agree that high-quality, educated people were the ones who could contribute to China's development into a wealthy, modern, middle-class, cosmopolitan, scientific nation. Birth control propaganda posters, political speeches, magazine advertisements and television commercials all concurred that high-quality people lived in cities, had plenty of money, enjoyed consumer products, and were very, very happy.

More importantly, *suzhi* ideology helped people make sense of market socialist China in a way that Maoist socialist ideology no longer could. It provided a moral framework for the market socialist economy. It explained why getting wealthy under certain circumstances was admirable while in other cases it was corrupt. Essentially, it offered a new and persuasive class hierarchy, where class position is determined by the amount of *suzhi*.[49] It taught people what they should do if they wanted to succeed in this new society; they should develop themselves through education. It gave people a way to believe that virtue was rewarded, and that contributing to the collective good resulted in benefits to the individual. As educational credentials became more admired, they also became more practically useful. More and more companies and organizations used educational credentials as their criteria for hiring and promotion. People wanted to patronize the businesses owned by well-educated people because they seemed more trustworthy than those with low levels of *suzhi*.[50]

When I conducted interviews in the northeastern city of Harbin in the late 1990s, the ideology of *suzhi* was already prevalent. Out of 82 interviewees, 62 told me that the most respected people in China were intellectuals, not political officials or business owners. A 22-year-old waitress explained that if someone went to school, "even if they don't have money, they'll have *suzhi*. Not like those people who dress in fancy clothes, but when they open their mouths, it's clear that they don't have culture." A restaurateur concurred: "There's a qualitative difference [literally, a difference in *suzhi*] between college graduates and other people." A low-level government worker said:

> Now intellectuals really have the respect of common people. They see them as "talent" and admire that. Because we all know that it's knowledge – that the state has developed to the certain level, but to go forward will need all kinds of knowledge, including agricultural development, high technology products.... Without culture, knowledge, you just can't do it.

When I interviewed people who had lower levels of education, they would often tell me, "You shouldn't talk to me. My quality is so low." Yet, like everyone else I interviewed, they believed that their children could become high-quality people through education. I asked a woman who ran a market stall what her hopes were for her 16-year-old son:

> Hope? Of course I hope he studies well, gets good grades, and gets into a good college.... Middle-aged people all would really like their kids – and it doesn't matter if they are boys or girls – to be devoted to their work, to progress in their studies, to get into college, and go overseas and study abroad. That's the path of glory we all want, isn't it?

At that point, she turned to the people sitting in the stalls nearby for confirmation, and they all nodded and murmured their agreement. For the parents I interviewed, the more education, the better. Over and over again, I heard the mantra, "a key high school, a famous college, and then go overseas for graduate school, Masters, PhD, go all the way."

(I have a PhD from an American university, and the fact that I had actually achieved "the path of glory" caused some of my interviewees to treat me with awe and respect. This is something I have never experienced in the United States. One high school student, the daughter of migrant workers, actually squealed, "I can't believe I'm talking to someone with a *doctorate*!" It was like being a very nerdy minor celebrity.)

Nor was it just talk; parents spent real money in their quest to imbue their children with *suzhi*. Even though most of the people I interviewed only had one child (a few had two), they reported investing half or more of their income in their offspring's education.[51] Working-class parents enrolled their children in extracurricular classes in English, computing, piano, and calligraphy. For example, in 1998, a Harbin factory worker told me that although he and his wife earned less than ¥900 a month (about US$110), they spent 60 percent of it on their son's studies. They paid ¥20 an hour for each of the boy's multiple tutors. "My wife says we will sell the house out from under ourselves to support his schooling. Most people are like this, now that we only have single children. You make money for your kids." I discovered that the most closed-mouthed interviewees would open up to me if they were parents and if I asked about their children's education. Previously shy or even hostile subjects would launch into detailed descriptions of their strategies for cultivating their offspring's quality, or pour out their concerns about their son or daughter's lack of progress despite parental efforts.

A world seen through the lens of *suzhi*

Suzhi, *stress, and discrimination*

The rise of a worldview based on *suzhi* has its costs. In too many cases in China, it has been used by people of "high quality" to treat people of "low quality" as second-class citizens. In rural areas, cadres have used it to justify policies that oppress their peasant constituents. In cities, middle-class urbanites have used *suzhi* ideology to rationalize a range of discriminatory and exploitative practices against migrants from the countryside.[52] An urban planning professor from one of Beijing's top universities snootily recommended that rural people should be screened through an examination before being permitted to migrate to the city. "If villagers enter the city, but their quality doesn't have a corresponding improvement, their consciousness doesn't have a corresponding change and they hold onto their original behaviors and habits," declared Professor Wen Guowei.[53] (It should be noted that this suggestion was met with outrage from many Chinese citizens, who pointed out that a better way to reduce the number of rural migrants would be to improve the "quality of life and opportunities in the countryside."[54])

These views spread from the cities to China's rural residents.[55] In 2008, I interviewed school administrators, teachers, parents, and students in seven rural counties across four different provinces (Yunnan, Hunan, Gansu, and Heilongjiang). Like my urban interviewees from a decade before, everyone seemed to agree that *suzhi* came from education and was associated with urban cosmopolitanism and capitalist wealth. Rural parents aspired for their children to get "as much education as possible," at least to attend university, but ideally to go to graduate school abroad. All of my interviewees concurred that if students passed the entrance examination to get into senior high school or college, their parents would find a way to pay for them to attend, even though those costs could add up to ten times their annual household income.[56]

A principal in Gansu province told me that none of the parents wanted their children to become farmers anymore. Indeed, not a single one of the students I interviewed at rural schools said that they wanted to work in agriculture when they grew up, despite the fact that the vast majority were the children of farmers. They explained that farmers were always poor and had to work too hard. Instead, they dreamt of white-collar professions, to become a teacher, doctor, or scientist. (There was also a contingent of aspiring police officers, and a few hopeful professional athletes, artists, and pop singers). When I asked them whether they would rather live in the city or countryside, the majority enthusiastically endorsed the city, although a vocal minority defended their hometowns. These children wanted to live Su Mingjuan's *suzhi* fairy tale, to go from being the poor country bumpkin to the glamorous professional in the city.

As many researchers have noted, *suzhi* ideology conveniently serves the interests of global capitalism at the cost of burdening China's children and their parents with immense anxiety and stress.[57] It convinces people to do all they can to make themselves and their offspring into the perfect capitalist employees: self-motivated, well-educated, highly disciplined, and technologically skilled. It also teaches them to want to shop a lot, to desire a cosmopolitan lifestyle with lots of consumer products, and to value the new and shiny over the old and traditional. After all, in the happy ending to Su Mingjuan's fairy tale, she did not end up as a princess in a ball gown, but as a bank employee in polished, professional clothes and accessories.

Suzhi versus self-esteem

Even if it served the interests of global capitalism, *suzhi* ideology also gave social entrepreneurs such as Xu Yongguang the leverage to develop Chinese NGOs and, as we shall see, to pressure the state to serve its people better. *Suzhi* ideology may justify many forms of discrimination: against the poor, the rural, the less educated. Yet it also insists that these peoples' shortcomings are not due to any inherent, internal flaws, but instead are the results of the inadequacies of society. It claims that their children can become adults of high quality, as long as they are given good health care, good schools, and good resources.

One way to highlight the difference between a worldview based on *suzhi* and one based more on Western individualism is to compare CYDF/Project Hope with another organization that tried to help poor rural children through education. Hua-Dan was founded by Caroline Watson, a British woman who grew up in Hong Kong, and it was staffed by young, educated people, both from Beijing and from foreign countries. Its mission was to empower migrant children in Beijing through the dramatic arts, using theater-based workshops to help the students build self-esteem, learn leadership skills, and to tap into their internal creativity. Hua-Dan members almost never spoke about the external circumstances affecting migrant children, such as the discriminatory policies that prevented them from attending public education in Beijing and forced them to attend shoddy, semi-legal migrant schools. Instead, they acted as though all the resources these migrant children needed were internal, and accessible through proper training and sufficient self-confidence.

The work that Hua-Dan members did was certainly valuable. Given the heavy burden of prejudice that these migrant children faced, they were powerfully affected by the attention and support showered upon them by the NGO's enthusiastic, highly-educated staff workers and volunteers. Hua-Dan's programs also gave migrant students an opportunity to build relationships with these high-status urbanites and foreigners, providing them with valuable social connections that would normally be out of their reach. Yet the self-focused ideology that drove Hua-Dan's activities precluded any active engagement with the economic and political institutions of inequality that contributed to the low-self-esteem, depression, and anger that they found in the migrant students they served.

Suzhi ideology assumes that individuals are the product of external social conditions, and that China's institutions must be transformed for its citizens to develop. It declares that the purpose of life is not personal fulfillment or even working for one's family, but instead to contribute to the community and the nation. Therefore, *suzhi* ideology served as a useful weapon for social entrepreneurs such as Xu Yongguang, who wanted to transform China. It armed them with a compelling argument to insist that both wealthy citizens and the state were responsible for improving the economic and social conditions of China's least privileged people. By using *suzhi* ideology to draw attention to the social problem of rural education, Xu Yongguang and his imitators transformed under-funded rural schools from an issue that no one cared about into a national crisis affecting the future of the nation. Those donors and charities who funded rural students or schools became heroes, seen as serving the innocent, helping the poor, and contributing to the future of China in one compact gesture.

Real results for rural education

By the time Xu Yongguang started CYDF and launched Project Hope, thanks to the prevalence of *suzhi* ideology, Chinese urban residents were well primed to believe that good education was the key to saving Su Mingjuan and the other poor but adorable children featured in those eye-catching black-and-white advertisements. They were also willing to accept the implicit argument that helping these children was also helping China move from its backward past into a more modern, economically-developed future. CYDF's Project Hope images implied that denying poor rural children the opportunity to develop their *suzhi* was a crime not only against these young people, but against China itself.

Project Hope's message struck a nerve. It not only managed to attract a lot of donors, but it spawned a national moral panic. The problem of rural education, ignored for decades, now commanded the attention of journalists, scholars, and political officials.[58] In 1999, one of China's most renowned filmmakers, Zhang Yimou, directed a heart-wrenching film called *Not One Less*, about a rural school so poor that every piece of chalk must be rationed. In the touching finale, Project Hope arrives with truckloads of school supplies donated by people from the city.

Although Project Hope never directly criticized the government, its campaign turned a spotlight onto government educational policies, and onto the failure of the party-state to serve its rural constituents well. In 1999, the State Council passed the "Resolution on *Suzhi* Education," requiring increased resources for smaller class sizes and better-trained teachers.[59] In 2005, Prime Minister Wen Jiabao announced at the opening of the annual National People's Congress that all tuition and school fees would be eliminated for the nine years of compulsory education (primary school and junior middle school) for rural students by 2007 and urban students by 2008. This policy change was not cheap; the government would be spending almost US$30 billion in the first year just for the rural schools. (At least in the rural areas where I conducted my research, this policy had been successfully implemented by 2008.)

At the same time, central, provincial, and local governments also began making grants available for school building and infrastructural improvement. In 2008, a Gansu Province administrator had told me that 70 schools in his district had been evaluated as below grade in their last assessment, but 30 of those schools had been rebuilt between 2006 and 2008 through either government grants or charitable donations from organizations such as Project Hope. (It is important to note that these policies and grants began several years before the 2008 Wenchuan earthquake, which brought international attention to the shoddy state of China's rural educational infrastructure when poorly-built schools collapsed and killed thousands of schoolchildren.) In 2008, the Chinese Ministry of Education also announced that the children of migrant workers would now be permitted to attend urban schools, which would be paid an incentive for admitting them. In doing so, it tore down one of the main obstacles migrant parents had for bringing their children to the city with them. It also removed the need for semi-legal migrant schools where Caroline Watson's NGO, Hua-Dan, served.

These government policies also undermined the need for CYDF/Project Hope, making its signature sponsorship programs redundant. As one CYDF employee pointed out to me, in the very first year it became illegal for schools to charge fees or tuition, the Chinese government invested more in rural education than Project Hope had managed to raise in three decades. Indeed, one could argue that these government policies were motivated in part by the desire of the Ministry of Education to reduce the power of CYDF and Project Hope, which were seen by some as causing embarrassment to the government. Although CYDF has launched campaigns for a number of years to address other social problems (AIDS, environmental protection), none of these ventures has been nearly as successful as Project Hope. Since 2009, the organization has had a much lower profile in China. (CYDF was also tarnished by a couple of minor financial scandals, although similar problems had arisen in the past without substantially diminishing the organization.) By this time, Xu Yongguang had been wooed to leave CYDF to run the government-sponsored China Charity Foundation. Since then, he has founded the Narada Foundation, which supports non-profits.

From another perspective, Xu Yongguang and CYDF had succeeded in accomplishing their central mission: to improve the accessibility and quality of education for children in poor rural areas. If the definition of a good citizen in a populist democracy is one who informs the state of the needs and concerns of the people and helps the state address those needs and concerns effectively, Xu Yongguang was a very good democratic citizen indeed. Through the Project Hope campaign, CYDF had pushed the state to implement policies that were neither shallow nor temporary, but instead costly and long term. Project Hope had inspired middle-class, urban citizens to care deeply about rural education. It had transformed the national conversation, shifting popular perceptions of the countryside and the role of education in development – and the role of the state and citizens in serving poor, rural children like Su Mingjuan. CYDF had also created a template for other citizens to use to address social issues dear to their hearts, as we shall see in the following chapters.

Notes

1 Xinhua News. "Star of Project Hope to enter college." September 7, 2002. *People's Daily*.
2 "La célèbre 'fille aux grands yeux', aidée par le Projet Espoir est aujourd'hui devenue col blanc." People's Daily Francais. http://french.peopledaily.com.cn/VieSociale/7136291.html.
3 Martin K. Whyte and William L. Parish, *Urban Life in Contemporary China* (Chicago: University of Chicago Press, 1984), 60.

4 Anita Chan, Richard Madsen, and Jonathan Unger, *Chen Village: Under Mao and Deng* (2nd ed.) (Berkeley: University of California Press, 1992).
5 Wu Wen and Daming Luo, "Heavy laden wings: Sad contemplations on China's education," *Chinese Education and Society* 28, no. 2 and 3 (1995): 3–96.
6 Accurate numbers are difficult to obtain. Earlier statistics tend to count only primary school students, while later ones include middle school students. Also, the Cultural Revolution seriously disrupted education from 1966 to 1969 and had effects for years afterward.
7 See, for example, Vivienne Shue, "State power and the philanthropic impulse in China today," in W. Ilchman, S. Katz, and E. Queen (Eds.), *Philanthropy in the World's Traditions* (Bloomington: Indiana University Press, 1998), 332–354.
8 Kang Xiaoguang, *Chuangzao Xiwang: Zhongguo Qingshaonian Fazhan Jijinghui Yanjiu (Creating Hope: A Study of the China Youth Development Foundation)* (Guilin: Lijiang Publishing House and Guangxi Normal University Publishing House, 1997); Yiyi Lu, *Non-Governmental Organizations in China: The Rise of Dependent Autonomy* (London; New York: Routledge, 2009).
9 For example, see the Spring Bud Program. See Heidi Ross, "Challenging the gendered dimensions of schooling: The state, NGOs, and transnational alliances," in G.A. Postiglione (Eds.), *Education and Social Change in China* (Armonk, NY: M.E. Sharpe, 2006), 25–50.
10 Stefan Landsberger, "The rise and fall of the Chinese propaganda poster," in A. Min, D. Duo, and S. Landsberger (Eds.), *Chinese Propaganda Posters* (Cologne: Taschen, 2003), 16–17.
11 Mao Zedong (Tse-tung), "Talks at the Yenan forum on literature and art," in *Selected Readings from the Works of Mao Tse-Tung: 1926–1963* (Honolulu: University Press of the Pacific, 2001 [1942]), 250–286, 260.
12 Anchee Min, Duo Duo, and Stefan Landsberger (Eds.), *Chinese Propaganda Posters* (Cologne: Taschen, 2003).
13 Lisa Rotondo, *Chinese Revolutionary Woodcuts: 1935–1948* (Hamilton, NY: Colgate University Picker Art Gallery, 1984); Joachim Homann (Ed.), *Woodcuts in Modern China: 1937–2008* (Hamilton, NY: Colgate University Picker Art Gallery, 2009).
14 Andrew Kipnis, "Homo Hierarchicus or Homo Neo-Liberalis? *Suzhi* discourse in the PRC," *Society for East Asian Anthropology* (2004); Carolyn L. Hsu, *Creating Market Socialism: How Ordinary People are Shaping Class and Status in China* (Durham, NC: Duke University Press, 2007); Ann Anagnost, "The corporeal politics of quality (*suzhi*)," *Public Culture* 16, no. 2 (2004): 189–208.
15 Mao Zedong (Tse-tung), "Remarks at spring festival," in S. Schram (Ed.), *Chairman Mao Talks to the People: Talk and Letters: 1956–1971* (New York: Pantheon Books, 1974 [1964]), 209.
16 Ross, *Challenging the Gendered Dimensions of Schooling: The State, NGOs, and Transnational Alliances*, 25–50, 29.
17 In modern China, "intellectuals" (*zhishi fenzi* – literally, "knowledgeable elements") is a term to designate those people who have a significantly higher level of formal education than the norm. By definition, then, as the average level of education in China has increased, the cutoff point for intellectuals has also risen. In the first half of the twentieth century, then, a person with a senior high school degree could be considered an intellectual. However, by the late twentieth century, most Chinese urbanites had finished senior high school, so to be considered an intellectual required at least some kind of college degree.
18 Carolyn L. Hsu, "The city in the school and the school in the city: Ideology, imagery, and institutions in Maoist and market socialist China," *Visual Studies* 23, no. 1 (2008): 20–33; Min, Duo and Landsberger, *Chinese Propaganda Posters*.
19 Hsu, *The City in the School and the School in the City: Ideology, Imagery, and Institutions in Maoist and Market Socialist China*, 20–33, 23.

92 The perfect suzhi fairy tale

20 Zhang Xinxin and Ye Sang, *Chinese Lives: An Oral History of Contemporary China*, W.J.F. Jenner and D. Davin (Trans.) (New York: Pantheon Books, 1987), 135–136.
21 For more on how families debated the merits of educational credentials versus political capital, see Susan L. Shirk, *Competitive Comrades* (Berkeley: University of California Press, 1982).
22 The term *suzhi* was used earlier, but meant something quite different. See Kipnis, "Homo Hierarchicus or Homo Neo-Liberalis? Suzhi discourse in the PRC."
23 Andrew Kipnis, "*Suzhi*: A keyword approach," *The China Quarterly* 186 (2006): 295–313, 297.
24 Paul R. Ehrlich, *The Population Bomb* (New York: Ballantine Books, 1976), 201.
25 Elizabeth Economy, *The River Runs Black* (2nd ed.) (Ithaca: Cornell University Press, 2010), 364.
26 For example, the groups that were exempt from the one child rule were ethnic minorities, rural families whose first child was a girl, and couples in which both parents had no siblings. According to some analyses, by the early twenty-first century, the one child rule applied to only about a third of Chinese families. See Susan Greenhalgh and Edwin A. Winckler, *Governing China's Population* (Stanford: Stanford University Press, 2005); Yadan Ouyang, "China relaxes its one-child policy," *The Lancet* 382, no. 9907 (2013): e28.
27 Kipnis, *Suzhi: A Keyword Approach*, 295–313, 297.
28 Ibid., 298.
29 Ibid., 300.
30 Deng Xiaoping, "Speech at the opening ceremony of the National Conference on Science," in *Selected Works of Deng Xiaoping*, Vol. 2 (Beijing: Foreign Language Press, 1984 [1978]), 98–111.
31 H. Lyman Miller, *Science and Dissent in Post-Mao China* (Seattle: University of Washington Press, 1996), 88ff.
32 Wang Jing, *High Culture Fever: Politics, Aesthetics, and Ideology in Deng's China* (Berkeley: University of California Press, 1996), 113.
33 Perry Link, *Evening Chats in Beijing: Probing China's Predicament* (New York: W.W. Norton & Company, 1992); Miller, *Science and Dissent in Post-Mao China*.
34 Fang Lizhi, *Bringing Down the Great Wall*, J.H. Williams (Trans.) (New York: W.W. Norton & Company, 1990).
35 Link, *Evening Chats in Beijing: Probing China's Predicament*, 74.
36 Hsu, *Creating Market Socialism: How Ordinary People are Shaping Class and Status in China*, Chapter 5.
37 Because of China's regulations, most foreign companies came into the country by developing joint ventures with Chinese firms.
38 Craig J. Calhoun, *Neither Gods nor Emperors: Students and the Struggle for Democracy in China* (Berkeley, CA: University of California Press, 1994), 246.
39 Ibid., 246–248.
40 Han Minzhu (Ed.), *Cries for Democracy; Writing and Speeches from the 1989 Chinese Democracy Movement* (Princeton: Princeton University Press, 1990), 275.
41 Suzanne Ogden et al. (Eds.), *China's Search for Democracy: The Student and the Mass Movement of 1989* (New York: M.E. Sharpe, Inc., 1992), 152.
42 Han, *Cries for Democracy; Writing and Speeches from the 1989 Chinese Democracy Movement*. 160.
43 Kathleen Hartford, "The political economy behind Beijing spring," in T. Saich (Ed.), *The Chinese People's Movement: Perspectives on Spring 1989* (Armonk, NY: M.E. Sharpe, Inc., 1990), 50–82, 72.
44 Calhoun, *Neither Gods nor Emperors: Students and the Struggle for Democracy in China*, 246–248.
45 Carolyn L. Hsu, "Political narratives and the production of legitimacy: The case of corruption in post-Mao China," *Qualitative Sociology* 24, no. 1 (Spring, 2001): 25–54.

46 Zhou Yongkang, was a former member of the Standing Committee of the Central Politburo of the CCP, which is understood to be the highest decision-making group in China. It has only seven members.
47 Hsu, "Political narratives and the production of legitimacy".
48 David S.G. Goodman, *Class in Contemporary China*, 27.
49 Carolyn L. Hsu, *Creating Market Socialism*.
50 Carolyn Hsu, "Cadres, Getihu, and good businesspeople: Making sense of entrepreneurs in early post-socialist China," *Urban Anthropology and Studies of Cultural Systems and World Economic Development* 35, no. 1 (Spring, 2006): 1–38, www.jstor.org/stable/40553488.
51 Nor was this unique to this particular city. See Cheng Li, *Rediscovering China: Dynamics and Dilemmas of Reform* (New York: Rowan & Littlefield Publishers, 1997).
52 Rachel Murphy, "Turning peasants into modern Chinese citizens: 'Population quality' discourse, demographic transition, and primary education," *The China Quarterly* 177 (2004): 1–20.
53 Wen Guowei, "People entering Beijing should first pass an examination," *Beijing Evening News* October 15, 2013.
54 Austin Ramzy, "Academic suggests entrance test for Beijing's migrant workers," *New York Times*, sec. Sinosphere, October 17, 2013. http://nyti.ms/1hulfk6.
55 Other scholars also observed this is different provinces. See, for example, Andrew Kipnis, "The disturbing educational discipline of 'peasants'," *The China Journal*, no. 46 (July, 2001): 1–24. www.jstor.org/stable/3182305.
56 State-funded education only covered six years of primary school and three years of middle school, not senior high school.
57 Yan Hairong, "Neoliberal governmentality and neohumanism: Organizing suzhi/value flow through labor recruitment networks," *Cultural Anthropology* 18, no. 4 (2003): 493–523; Anagnost, "The corporeal politics of quality (suzhi)," 189–208.
58 Rui Xiao, "Project Hope provides financial assistance to more than a million out-of-school children," *Chinese Education and Society* 30, no. 2 (1997): 63–64; Wu and Luo, *Heavy Laden Wings: Sad Contemplations on China's Education*, 3–96.
59 Murphy, "Turning peasants into modern Chinese citizens: 'Population quality' discourse, demographic transition, and primary education," 1–20; Yi Lin, "Turning rurality into modernity: *Suzhi* education in a suburban public school of migrant children in Xiamen," *The China Quarterly* 206 (2011): 313–330. http://dx.doi.org/10.1017/S0305741011000282.

Bibliography

Anagnost, A. 2004. The corporeal politics of quality (*suzhi*). *Public Culture*, 16(2), pp. 189–208.
Calhoun, C.J. 1994. *Neither Gods nor Emperors: Students and the Struggle for Democracy in China*. Berkeley, CA: University of California Press.
Chan, A., Madsen, R., and Unger, J. 1992. *Chen Village: Under Mao and Deng* (2nd ed.). Berkeley: University of California Press.
Deng, X. 1984 [1978]. Speech at the opening ceremony of the National Conference on Science. *Selected Works of Deng Xiaoping*. Beijing: Foreign Language Press, pp. 98–111.
Economy, E. 2010. *The River Runs Black* (2nd ed.). Ithaca: Cornell University Press.
Ehrlich, P.R. 1976. *The Population Bomb*. New York: Ballantine Books.
Fang, L. 1990. *Bringing Down the Great Wall*. New York: W.W. Norton & Company.
Goodman, D.S.G. 2014. *Class in Contemporary China*. Cambridge, UK: Polity Press.

Greenhalgh, S. and Winckler, E.A. 2005. *Governing China's Population.* Stanford, CA: Stanford University Press.
Han, M. (Ed.). 1990. *Cries for Democracy; Writing and Speeches from the 1989 Chinese Democracy Movement.* Princeton: Princeton University Press.
Hartford, K. 1990. The political economy behind Beijing spring. In: T. Saich (Ed.), *The Chinese People's Movement: Perspectives on Spring 1989.* Armonk, NY: M.E. Sharpe, pp. 50–82.
Homann, J. (Ed.). 2009. *Woodcuts in Modern China: 1937–2008.* Hamilton, NY: Colgate University Picker Art Gallery.
Hsu, C.L. 2001. Political narratives and the production of legitimacy: The case of corruption in post-Mao China. *Qualitative Sociology,* 24(1), pp. 25–54.
Hsu, C. 2006. Cadres, Getihu, and good businesspeople: Making sense of entrepreneurs in early post-socialist China. *Urban Anthropology and Studies of Cultural Systems and World Economic Development,* 35(1), pp. 1–38.
Hsu, C.L. 2007. *Creating Market Socialism: How Ordinary People are Shaping Class and Status in China.* Durham, North Carolina: Duke University Press.
Hsu, C.L. 2008. The city in the school and the school in the city: Ideology, imagery, and institutions in Maoist and market socialist China. *Visual Studies,* 23(1), pp. 20–33.
Kang, X. 1997. *Chuangzao Xiwang: Zhongguo Qingshaonian Fazhan Jijinghui Yanjiu (Creating Hope: A Study of the China Youth Development Foundation).* Guilin: Lijiang Publishing House and Guangxi Normal University Publishing House.
Kipnis, A. 2001. The disturbing educational discipline of "peasants." *The China Journal,* (46), pp. 1–24.
Kipnis, A. 2004. Homo Hierarchicus or Homo Neo-Liberalis? *Suzhi* discourse in the PRC. *Society for East Asian Anthropology,* Berkeley, CA.
Kipnis, A. 2006. *Suzhi*: A keyword approach. *The China Quarterly,* 186, pp. 295–313.
Landsberger, S. 2003. The rise and fall of the Chinese propaganda poster. In: A. Min, D. Duo, and S. Landsberger (Eds.), *Chinese Propaganda Posters.* Cologne: Taschen, pp. 16–17.
Li, C. 1997. *Rediscovering China: Dynamics and Dilemmas of Reform.* New York: Rowan & Littlefield Publishers.
Lin, Y. 2011. Turning rurality into modernity: *Suzhi* education in a suburban public school of migrant children in Xiamen. *The China Quarterly,* 206, pp. 313–330.
Link, P. 1992. *Evening Chats in Beijing: Probing China's Predicament.* New York: W.W. Norton & Company.
Lu, Y. 2009. *Non-governmental Organizations in China: The Rise of Dependent Autonomy.* London; New York: Routledge.
Mao, Z. 1974 [1964]. Remarks at spring festival. In: S. Schram (Ed.), *Chairman Mao Talks to the People: Talk and Letters: 1956–1971.* New York: Pantheon Books, pp. 209.
Mao, Z. 2001 [1942]. Talks at the Yenan forum on literature and art. *Selected Readings from the Works of Mao Tse-tung: 1926–1963.* Honolulu: University Press of the Pacific, pp. 250–286.
Miller, H.L. 1996. *Science and Dissent in Post-Mao China.* Seattle: University of Washington Press.
Min, A., Duo, D., and Landsberger, S. (Eds.). 2003. *Chinese Propaganda Posters.* Cologne: Taschen.
Murphy, R. 2004. Turning peasants into modern Chinese citizens: "Population quality" discourse, demographic transition, and primary education. *The China Quarterly,* 177, pp. 1–20.

Ogden, S., Hartford, K., Sullivan, L., and Zweig, D. (Eds.). 1992. *China's Search for Democracy: The Student and the Mass Movement of 1989.* New York: M.E. Sharpe.

Ouyang, Y. 2013. China relaxes its one-child policy. *The Lancet*, 382(9907), p. e28.

Ramzy, A. 2013. Academic suggests entrance test for Beijing's migrant workers. *New York Times* Sinosphere, October 17, 2013..

Ross, H. 2006. Challenging the gendered dimensions of schooling: The state, NGOs, and transnational alliances. In: G.A. Postiglione (Ed.), *Education and Social Change in China.* Armonk, NY: M.E. Sharpe, pp. 25–50.

Rotondo, L. 1984. *Chinese Revolutionary Woodcuts: 1935–1948.* Hamilton, NY: Colgate University Picker Art Gallery.

Shirk, S.L, 1982. *Competitive Comrades.* Berkeley: University of California Press.

Shue, V. 1998. State power and the philanthropic impulse in China today. In: W. Ilchman, S. Katz, and E. Queen (Eds.), *Philanthropy in the World's Traditions.* Bloomington: Indiana University Press, pp. 332–354.

Wang, J. 1996. *High Culture Fever: Politics, Aesthetics, and Ideology in Deng's China.* Berkeley: University of California Press.

Wen, G. 2013. People entering Beijing should first pass an examination. *Beijing Evening News*, October 15, 2013.

Whyte, M.K. and Parish, W.L. 1984. *Urban Life in Contemporary China.* Chicago: University of Chicago Press.

Wu, W. and Luo, D. 1995. Heavy laden wings: Sad contemplations on China's education. *Chinese Education and Society*, 28(2 and 3), pp. 3–96.

Xiao, R. 1997. Project Hope provides financial assistance to more than a million out-of-school children. *Chinese Education and Society*, 30(2), pp. 63–64.

Xinhua News. 2002. Star of Project Hope to enter college. *People's Daily*, September 7. 2002.

Yan, H. 2003. Neoliberal governmentality and neohumanism: Organizing suzhi/value flow through labor recruitment networks. *Cultural Anthropology*, 18(4), pp. 493–523.

Zhang, X. and Sang, Y. 1987. *Chinese Lives: An Oral History of Contemporary China.* New York: Pantheon Books.

5 Getting in bed with the state

A social entrepreneur comes to the rescue

Heilongjiang is China's northernmost province. Bordering Russia's Siberia, it is known for its harsh winters and abundant natural resources. Gu Wei grew up in its capital city, Harbin. He was the son of a government cadre. In 1966, when he was ten years old, the Cultural Revolution shut down his school and he joined his classmates to "make revolution." However, he explained, as soon as formal education became available again, he "grasped the opportunity" and earned a teaching degree. Like Chapter 4's Xu Yongguang, the founder of Project Hope, this bright and politically enthusiastic young man caught the eye of the Communist Youth League. Gu Wei became a Youth League cadre at his school, then was promoted to the provincial level offices of the Heilongjiang Provincial Youth League to work in the Department of Propaganda. He was 24 years old, and his career prospects looked bright.

What Gu Wei could not anticipate was that at the very moment his political career was taking off in Heilongjiang, in Beijing Deng Xiaoping was launching a series of market socialist reforms that would complicate his future. The purpose of the Youth League's Department of Propaganda was to inspire political zeal, but Deng's regime denigrated this type of ideological enthusiasm and argued that it was far less valuable than the educational credentials and technical skills that were the characteristics of *suzhi*. By the mid-1980s, the Department of Propaganda seemed completely out of touch with the rest of Chinese society, and young people were losing interest in the Youth League. Gu Wei felt that the work he was doing was no longer useful. "It didn't solve practical problems," he complained. To make things worse, the Ministry of Finance also appeared to believe that the Communist Youth League might be obsolete, since it froze the organization's funding.

In 1988, the leaders of the Heilongjiang Youth League decided to take serious action. They would start a market venture, an affiliated, for-profit business firm that would earn enough money for the parent organization so that the Heilongjiang Youth League could launch new, interesting projects.[1] Gu Wei volunteered to take charge of the new firm, even though this meant losing his government salary. He would become an entrepreneur. The Provincial Party Committee provided a start-up loan of ¥10,000 (about US$1600).

For four years, Gu Wei ran the market venture with partial success. He was able to make enough money to keep the firm afloat, pay a dozen employees, and contribute ¥10,000 to the Heilongjiang Youth League annually. However, his company was never able to establish a long-term business strategy. Instead, it made money in fits and starts when opportunities arose, usually through personal connections (*guanxi*). At one point, it published a set of pamphlets on traffic safety. Later, it translated some Russian books into Chinese and sold them. It arranged study tours for aspiring entrepreneurs interested in doing business in Russia. Gu Wei admitted that he felt out of his depth: "I found running a business full of hardship. If you're not careful, you lose money. We are not businessmen." After four years, the market venture had not made much progress in solving the Heilongjiang Youth League's central identity crisis. Gu Wei's firm did not make enough profit to solve its financial difficulties. Even worse, no one came up with any good ideas for innovative or interesting projects. Gu Wei had confirmed the research findings of organizational sociologists: startups are hard and have a very high rate of failure, especially if they are attempting to do something new and innovative.[2]

In 1992, Gu Wei concluded that the best way to solve the organization's difficulties would be to franchise a branch of Project Hope from the China Youth Development Foundation (CYDF). As described in the previous chapter, CYDF was China's most successful charity due to its Project Hope campaign for rural education – the one that featured black-and-white photos of poor peasant children. CYDF needed staff and offices at the local level to collect donations, identify needy students and schools, and to channel Project Hope donations to the correct recipients. If the Heilongjiang Communist Youth League provided the offices and staff, it would have plenty of work to do. More importantly, Project Hope would help the Youth League solve its identity problem. It would still be carrying out its traditional mission of serving the youth, but in a way that fit the *suzhi*-based worldview of a new China.

Unfortunately, there was a reason why CYDF had not yet established a Project Hope campaign in Heilongjiang Province. Its policy was to set up Project Hope sponsorship programs only in government-designated poverty-stricken counties. Although Heilongjiang had poverty-stricken areas, no county in the province was quite poor enough to qualify for the designation. In 1992, CYDF changed its policy: provinces such as Heilongjiang could run Project Hope campaigns if they agreed to hand over 10 percent of all donated funds every year to CYDF for use in more impoverished areas. Gu Wei traveled to Beijing to meet with Xu Yongguang and sign a contract. The Heilongjiang Communist Youth League would run the Heilongjiang Youth Development Foundation (HYDF), which was permitted to franchise Project Hope for a fee as long as it followed the central organization's protocols.[3] By 2008, HYDF Project Hope had a dedicated staff of 12 and supported 150,000 students in the province.

98 *Getting in bed with the state*

In essence, the Heilongjiang Communist Youth League turned to a social entrepreneur to solve its political difficulties. In turn, CYDF outsourced its labor needs to a department of the party-state. This transaction offers a glimpse into the complicated relationships that developed between the Chinese government (which was filled with bureaucrats with their own problems to solve) and Chinese social entrepreneurs (who were willing to sell solutions to those problems as long as the end result would further their social missions – and serve the interests of their NGOs).

The Chinese government's official position on NGOs (versus what Chinese officials actually do)

Unfriendly laws

Close relationships and even partnerships between Chinese party-state bureaucrats (such as Gu Wei), and Chinese NGOs (such as CYDF/Project Hope), became surprisingly common in the 1990s and early twenty-first century. They flourished despite the fact that the Chinese government's official position on social entrepreneurs and NGOs was rather antagonistic. The Chinese Communist Party's vision for the People's Republic of China never included a role for social entrepreneurs or NGOs, regardless of whether it was Mao Zedong's version or Deng Xiaoping's version. Citizen organizations flourished briefly in the 1980s, but the crackdown following the 1989 Tiananmen Protests put an end to that.[4]

When social entrepreneurship emerged a decade later, it became clear that the Chinese legal system was designed to hinder rather than facilitate the rise of a vibrant NGO sector. Regulations were promulgated in 1998 and 2004, but both sets were confusing and obstructionist. All Chinese NGOs were required to register with the Ministry of Civil Affairs, a process that was confusing and often difficult. To register, an NGO had to have a "supervisory agency": a government institution or GONGO that would be responsible for keeping the NGO in line.[5] Chinese NGOs sarcastically called these supervisory agencies "mothers-in-law," and social entrepreneurs without *guanxi* connections with government officials struggled to find an agency to sponsor them.[6] Supposedly "nonprofit public welfare institutions" could be certified to raise funds domestically, but only a few state-connected organizations were ever granted permission.[7] All NGO funds were supposed to be regularly audited, but there was no system to carry this out.[8]

Because the regulations were so unfriendly during this time period, the majority of NGO-like organizations in China never officially registered as NGOs.[9] Some organizations registered as for-profit businesses. Others never registered with the government at all. Compliance with other regulations was similarly uneven. As a result, most Chinese NGOs operated in a legal gray area. Like speeding drivers on a US highway, the majority were technically in violation of the law, hoping that they would never get caught. In 2013, legal policies were revised with clearer and friendlier regulations for domestic NGOs, a sign that the state was finally acknowledging the growing role of social entrepreneurship in China.[10] In 2016, the Chinese government passed a Charity Law that incorporated input from the NGO sector and was viewed as a step forward for civil society.[11] However, in the same year, it also passed a law regulating foreign NGOs that put them under the purview of the Public Security Bureau, and authorities punished or shut down a number of organizations deemed potential sites of dissidence.[12]

Chinese government officials were well aware that the state's official position on social entrepreneurship ranged between lukewarm and hostile. Yet a substantial number of party-state bureaucrats found it worth their while to enter into alliances with social entrepreneurs and NGOs. To understand why, we need to look more closely at the complex conglomeration of departments, bureaus, and offices that make up the Chinese party-state bureaucracy.

Government organizations have problems, too

When Westerners discovered that Chinese social entrepreneurs often had close relationships with Chinese party-state officials, most presumed that this meant that the government controlled the NGOs. In many ways, this assumption is reasonable, given the vast power differential between the Chinese party-state and Chinese NGOs. As many social entrepreneurs explained in interviews, China is a "strong government nation," where the single-party state holds more autocratic power than governments do in multiparty democratic countries. China's government is also more centralized in comparison to many other large nations.[13] It is easy to view the Chinese government as an all-powerful monolith, controlling the entire country from the center.

Yet when we view the Chinese government as a monolith, we ignore the reality that the party-state bureaucracy is a collection of commissions, ministries, bureaus, departments, and offices, each with its own agendas and concerns. They may all be part of the same government, but their different interests often lead to tension or even conflict between various organizations.[14] Although these state agencies are not independent firms, they share certain characteristics with autonomous organizations. All organizations, whether they are private businesses, NGOs, or government departments, need to maintain a constant supply of resources to survive.[15] A private business must persuade enough customers to buy its products so that sufficient revenue will keep flowing. An NGO needs to persuade enough donors to offer contributions so its operating expenses will be covered. A government department needs to persuade the people above it in the bureaucracy that it deserves its share of the budget every cycle.[16] Besides money, organizations also require other resources, such as staffing and access to information or opportunities.[17]

Although businesses and NGOs have higher rates of failure than government departments, it is possible for state agencies to be reduced in size and even closed down altogether. There are two circumstances that make them especially vulnerable: first, when government budgets shrink, state agencies find themselves fighting each other for smaller pieces of a smaller pie. Depending on the extent of the financial cuts, departments may find themselves downsized, merged, or even disbanded. Second, government agencies prove their importance by demonstrating results that match the priorities of those above them in the bureaucracy. When those priorities change dramatically, departments may find themselves obsolete and at risk for the chopping block. Deng Xiaoping's 1979 market socialist reforms, combined with the rise of a new worldview based on *suzhi*, created both of these conditions. Many government offices found themselves in trouble. These included the Communist Youth League, an organization with an explicitly ideological mission in a time period when ideology had gone out of style. No wonder Gu Wei was willing to seek creative solutions.

Organizations not only need a constant supply of financial resources to survive, they also need to be able to attract qualified staff. Under Mao, it had been easy to attract smart, ambitious, hard-working young people because the party-state bureaucracy held a monopoly on the most attractive jobs in the PRC. But after the market reforms, this changed. In the 1980s, cadres such as Gu Wei of the Heilongjiang Youth League found it increasingly difficult to find good people to hire. A *suzhi* worldview not only taught Chinese citizens to admire scientists and entrepreneurs, but also to associate government cadres with incompetence and corruption. A Harbin department store manager told me,

> People used to think, "oh, he's a high official, he must have ability." Now they just think that those officials must have had good opportunities. That's what I think, that high officials are not necessarily better or smarter than lower officials. You don't actually rise on ability.

By the 1990s, many young people were turned off from government positions by this dismal reputation.

Even if government agencies successfully hired staff members, some of them struggled to keep them. In order to move up the career ladder in the party-state bureaucracy, individual cadres had to be able show off a list of accomplishments. They needed a résumé that demonstrated their contributions to the government's overall goals. In a department that was losing its funding and unsure of its mission, what could an ambitious cadre accomplish? With a more open labor market, people could leave for other state organizations or even the private sector if they believed that their own department was a sinking ship. Gu Wei's department kept losing staff members who decided to leave the cadre track for the business world. Without talented staff members, how could a party-state department reinvent itself for a new China?

Social entrepreneurs offer their services

Although government organizations did not advertise their problems, many Chinese social entrepreneurs were still aware of these issues. This was because, at the turn-of-the-century, a significant proportion of social entrepreneurs were former party-state cadres themselves. (Both Peter Xu of Golden Key and Xu Yongguang of CYDF had been cadres before starting their organizations.) There were many reasons for this: from the 1950s through to the 1980s, to be a cadre was the most desirable career in China. Social entrepreneurs share many of the traits that the government sought out when recruiting cadres: intelligence, ambition, self-discipline, perseverance, and leadership skills. In addition, social entrepreneurship is a risky endeavor, so it is more likely to attract people with excellent connections, access to resources, relevant expertise, and substantial self-confidence. For Chinese people of a certain age, it was likely these conditions could only be met through a cadre career in the party-state bureaucracy.

These former cadres-turned-social entrepreneurs knew firsthand about the general pressures that state organizations were facing in the market socialist era of government downsizing. More importantly, they would know about some of the specific problems that specific party-state agencies were facing because of personal experience or personal relationships. A social entrepreneur did not need to build an alliance with "the Chinese government" as a whole. Instead, he or she needed to develop relationships with specific officials in specific offices and help these particular people achieve their particular goals.[18] The former-cadres-turned-social entrepreneurs still had friends and acquaintances in government agencies. Or, to put it in Chinese terms, they still had *guanxi* there. As I explained in Chapter 3, a *guanxi* relationship is the foundation for an exchange of gifts and favors, including information and introductions. Through the "chain of favors" rule of Chinese *guanxi*, a social entrepreneur could begin with a few relationships with a few state actors, and expand it out into a social network, reaching more deeply throughout the party-state bureaucracy.

These connections were only useful if social entrepreneurs had something to offer state actors and agencies. Specifically, social entrepreneurs could enter into a *guanxi* gift exchange with cadres if they could demonstrate a way to produce better results – results that would impress bureaucrats higher up in the hierarchy – without needing more state resources. On the simplest level, social entrepreneurs could help government agencies access alternative sources of resources besides government funding, such as private donors or international foundations. Another strategy for Chinese NGOs was to develop more efficient techniques, and then offer these techniques to state organizations to adopt. In essence, the NGO would act as the government agency's unpaid research and development lab. Some social entrepreneurs went even further. For party-state organizations on the verge of obsolescence, they could create a whole new mission and identity, one more in line with the ruling regime's new priorities.

Chinese social entrepreneurs, at least those who were former cadres, knew that these approaches would be effective because of their own experience in government organizations. They were all well aware that the ponderous and conservative nature of the Chinese state bureaucracy made it difficult for state actors to find creative solutions, even when their organizational survival depended on it. One social entrepreneur, Jin Jiaman of the Global Environmental Institute, explained to me, "...there are various regulations, and there are position ranks and levels, and all of these will control what you want to do. So actually, if you have some ideas and you want to implement them, it is almost impossible." She would know; she had spent most of her career at a state research academy.

Innovative entrepreneurship has a high rate of failure.[19] Jin Jiaman pointed out that at her NGO, it was normal to have more than 50 percent of project ideas fail. She was willing to accept that as the price for finding new and effective solutions. However, such a failure rate would never be tolerated at a state agency. Party-state cadres were rewarded for being risk-averse and obedient, rather than bold and experimental. Gu Wei's story at the Heilongjiang Youth League reveals that even a smart and ambitious cadre may not have the skill set (or the luck or the *guanxi*) to succeed as an entrepreneur. NGOs could run the risks that state organizations could not take in order to test potential solutions to social problems.

In return, social entrepreneurs would gain access to state-controlled resources for their NGOs. For example, NGOs often needed government permission to access client populations. If they were fortunate, they could even serve those client populations with state resources. If an NGO developed a successful model for solving the social problem, the state agency could adopt it and implement it on a wide scale, at no cost to the NGO. Last, but not least, an alliance with a state agency provided social entrepreneurs and their NGOs with protection. They were much less likely to face legal charges or government suppression if everyone knew they had powerful friends in the party-state bureaucracy.

The rest of this chapter explores the complicated world of NGO–state alliances through two case studies: one about rural schools, and one about the Chinese Youth League.

Case 1 Rural schools fight for market share

Declining enrollments

Even in the early twentieth century, almost all schools in China's countryside were run by the government and therefore were part of the party-state bureaucracy. The rise of a worldview based on *suzhi* brought a number of benefits to these rural school districts. As we saw in the previous chapter, social entrepreneurs such as Xu Yongguang successfully persuaded the Chinese population to believe that (a) education was the key to China's development, and that (b) rural education was in crisis. After the turn of the century, it became fashionable for charities and philanthropists to donate money to rural schools. State officials increased investment in rural education as the political benefits of caring about the topic (and the political costs of looking indifferent) increased. The combination of increased government/private funding and *suzhi* ideology meant that educators benefited from both better compensation and higher social status.

Ironically, just when *suzhi* ideology and increased funding began substantially improving conditions for rural education, schools faced a new crisis: declining enrollments. After rising for decades, the Chinese school-age population began to drop, especially in the countryside (see Figure 5.1).

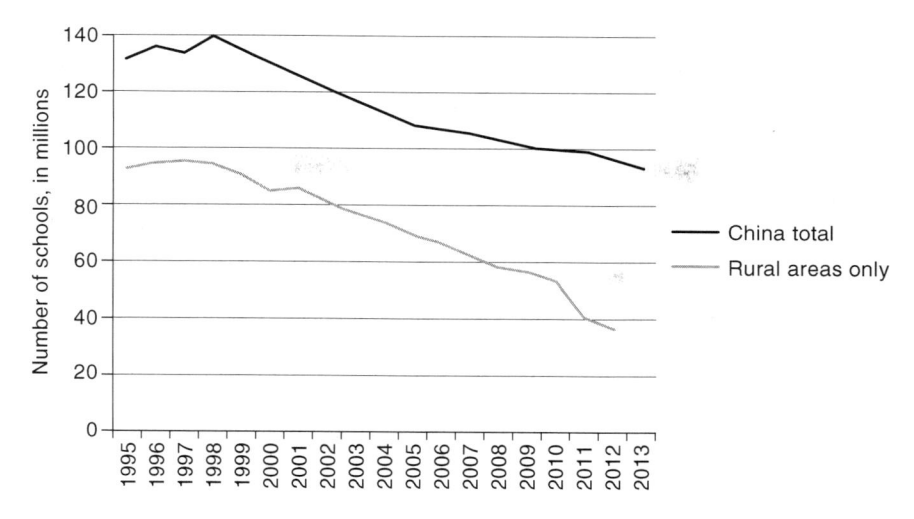

Figure 5.1 Primary school student population, in millions, from 1995–2013.

Source: National data from the All China Data Center. Rural data compiled from the Rural Statistical Yearbook of China, 1997 through 2013, "Number of Students and Teachers of Middle School and Primary School in Rural Areas." Both sources accessed through China Data Online.

China's Birth Planning Policy (known in the West as the "One-Child Policy") was one major source of the decline. Launched in 1980, the policy itself restricted rural families to having only one or two children, depending on their circumstances.[20] However, the decreasing school age population was not just a result of oppressive state regulations, but also of cultural change. When I visited rural Anhui in 1993, many of the families I met had illegal second or third children in order to maximize the number of sons in the family. But by 2008, when I studied rural school districts in four Chinese provinces, rural families were *voluntarily* restricting themselves to a single child even if they could legally apply to have a second one. Although many of the students in the middle and high school had siblings, the children in the lower grades of primary school were almost all singletons.

Why would parents choose to have only one child, even if they were permitted to have a second one? *Suzhi* ideology had taught rural residents to value "quality over quantity," as propaganda from the Birth Planning Policy proclaimed. In the twenty-first century, rural parents had new aspirations for their children: the "path of glory" of higher education and white-collar professions. These new dreams required a new mode of parenting that involved a much greater investment of time and money than anything previous generations had experienced. For young couples inculcated in *suzhi* ideology, raising one child according to these expectations was daunting enough. To try to do it for two or more children seemed too overwhelming to imagine. In my interviews, when I asked young women if they would consider having two children, they looked at me as though I were insane.

The decline in the rural school age population was exacerbated by rural-to-urban migration. In the 1990s, there were an estimated 60–70 million rural migrant workers in Chinese cities. By 2010, that number had risen to over 150 million.[21] Most of these were young adults, seeking jobs in construction or manufacturing, at or near the age of marriage and parenthood. Before 2008, they faced a difficult decision when their offspring reached school age: should they keep their children with them in the city or send them back to their rural hometowns to be raised by their grandparents? Because most rural migrants did not possess an official resident's card (*hukou*) for the city in which they worked, they were legally ineligible for local services. This included local schools. Some urban schools would allow nonresidents in if they paid tuition, but the prices were much too high for ordinary people.[22] In cities where this rule was strictly enforced, such as Beijing, migrants would have to send their children to semi-legal schools that were unregulated by the state. However, in August 2008, the Ministry of Education announced that urban schools would accept all children, regardless of *hukou*. With this barrier removed, rural migrants lost a major incentive to keep their children in their village schools, and the speed of rural population decline increased.

For small rural schools, the number of students could fall precipitously in a very short period. In Lanxi County, Heilongjiang Province, one primary school declined from 200 students to 154 between 2003 and 2008. That was nothing compared with Mei Hu Primary School in Hunan Province, which dropped from 200 to 89 students in the same time period (see Figure 5.2). Because Chinese schools were funded on a per-pupil basis, declining enrollments meant shrinking budgets. By 2008, Mei Hu Primary School could only hire four teachers and could only offer classes in three grades: second, third, and fourth. Even worse, as the school-age population dropped in the countryside, a number of schools had to be shut down entirely. Mei Hu's village had already lost its middle school. The primary school was slated to merge with three other declining institutions, and even the new combined school would have only 120 pupils.

Social entrepreneurs can help save your school

Although rural China was experiencing a decline in the school age population in general, not all school districts were affected equally. Some schools were actually flourishing. One reason was that rural China was urbanizing. While many places were losing people, certain villages were growing into towns and certain towns were growing into cities, either because of market forces, government intervention, or a combination of both.[23] The schools in these new population centers prospered at the expense of other locations.

Schools could themselves become the attractions creating population growth. Although rural students faced restrictions when trying to attend city schools until 2009, they were always permitted to switch between rural schools with little difficulty. After 2007, rural schools were not allowed to charge out-of-district students any fees, making it even easier to jump school districts. In a society

Figure 5.2 Mei Hu primary school, Hunan Province, 2008.
Source: author's photo.

inculcated with *suzhi* ideology, many parents were quite willing to move their children to new schools on the basis of reputation, even if that meant the child would be separated from the rest of the family. As a result, high-status schools attracted more and more students, while other schools found themselves losing market share. Unfortunately, the schools that lost students also lost funding, making it more difficult for them to compete with desirable schools.

This is where social entrepreneurs could step in. They could offer local school administrators a way to slow or stop the rate of decline, or even transform a dying school into a thriving school. For example, Peter Xu's Golden Key developed inexpensive learning aids and teacher training modules so that even poorly educated rural teachers could serve blind and visually-impaired children. It lobbied cadres to adopt these materials. For education cadres and school administrators, it was a good deal. Golden Key materials were cheap and they helped bureaucrats look effective at serving the people. They also helped declining rural schools tap into an underserved population of students, boosting their numbers and giving their administrators ammunition for requesting increased budgets.

Project Hope helped rural schools by sponsoring students, so children at risk of dropping out of school stayed in the classroom. Even better, Project

Hope improved, renovated, and built the schools themselves. A new library, basketball court, or computer lab could make a rural school much more attractive to families, and perhaps even persuade migrant parents to leave their children in the village rather than to take them to the city. With a whole new school building, a school could even draw in students from outside of the district. In Yunnan Province, the proud principal gave me a tour of Lei Feng Hope School in Xundian County. Because it was the first Hope School in the province, it was Project Hope's showpiece. The organization's contributions were visible everywhere: the new building, the computers, and even the soymilk maker in the cafeteria kitchen. Before Project Hope came in 1997, the school had only 170 students. By the time I visited, in 2008, it had 372, including 50 children who came from so far away that they had to board in the school's dormitory.

Nor was Project Hope the only non-governmental source of transformative resources. In 2008, Shaoshan Key School in Hunan Province boasted 1500 students and an annual student growth rate of 10 to 20 percent. Its dormitory housed hundreds of boarders. Shaoshan Key School was once just a small village school. A 1993 merger brought the students from three other schools to this location. The turning point came in 2003, when a Hong Kong charity donated a four-storey building, containing a computer lab and recording studio, transforming the school into a magnet for the region (see Figure 5.3). In 2006, donors funded an additional building for the primary school, plus a beautiful kindergarten nearby.

Figure 5.3 Shaoshan key school, Hunan Province, 2008.
Source: author's photo.

Ironically, success bred success, even in terms of attracting charitable donations designed to alleviate rural poverty. Both Lei Feng Hope School and Shaoshan Key School attracted more impressive contributions in the years following their first donation. This was in part because, after the initial transaction, they now had a relationship with a wealthy patron and/or a charitable organization. Through the rules of *guanxi* networks, this meant that they were in a position to build relationships with their patron's rich friends and acquaintances, some of whom would be brought by their patron to visit the site. These new relationships could be converted into additional donations.

Conversely, the schools that were truly in need encountered many obstacles in attracting charitable donations. We can see this in the case of one of the victims of Shaoshan Key School's success: Mei Hu Primary School (Figure 5.2), the school whose numbers had dropped from 200 to 89 students. All the local families with ambition and money had moved their children to Shaoshan Key School.[24] As one of its remaining teachers explained, Mei Hu not only had trouble attracting students, but also staff. Its students required "more work" because they were "the poor ones" whose parents had left them with their grandparents to go to work in cities. Their grandparents tended to have an even lower level of education than their parents, so the children received very little educational support at home. Yet it was Shaoshan Key School that had the resources to hire the best teachers, boasting that its entire faculty had "high-level" credentials.

Ironically, Mei Hu Primary School received no charitable contributions. It had no connections with Hong Kong business tycoons, perhaps in part because it was inaccessible to a Mercedes-Benz. To get to it, I had to travel on dirt roads, some of which were causeways barely more than a meter wide between sunken flooded fields. Because these causeways were too narrow for cars, I was taken to Mei Hu on the back of a motorcycle. (I clung to my "chauffer" with absolutely no dignity, eyeing the two meter drop on either side of the "road" with great trepidation.) Although Project Hope tried to target the neediest schools, Mei Hu was ineligible to become a Hope school. The reason was because Project Hope would only invest in schools that had at least 160 students and were projected to remain viable for at least the next 20 years. After all, social entrepreneurs are practical, and want their charitable contributions to be "effective." Investing in small, dying schools simply did not make sense. By building alliances with healthy local school districts, the social entrepreneurs could not only serve a larger number of children, but they could also compile reams of good-looking statistics with which to impress potential donors.

Case 2 What do you do when ideology goes out of style?

Although rural schools struggled with the problem of declining school populations, at least everyone agreed that education itself was important, thanks to the persuasive power of *suzhi* ideology. By contrast, the Communist Youth League (CYL) found itself struggling with its very purpose and identity in the market socialist era. The Youth League was founded in 1920 by young Marxists dedicated to bringing a socialist revolution to China.[25] After the establishment of the People's Republic of China, the Youth League became the junior partner of the Communist Party. Its purpose was to socialize the youth of China into the correct political ideology. It also served a second purpose of identifying and grooming the young people who had the best potential to become Communist Party members and party-state cadres.

By the late twentieth century, the CYL was a huge organization, rivaling the size of the Communist Party. In China, Communist Party membership is only open to adults, but Youth League membership is available to adolescents as young as 14. Like the Communist Party, the Youth League is a national organization with separate branches in each of China's provinces and regions, as well as offices at the county and local level. For the politically ambitious, the Communist Youth League was seen as a path to power in the Communist Party. Because the organization serves young people, cadres leave the Youth League when they reach middle age and are appointed to positions in the Communist Party or the government. A number of cadres who started off their careers in the Youth League have risen to positions of political prominence in China, including Hu Jintao, who became China's President, and Li Keqiang, its Premier.

However, in the 1980s, thanks to Deng Xiaoping's market socialist reforms and the rise of *suzhi* ideology, the Communist Youth League found itself facing challenges at the national, provincial, and local level. The national organization struggled with defending its relevance and jostling for power among the other big players in the party-state bureaucracy. At the provincial level, cadres like Gu Wei of the Heilongjiang Communist Youth League found themselves dealing with frozen funding, staffing problems, and (on a personal level) stalled career trajectories. Meanwhile, CYL offices at the county and township levels faced the threat of downsizing and layoffs.

Fortunately for the Youth League, Xu Yongguang of CYDF/Project Hope offered a solution to its problems, although he demanded a great deal in return. The resulting relationship between the Communist Youth League and the NGO was symbiotic and complicated, and nothing at all like the simplistic images of government oppression that many Westerners hold of China and its NGOs.

New missions through moral panics

How could social entrepreneurs help government organizations, like the Youth League, whose original purpose no longer matched government priorities? They could do so through a strategy of creating new missions for the old organizations, missions that would coincidentally further the goals of the social entrepreneurs' own NGOs.

First, social entrepreneurs would draw public attention to a social problem. They would generate publicity to persuade Chinese citizens, especially urban, middle-class citizens, to focus on this particular concern. Ideally, social entrepreneurs would whip the populace up into what sociologists call a moral panic.

They would convince people that this particular social issue was a "threat to societal values and interests," and that it demanded the attention of journalists, experts, authority figures, and all right-thinking people.[26] Given its self-proclaimed identity as a populist democracy, Chinese political leaders legitimized their authority by claiming to serve their people and to respond to their concerns. Government leaders who ignored the citizens' popular concerns would be at risk of losing their legitimacy, as the 1989 Tiananmen Square protesters revealed when they successfully persuaded Chinese urbanites into a moral panic about political corruption.[27]

As we saw in Chapter 4, Xu Yongguang, through Project Hope's powerful media campaign, successfully instigated a moral panic about rural education. Similarly, environmentalist social entrepreneurs taught Chinese citizens to notice previously ignored environmental threats. For example, even in the late 1990s, urbanites in China's smoggiest cities paid very little attention to air pollution. To persuade them to notice the air pollution, environmental NGOs led bird-watching expeditions and nature photography workshops to change the way people looked at their surroundings.[28] In Beijing, an organization called Green Beagle handed out portable air quality monitors to volunteers and published the data on the web, in its "I Monitor Air for My Country" campaign.[29] Other organizations copied the campaign in other Chinese cities. Thanks in part to these efforts, urban air pollution became a significant public issue, the topic of mass media articles, internet blog rants, and anxiety-filled ordinary conversations.

Second, the social entrepreneur would offer the government agency a way to address this social problem. This set of actions would be designed to make the state organization look not just aware and concerned about the issue, but also innovative, effective, virtuous, and vitally necessary to the common good. These, of course, were the virtues the Chinese government aspired to display, and therefore the characteristics that would allow this particular government office to be looked upon with favor by bureaucrats higher up in the party-state hierarchy.

The set of actions would also be designed to require the state organization to serve the interests of the social entrepreneurs' NGO, either directly or indirectly. It could require the government agency to partner directly with the NGO on the project. It could steer the government to purchase goods or services from the NGO, as in the case of Golden Key. The state may have to take on members of the NGO as consultants for the project, and even for designing government policies. The NGO may simply benefit from the fact that the state was now carrying out its mission, so that many more people in its target population could be served than if the NGO tried to reach them directly. If nothing else, it established or deepened the *guanxi* relationships between the members of the state organization and the NGO, making it much more likely that the former would implement the latter's ideas in the future. Moreover, the government organization now had an incentive to both publicize the social problem and to protect the NGO from interference from other party-state agencies.

Outsourcing Project Hope to the Youth League

By the late 1980s, the Communist Youth League had a problem. It was an expensive nationwide organization with branches in almost every county and most townships in China, but it was struggling to justify its existence, much less the need for so many offices and employees. Xu Yongguang offered a solution to this problem: Project Hope. If the Youth League helped CYDF carry out Project Hope, it would no longer be an obsolete state institution with little purpose. Instead, it would be a vital organization addressing one of the most important social problems of the day: the crisis in rural education.

This partnership also benefited Xu Yongguang and CYDF. Implementing a charitable program like Project Hope across China would require an enormous number of staff members working at the county and village levels. Someone needed to identify qualified students and schools with accuracy, and someone needed to funnel resources to the students and schools consistently, efficiently, and honestly over many years. To run such a program alone, an NGO would have to be enormous, and enormously expensive. Xu avoided the cost of establishing local offices by turning over all the ground-level work to the Communist Youth League. After all, the Youth League already had county- and township-level offices all over China, with staff members collecting data about young people. By outsourcing its local-level work to the Youth League, CYDF could implement a nationwide charitable campaign serving millions of students with a staff of just a few dozen employees. It could also please its donors by keeping its administrative overhead low, since Youth League staff members were paid by the Communist Party, not CYDF.

Meanwhile, the Communist Youth League was transformed from an organization that did work that almost nobody believed was important (promoting political ideology) into one that did work that almost everyone agreed was vital to China's future (improving rural education). Project Hope work drew a lot of media attention and generated excellent press, through high-profile fund-raising events and photo ops in front of shiny new Hope Schools or with adorable Project Hope schoolchildren. It also impressed people in power, unlike most of the rest of the Youth League's endeavors. As one Youth League cadre complained:

> When the General Secretary of the [Chinese Communist] Party tries to name the achievements of the Communist Youth League, the only thing he can think of is Project Hope. He does not remember any other work which the Communist Youth League has done.[30]

Project Hope helped the Communist Youth League solve its financial and staffing problems. It is important to note that Project Hope funds were reserved for charity work and could not be used by Youth League offices for their own staff or needs. However, running Project Hope helped the Youth League fend off budget cuts and justified its requests for increased government funding. No one would question the need for all those local level staff members and offices if they were working hard for Project Hope. The charitable campaign also helped the Youth League attract members and staff. I interviewed a Youth League cadre who worked for Yunnan Project Hope. Well-educated and articulate, he told me that his parents were wealthy enough that he did not need to work for a living. He was the very embodiment of *suzhi*. This young man explained to me that he chose to work for the Youth League because of Project Hope; he wanted a career with meaning. Research reveals that working on Project Hope campaigns helped Youth League cadres in their official careers, allowing them to list impressive achievements and gain good positions when reassigned to the Communist Party or government.[31]

The Youth League basked in the moral glow of Project Hope. This was especially true at the local level in the countryside, where everyone assumed that Project Hope was run by the Communist Youth League (or the government) and had no idea it was connected to an NGO. I interviewed cadres, school administrators, teachers, students, volunteers and parents at 13 rural schools, half of which were Project Hope beneficiaries. None of these people thought that the charity was connected to an NGO. Part of this confusion no doubt stemmed from the fact that few people in China knew what an NGO was, even in 2008–2009. But given CYDF's considerable skills with media and marketing, it certainly could have done more to correct this misconception. Instead, it did the opposite, downplaying its own role and allowed all the credit to go to the Communist Youth League.

Nor was CYDF unusual in this; many Chinese NGOs allowed the state to take credit for their initiatives.[32] By allowing government organizations to take all the credit for their initiatives, NGOs not only gained access to government resources, but to legitimacy and local cooperation in places where NGOs were an unfamiliar concept. Even as late as 2015, survey research revealed that Chinese citizens had very little trust for NGOs, but high levels of trust for the government.[33] Rural Chinese citizens would react to strangers coming into their communities and offering benefits with suspicion and hostility. However, they were accustomed to the idea of government organizations serving citizens and solving social problems.

GONGO (Government-Organized NGO) or GENGO (Government-Exploiting NGO)?

By partnering with the Communist Youth League, CYDF could outsource most of the labor necessary for carrying out its work to the Chinese government. These were not the only benefits it gained from its partnership with the Youth League. It also gained the protection of a powerful party-state organization, which allowed CYDF to maintain its autonomy and establish innovative programs without government interference – including, surprisingly enough, interference from the Youth League itself. This autonomy is especially surprising given the complicated, even convoluted relationship between the two organizations.

Many Chinese people, and quite a few China scholars, would argue that CYDF has had such a close relationship with the Communist Youth League because CYDF is part of the Youth League, rather than an independent organization. These people have insisted that CYDF is not an NGO, but a GONGO (government-organized NGO) that is a subsidiary of a party-state organization.[34] According to one version of CYDF's history, the Communist Youth League, became concerned about threats to its organizational future and founded CYDF in 1989.[35] The Youth League provided CYDF's initial operating budget and office space, and staffed it with its own cadres, including Xu Yongguang. In this story, Xu is not a social entrepreneur at all, but just another state employee following orders.

However, Xu Yongguang and many of CYDF's administrators told me a different version of the origins of their organization. According to them, Xu was a social entrepreneur who left the safety of the government bureaucracy in order to start CYDF because of his deep concern about the plight of poor rural children. When interviewed, he emphasized the riskiness of his choice. Like Gu Wei, who was profiled at the beginning of this chapter, he felt like he was leaving the safety net of the state bureaucracy when he made this move. He was in his late 30s at the time, and everyone expected him to transition out of the Youth League into the government because of his age. It was 1989, Xu pointed out, when no one in their right mind would turn down a safe and prestigious government job. Xu did note that he started the organization with several colleagues from the Youth League, but he implied they joined CYDF voluntarily. He also agreed that the Youth League gave the original RMB100,000 (about US$16,000) to register the foundation, but Xu made it sound like one donation among many. He pointed out that CYDF sent out 500,000 letters soliciting donations from enterprises and departments all over China, and raised RMB1 million. In this version of the founding narrative, CYDF began as an NGO that could operate with relative autonomy from the party-state. The Communist Youth League was simply one of its best supporters, as well as its legally-mandated supervisory agency.

Is it possible to reconcile these two stories? If, in the late-1980s, Xu Yongguang decided that he wanted to create an effective, innovative organization to address the social problem of rural education, how would he do it? As a cadre, it would be a reasonable strategy for him to exploit the fact that the Communist Youth League needed to do something to re-brand itself in the post-Mao era and to offer it a solution that aligned with his own goals. As the head of a new organization, he would need office space and funding, and he would presumably know how to extract those resources out of the Youth League. He would also poach talented staff members from the people he knew there. Over the next two decades, he would use his considerable *guanxi* at the Youth League to gain access to the resources CYDF needed to flourish and to avoid sanctions. From an outsider's perspective, it would look like the Communist Youth League set up CYDF as its GONGO and had it under its control. How could anyone tell how much autonomy CYDF had until it exercised it?

When we look at the actual history of CYDF, we find that in fact it exercised considerable autonomy and operated more like an independent NGO than a subsidiary of the Youth League. It was able to carry out its own agenda even in cases when its actions angered powerful government departments. CYDF has been the most-studied charity in recent Chinese history, and yet researchers find no evidence that the Communist Youth League ever interfered with CYDF's hiring or management of its staff, or in the development and implementation of its projects.[36] On paper, the Youth League created an office to supervise the Project Hope funds, yet this supervisory office was not only funded by CYDF, but it was also housed in CYDF offices.[37]

In the 1990s, some provincial Youth League organizations tried to use the "Project Hope" label for their activities without CYDF permission, claiming that the campaign belonged to the Youth League. CYDF complained, and the national Communist Youth League forced its provincial departments to stop.[38] CYDF also successfully refused to allow the provincial Youth League offices to manage Project Hope money, despite their efforts to take over provincial Project Hope budgets. CYDF insisted that all Project Hope money belonged to the national Project Hope Fund and therefore fell under the jurisdiction of CYDF. Donations were collected and distributed by special Project Hope Fund offices, headed up by managers appointed by CYDF, not the Youth League.

Indeed, it is easier to find examples where the Communist Youth League appeared to do the bidding of CYDF than the reverse. For instance, the Youth League arranged for important officials to show up at Project Hope events. This allowed CYDF to secure big donations from corporations and enterprises which sought access to those officials in order to build *guanxi* connections.[39] (Eventually, Project Hope was famous enough that CYDF no longer needed the Youth League to secure the presence of top officials.) The Youth League did more than provide visits by high-level cadres to help CYDF. Powerful officials pressured cadres throughout the party-state bureaucracy to make "voluntary" contributions to Project Hope to ensure successful campaigns.[40]

In its first two decades, CYDF defied government departments or state policy on several occasions without incurring sanctions, most likely because it was being protected by the Communist Youth League. In the fall of 1989, when Xu Yongguang launched Project Hope, it was only a few months after the Tiananmen Protests and massacre. China's mass media was under instruction from the Party to report only on positive achievements for the nation's fortieth anniversary. The sad plight of rural dropouts and decrepit schools certainly did not fit this mandate. Yet CYDF managed to hold a news conference attended by all the major news media in China.[41] The powerful Ministry of Education was insulted by the very idea of Project Hope because it claimed that outside donations were needed to rescue China's education system. Yet it was unable to prevent the campaign from becoming enormously successful. In 1991, the CCP Central Committee and the State Council jointly decreed that no new foundations would be approved, and no existing foundations would be permitted to set up local branches. Yet CYDF went ahead and established local branches of Project Hope and apparently incurred no penalty for these actions.[42]

Guanxi was a key component of CYDF's success. Through his high-level ties with the Communist Youth League, Xu Yongguang could also develop supportive relationships with other departments of the government. CYDF would not have been able to create a moral panic around the problem of rural school dropouts and decrepit school infrastructure without the complicity of the state-run media. CYDF was very effective in developing powerful images and stories, but these would not have mattered if the propaganda apparatus of the party-state had not printed, published, and aired them frequently. The state media also provided legitimacy. When CYDF first started out, people who received its mass mailings reacted with suspicion that it was a scam, even going as far as contacting the police. Then China's top state-run newspaper, the *People's Daily*, carried an advertisement for Project Hope. According to CYDF staff members, this completely changed the popular perception of the organization:

> Just imagine. Even the *People's Daily* has carried an advertisement for CYDF and Project Hope, so there can be no doubt that it is not a sham.... Afterwards we never heard people writing to the police asking them to check out the CYDF again.[43]

There is no doubt that from its birth CYDF was entangled with the Communist Youth League in a complicated relationship. However, it would be erroneous to assume that the government organization controlled the NGO as its GONGO. Instead, Xu Yongguang appears to have exploited his relationship with the Communist Youth League to gain substantial benefits for his organization, while managing to maintain significant autonomy from interference. Instead of a GONGO (government-organized NGO), perhaps it will be more accurate to view CYDF as a GENGO (government-exploiting NGO).[44]

The price of state alliances

CYDF was an unusually successful Chinese NGO, and Xu Yongguang has been an unusually successful Chinese social entrepreneur. Yet the strategy of building a mutually beneficial partnership with a government department was quite common among early twenty-first century social entrepreneurs, especially if they had previously worked in the party-state bureaucracy.[45] As Jin Jiaman of GEI (Global Environmental Institute) explained to me,

> I feel that what a Chinese NGO can do is come up with a new concept or a new idea, and you want to apply that locally. You first make a demonstration model. You do it on a small scale. When you have enough experience and get the model to work well, you can then inform the government, and provide the government with something to copy and paste. So eventually,

when the government is copying your model and promoting it on a large scale, it will have a huge effect...

Although state alliance strategies offered many benefits to organizations, they also had their costs. Social entrepreneurs who partnered with party-state cadres all had to follow the same set of unspoken rules: avoid highly controversial political topics; push for social transformation, but not for political change; and never directly criticize state officials in power. Chinese NGOs that failed to comply with these constraints could be cut off from their supply of resources, denied access to potential clients, and even prematurely shut down. As Xu Yongguang admitted, "We must never do anything that the government would find objectionable. If we insist on doing such things, then there can be only one outcome, and that is failure."[46]

The relationships between NGOs and state organizations were almost never formalized. Most NGOs did not receive government contracts for this work. Instead, their connection with state officials was based on personal *guanxi*, and the relationships were between people, not the organizations.[47] Because nothing was official, when government agencies "cut and pasted" an NGO's project, the NGO usually received no credit. Chinese social entrepreneurs claimed that they were at peace with this. One environmental activist, Kang Yuanyou, explained:

> After all the hard work, of course we would be happy to see our name appear on the publications alongside the local government. But it would be better if the government totally forgot about us, and framed it as if it were their own initiative and their own idea. Because that means an ENGO [environmental NGO] initiative has transformed into a government commitment. This is important, because even international NGOs can rarely sustain a long-term operation at any particular location. The best scenario is to pass on the torch to the local institutions ... as long as the initiative is adopted, our goal is achieved.[48]

In other words, the "best scenario" was if the NGO conducted all the necessary work of research and development and then allowed a state organization to take all the credit for this work and implement the project on a larger scale. Although this strategy may have helped Chinese NGOs maintain good relationships with government officials, it prevented Chinese citizens from learning about the work of these voluntary organizations and social entrepreneurs. Hiding their light under a bushel may have been the most pragmatic tactic for solving a particular social problem, but in the long run it reduced the influence of the NGO sector as a whole. No wonder Chinese citizens trusted the government more than they trusted NGOs, according to survey data.[49] Chinese NGOs were allowing the government to take credit for all of their hard work.

By developing such close relationships with the state organization, these NGOs were also at risk of harm whenever their government patron encountered problems or misbehaved. For example, on several occasions, the Hong Kong media reported instances when Project Hope funds were mishandled and embezzled by Youth League staff. When mainland media sources attempted to pick up the story, they were suppressed by the government. This may seem like a benefit to the organization, but Xu Yongguang and other CYDF administrators felt that this kind of government overprotection was actually detrimental to the organization. The stories always leaked out anyway so the NGO's reputation inevitably incurred damage. The suppression only served to give everybody the impression that the organization must be covering up other sins that are even more terrible than the ones exposed. Moreover, the NGO lost an opportunity to demonstrate its internal disciplinary measures, or to provide a very public warning to its own staff members to stay in line.

Ironically, state partnerships may also harm Chinese NGOs when they succeed too well. The strategies are designed to transform state behavior, but at the price of allowing the state to take most of the credit for the results. Golden Key used alliances with state organizations to get its training materials and learning aids to an increasing number of blind and visually impaired schoolchildren over the years. Yet the organization itself never had a public profile or reputation, and it never grew beyond four overworked, underpaid staff members in a tiny office. When founder Peter Xu retired, a government agency took over the organization. Similarly, CYDF and other similar charities successfully managed to generate a moral panic over rural education in China. Through partnerships with state organizations, they taught the Chinese government how to deliver a higher quality of schooling to children in the countryside. Eventually, state agencies became sufficiently pressured and sufficiently competent to deliver educational reforms without the help of NGOs like CYDF.

The strategy of state partnership also limited the scope of social entrepreneurial activity. It only worked when NGO goals coincided with the goals of state actors and agencies. Although they could and did expand the purview of state concern, Chinese NGOs that relied on state partnerships could not advocate for social changes that would limit or reduce the power of the government. Indeed, their underlying strategy arguably increased the power of the state rather than reduced it – their mission was to push the state to address more social problems, pass more regulations, and provide more benefits. Yet these social entrepreneurs also offered a method for real political change in a populist democracy, a way for citizens to transform the Chinese party-state to make it less incompetent and corrupt, and more effective and responsive to its citizens' needs.

Notes

1 Market ventures were for-profit businesses run by state organizations, such as government offices, state universities, and even the military. The government encouraged them as a way to reduce dependency on state funds. For a while, the hottest discos in Beijing were run by the People's Liberation Army. Carolyn L. Hsu, "Market ventures, moral logics, and ambiguity: Crafting a new organizational form in post-socialist China," *The Sociological Quarterly* 47, no. 1 (2006): 62–92.

2 Heather Haveman, "Between a rock and a hard place: Organizational change and performance under conditions of fundamental environmental transformation," *Administrative Science Quarterly* 37 (1992): 48–72.
 3 Gu reports that HYDF only paid CYDF for two years. After that "We stopped paying it, and they never said anything."
 4 Mun Tsang, "Intergovernmental grants and the financing of compulsory education in China" (Peking University, Beijing, China, May 17–19, 2001, 2001); Jennifer Adams and Emily Hannum, "Children's social welfare in China, 1989–1997: Access to health insurance and education," *China Quarterly* no. 181 (2005): 100–121; Deborah Davis, "Chinese social welfare: Policies and outcomes," *China Quarterly* no. 119 (1989): 577–597; Jude Howell, "NGO-state relations in post-Mao China," in D. Hulme and M. Edwards (Eds.), *NGOs, States and Donors* (New York: St. Martin's Press, 1996), 202–215, 205–207.
 5 Qiusha Ma, *Non-Governmental Organizations in Contemporary China* (New York: Routledge, 2006), Chapter 2; Karla W. Simon, *Civil Society in China: The Legal Framework from Ancient Times to the "New Reform Era"* (Oxford: Oxford University Press, 2013), Chapter 8.
 6 Katja M. Yang and Björn Alpermann, "Children and youth NGOs in China: Social activism between embeddedness and marginalization," *China Information* 28, no. 3 (November 1, 2014): 311–337.
 7 Karla W. Simon, *Civil Society in China: The Legal Framework from Ancient Times to the "New Reform Era"* (Oxford: Oxford University Press, 2013), 255–257.
 8 Ibid., 204.
 9 Shawn Shieh et al., *Chinese NGO Directory (251 NGO Profiles and Special Report): China's Civil Society in the Making* (Beijing: China Development Brief, 2013), xii; Timothy Hildebrandt, "The political economy of social organization registration in China," *The China Quarterly* 208 (2011): 970, http://dx.doi.org/10.1017/S0305741 011001093.
10 Karla W. Simon, "Meaningful changes in the legal environment for civil society organizations: Their relationship to larger trends in China's 'new' governance" (University of Alberta, Edmonton, CA, August 16, 2013). https://docs.google.com/a/colgate.edu/file/d/0BxzGT6Btpa-kTnN1UzdNMVNkVE0/edit.a.
11 Shawn Shieh, "China's charity law passes, finally!" *NGOs in China*, March 20, 2016. http://ngochina.blogspot.com/2016/03/chinas-charity-law-passes-finally-civil.html.
12 Carolyn L. Hsu and Jessica C. Teets. "Is China's new overseas NGO management law sounding the death knell for civil society? Maybe not." *Asia-Pacific Journal* 14, no. 4 (2016): 3. Shawn Shieh, "The overseas NGOs law is now official," *NGOs in China* April 29, 2016. http://ngochina.blogspot.com/2016/04/the-overseas-ngo-management-law-is-now.html.
13 Most of the other large nations of the world are federal states where the central government shares power with provincial/regional governments; for example, Russia, India, the United States, and Canada. The PRC is a unitary state where even the governors of its provinces and the mayors of its largest cities are appointed by the central government in Beijing.
14 For a vivid description of the kind of disputes that may arise between state organizations, see Andrew Mertha, *China's Water Warriors: Citizen Action and Policy Change* (paperback ed.) (Ithaca: Cornell University Press, 2010), 168. It depicts, in fascinating detail, several cases of environmental controversy where different government agencies ended up on different sides of the fight.
15 Jeffrey Pfeffer and Gerald R. Salancik, *The External Control of Organizations: A Resource Dependence Perspective* (New York: Harper & Row, 1978); Joseph Galaskiewicz and Wolfgang Bielefeld, *Nonprofit Organizations in an Age of Uncertainty* (Hawthorne, NY: Aldine de Gruyter, 1998).

118 Getting in bed with the state

16 In social science parlance, organizations must be able to offer persuasive "institutional accounts" – arguments to potential clients, suppliers, staff and partners that the organization produces desirable, important services using innovative, reliable, and legitimate methods. See Paul DiMaggio, "Interest and agency in institutional theory," in L. Zucker (Ed.), *Institutional Patterns and Organizations* (Cambridge, MA: Ballinger Publishing, 1988), 3–22.
17 John W. Meyer and Brian Rowan, "Institutionalized organizations: Formal structure as myth and ceremony," in W.W. Powell and P.J. DiMaggio, *The New Institutionalism in Organizational Analysis* (Chicago: University of Chicago Press, 1991), 41–62; Roger Friedland and Robert R. Alford, "Bringing society back in: Symbols, practices, and institutional contradictions," in W. Powell and P. DiMaggio (Eds.), *The New Institutionalism in Organizational Analysis* (Chicago: University of Chicago Press, 1991), 232–263; Robin Stryker, "Legitimacy processes as institutional politics," *Research in the Sociology of Organizations* 17 (2000): 179–223; Carolyn L. Hsu, "Beyond civil society: An organizational perspective on state-NGO relations in the People's Republic of China," *Journal of Civil Society* 6, no. 3 (2010): 259–278; Carolyn L. Hsu and Y. Jiang "An institutional approach to Chinese NGOs: State alliance versus state avoidance resource strategies," *The China Quarterly* 221 (2015): 100–122.
18 According to a survey of Chinese NGOs, the majority of respondents saw local government offices as more helpful and approving of NGOs than the central government. This is notable since public opinion polls in China have consistently shown that, in general, citizens have higher approval ratings of the central government than local governments. Timothy Hildebrandt, *Social Organizations and the Authoritarian State in China* (Cambridge; New York: Cambridge University Press, 2013). 41.
19 Heather Haveman, "Between a rock and a hard place: Organizational change and performance under conditions of fundamental environmental transformation," *Administrative Science Quarterly* 37 (1992): 48–72.
20 In farming families, if the first child was a girl, a second child was permitted. Ethnic minorities and couples where both parents were singletons were also allowed to have second children. According to some analyses, by the early twenty-first century, the one child rule only applied to only about a third of Chinese families. Susan Greenhalgh and Edwin A. Winckler, *Governing China's Population* (Stanford: Stanford University Press, 2005); Yadan Ouyang, "China relaxes its one-child policy," *The Lancet* 382, no. 9907 (2013): e28.
21 Kam Wing Chan, "China, internal migration," in I. Ness and P. Bellwood (Eds.), *The Encyclopedia of Global Human Migration* (Indianapolis: Wiley, 2013).
22 In January, 2008, I paid over US$4000 for my daughter to attend one semester first-grade at a Beijing public school.
23 Andrew Kipnis, "Urbanisation in between: Rural traces in a rapidly growing and industrialising county city," *China Perspectives* 2013, no. 3 (2013): 5–12. http://search.ebscohost.com/login.aspx?direct=true&db=aph&AN=90082893&site=ehost-live; Him Chung and Jonathan Unger, "The Guangdong model of urbanisation," *China Perspectives* 2013, no. 3 (2013): 33–41. http://search.ebscohost.com/login.aspx?direct=true&db=aph&AN=90082896&site=ehost-live; Yu Zhu et al., "The extent of in situ urbanisation in China's county areas," *China Perspectives* 2013, no. 3 (2013): 43–52. http://search.ebscohost.com/login.aspx?direct=true&db=aph&AN=90082897&site=ehost-live.
24 Although after 2007 schools were not allowed to charge extra fees to out-of-district students, families would still have to pay for commuting costs, meal money, and dormitory rooms, if their children had to board.
25 Kerry Brown, "Communist youth league," in *Berkshire Encyclopedia of China*, Vol. 1 (Great Barrington, MA: Berkshire Publishing Group, 2009), 460–461.
26 For more on the concept of moral panics, see *Understanding Media: The Extensions of Man*, directed by Marshall McLuhan (New York: McGraw-Hill, 1964); Stanley

Cohen, *Folk Devils and Moral Panics: The Creation of the Mods and Rockers* (New York: Routledge, 2011).

27 Carolyn L. Hsu, "Political narratives and the production of legitimacy: The case of corruption in post-Mao China," *Qualitative Sociology* 24, no. 1 (Spring, 2001): 25–54.

28 Joy Yueyue Zhang and Michael Barr, *Green Politics in China: Environmental Governance and State-Society Relations* (London: Pluto Press, 2013), 159. Chapter 2.

29 Ibid., 70.

30 Liping Sun et al., *Dongyuan Yu Canyu: Disanbumen Mujuan Jizhi Ge'an Yanjiu (Mobilization and Participation: A Case Study of Third Sector Fundraising)* (Hangzhou: Zhejiang People's Publishing House, 1999), 120.

31 Ibid.; Yiyi Lu, *Non-Governmental Organizations in China: The Rise of Dependent Autonomy* (London; New York: Routledge, 2009).

32 Hildebrandt, *Social Organizations and the Authoritarian State in China*, p. 88.

33 Bruce J. Dickson, "The Xi Jinping administration: A comprehensive assessment," *Association of Asian Studies Annual Meeting*, Friday, April 1, 2016.

34 Technically, CYDF would be a PONGO (Party-organized NGO) rather than a GONGO. See Patricia M. Thornton, "The advance of the party: Transformation or takeover of urban grassroots society?" *The China Quarterly* 213 (2013): 1–18. http://search.proquest.com/docview/1318560733?accountid=10207.

35 Xiaoguang Kang, *Chuangzao Xiwang: Zhongguo Qingshaonian Fazhan Jijinghui Yanjiu (Creating Hope: A Study of the China Youth Development Foundation)* (Guilin: Lijiang Publishing House and Guangxi Normal University Publishing House, 1997); Ma, *Non-Governmental Organizations in Contemporary China*; Lu, *Non-Governmental Organizations in China: The Rise of Dependent Autonomy*.

36 Kang, *Chuangzao Xiwang: Zhongguo Qingshaonian Fazhan Jijinghui Yanjiu (Creating Hope: A Study of the China Youth Development Foundation)*; Sun et al., *Dongyuan Yu Canyu: Disanbumen Mujuan Jizhi Ge'an Yanjiu (Mobilization and Participation: A Case Study of Third Sector Fundraising)*; Lu, *Non-Governmental Organizations in China: The Rise of Dependent Autonomy*.

37 Kang, *Chuangzao Xiwang: Zhongguo Qingshaonian Fazhan Jijinghui Yanjiu (Creating Hope: A Study of the China Youth Development Foundation)*, 160.

38 Lu, *Non-Governmental Organizations in China: The Rise of Dependent Autonomy*, p. 33.

39 Sun et al., *Dongyuan Yu Canyu: Disanbumen Mujuan Jizhi Ge'an Yanjiu (Mobilization and Participation: A Case Study of Third Sector Fundraising)*, 162.

40 This is known as the "administrative method of fundraising." To be fair, CYDF did work hard to reduce its dependence on this kind of contribution and to increase its funding from voluntary, nongovernmental sources. Ibid., 126–133.

41 Xu Yongguang interview. Also see Ibid., 35.

42 Kang, *Chuangzao Xiwang: Zhongguo Qingshaonian Fazhan Jijinghui Yanjiu (Creating Hope: A Study of the China Youth Development Foundation)*, 89–90.

43 Lu, *Non-Governmental Organizations in China: The Rise of Dependent Autonomy*, 53.

44 Carolyn L Hsu, "China Youth Development Foundation: GONGO (Government-organized NGO) or GENGO (Government-exploiting NGO)?" In R. Hasmath and J.Y.J. Hsu (Eds.), *NGO Governance and Management in China* (Oxford: Routledge, 2015).

45 Carolyn L. Hsu and Yuzhou Jiang, "An institutional approach to Chinese NGOs: State alliance versus state avoidance resource strategies," *The China Quarterly* 221 (2015): 100–122; Hsu, *Beyond Civil Society: An Organizational Perspective on State-NGO Relations in the People's Republic of China*, 259–278.

46 Kang, *Chuangzao Xiwang: Zhongguo Qingshaonian Fazhan Jijinghui Yanjiu (Creating Hope: A Study of the China Youth Development Foundation)*, 387.

47 Timothy Hildebrandt, *Social Organizations and the Authoritarian State in China* (Cambridge; New York: Cambridge University Press, 2013). 150.
48 Joy Yueyue Zhang and Michael Barr, *Green Politics in China: Environmental Governance and State-Society Relations* (London: Pluto Press, 2013), 101.
49 Dickson, *The Xi Jinping Administration: A Comprehensive Assessment.*

Bibliography

Adams, J. and Hannum, E. 2005. Children's social welfare in China, 1989–1997: Access to health insurance and education. *China Quarterly*, (181), pp. 100–121.

Brown, K. 2009. Communist Youth League. *Berkshire Encyclopedia of China*. Great Barrington, MA: Berkshire Publishing Group, pp. 460–461.

Chan, K.W. 2013. China, internal migration. In: I. Ness and P. Bellwood (Eds.), *The Encyclopedia of Global Human Migration*. Indianapolis: Wiley.

Chung, H. and Unger, J. 2013. The Guangdong model of urbanisation. *China Perspectives*, 2013(3), pp. 33–41.

Cohen, S. 2011. *Folk Devils and Moral Panics: The Creation of the Mods and Rockers*. New York: Routledge.

Davis, D. 1989. Chinese social welfare: Policies and outcomes. *China Quarterly*, (119), pp. 577–597.

Dickson, B.J. 2016. The Xi Jinping administration: A comprehensive assessment, *Association of Asian Studies Annual Meeting*, Friday, April 1, 2016.

DiMaggio, P. 1988. Interest and agency in institutional theory. In: L. Zucker (Ed.), *Institutional Patterns and Organizations*. Cambridge, MA: Ballinger Publishing, pp. 3–22.

Friedland, R. and Alford, R.R. 1991. Bringing society back in: Symbols, practices, and institutional contradictions. In: W. Powell and P. DiMaggio (Eds.), *The New Institutionalism in Organizational Analysis*. Chicago: University of Chicago Press, pp. 232–263.

Galaskiewicz, J. and Bielefeld, W. 1998. *Nonprofit Organizations in an Age of Uncertainty*. Hawthorne, NY: Aldine de Gruyter.

Greenhalgh, S. and Winckler, E.A. 2005. *Governing China's Population*. Stanford: Stanford University Press.

Haveman, H. 1992. Between a rock and a hard place: Organizational change and performance under conditions of fundamental environmental transformation. *Administrative Science Quarterly*, 37, pp. 48–72.

Hildebrandt, T. 2011. The political economy of social organization registration in China. *The China Quarterly*, 208, pp. 970.

Hildebrandt, T. 2013. *Social Organizations and the Authoritarian State in China*. Cambridge; New York: Cambridge University Press.

Howell, J. 1996. NGO-state relations in post-Mao China. In: D. Hulme and M. Edwards (Eds.), *NGOs, States and Donors*. New York: St. Martin's Press, pp. 202–215.

Hsu, C.L. 2001. Political narratives and the production of legitimacy: The case of corruption in post-Mao China. *Qualitative Sociology*, 24(1), pp. 25–54.

Hsu, C.L. 2006. Market ventures, moral logics, and ambiguity: Crafting a new organizational form in post-Socialist China. *The Sociological Quarterly*, 47(1), pp. 62–92.

Hsu, C.L. 2010. Beyond civil society: An organizational perspective on state-NGO relations in the People's Republic of China. *Journal of Civil Society*, 6(3), pp. 259–278.

Hsu, C.L. 2015. China Youth Development Foundation: GONGO (Government-organized NGO) or GENGO (Government-exploiting NGO)? In: R. Hasmath and J.Y.J. Hsu (Eds.), *NGO Governance and Management in China*. Oxford: Routledge.

Hsu, C.L. and Jiang, Y. 2015. An institutional approach to Chinese NGOs: State alliance versus state avoidance resource strategies. *The China Quarterly*, 221, pp. 100–122.

Hsu, C.L. and Teets, J.C. 2016. Is China's new overseas NGO management law sounding the death knell for civil society? Maybe not. *Asia-Pacific Journal*, 14(4), pp. 3.

Kang, X. 1997. *Chuangzao Xiwang: Zhongguo Qingshaonian Fazhan Jijinghui Yanjiu (Creating Hope: A Study of the China Youth Development Foundation)*. Guilin: Lijiang Publishing House and Guangxi Normal University Publishing House.

Kipnis, A. 2013. Urbanisation in between: Rural traces in a rapidly growing and industrialising county city. *China Perspectives*, 2013(3), pp. 5–12.

Lu, Y. 2009. *Non-governmental Organizations in China: The Rise of Dependent Autonomy*. London; New York: Routledge.

Ma, Q. 2006. *Non-Governmental Organizations in Contemporary China*. New York: Routledge.

McLuhan, M. 1964. *Understanding Media: The Extensions of Man*. New York: McGraw-Hill.

Mertha, A. 2010. *China's Water Warriors: Citizen Action and Policy Change* (paperback ed.) Ithaca: Cornell University Press.

Meyer, J.W. and Rowan, B. 1991. Institutionalized organizations: Formal structure as myth and ceremony. In: W.W. Powell and P.J. DiMaggio (Eds.), *The New Institutionalism in Organizational Analysis*. Chicago: University of Chicago Press, pp. 41–62.

Ouyang, Y. 2013. China relaxes its one-child policy. *The Lancet*, 382(9907), pp. e28.

Pfeffer, J. and Salancik, G.R. 1978. *The External Control of Organizations: A Resource Dependence Perspective*. New York: Harper & Row.

Shieh, S. 2016. Last update, China's charity law passes, finally! (Civil society 2, National security 2 halftime). March 20, 2016. Available: http://ngochina.blogspot.com/2016/03/chinas-charity-law-passes-finally-civil.html.

Shieh, S. 2016. The overseas NGOs law is now official. In *NGOs in China*, April 29, 2016. http://ngochina.blogspot.com/2016/04/the-overseas-ngo-management-law-is-now.html

Shieh, S., Liu, H., Zhang, G., Brown-Inz, A., and Gong, Y. 2013. *Chinese NGO Directory (251 NGO Profiles and Special Report): China's Civil Society in the Making*. Beijing: China Development Brief.

Simon, K.W. 2013. *Civil Society in China: The Legal Framework from Ancient Times to the "New Reform Era"*. Oxford: Oxford University Press.

Simon, K.W. 2013. Meaningful changes in the legal environment for civil society organizations: Their relationship to larger trends in China's "new" governance, *Forum on NGO Governance and Management in China*, August 16, 2013.

Stryker, R. 2000. Legitimacy processes as institutional politics. *Research in the Sociology of Organizations*, 17, pp. 179–223.

Sun, L., Jin, J., He, J., and Bi, X. 1999. *Dongyuan yu Canyu: Disanbumen Mujuan Jizhi Ge'an Yanjiu (Mobilization and Participation: A Case Study of Third Sector Fundraising)*. Hangzhou: Zhejiang People's Publishing House.

Thornton, P.M. 2013. The advance of the party: Transformation or takeover of urban grassroots society? *The China Quarterly*, 213, pp. 1–18.

Tsang, M. 2001. Intergovernmental grants and the financing of compulsory education in China, *International Conference on Economics of Education*, May 17–19, 2001.

Yang, K.M. and Alpermann, B. 2014. Children and youth NGOs in China: Social activism between embeddedness and marginalization. *China Information*, 28(3), pp. 311–337.

Zhang, J.Y. and Barr, M. 2013. *Green Politics in China: Environmental Governance and State-Society Relations*. London: Pluto Press.

Zhu, Y., Lin, M., Lin, L., and Chen, J. 2013. The extent of in situ urbanisation in China's county areas. *China Perspectives*, 2013(3), pp. 43–52.

6 Environmental NGOs
Foreign funding and Chinese connections

A journey to the West

In 1996, a middle-aged researcher at a Chinese state-run environmental institute was given the opportunity to travel to the United States to learn about NGOs. As part of the trip, Jin Jiaman visited over two dozen American NGOs. In her interview, she smiled as she recalled her excitement:

> Big ones and small ones – there was even one with just one person! That one just provided information online. I felt like it was so refreshing because NGOs, they could have their independence. Because in China then, you know how we were educated.... If you were sent to the countryside, you went to the countryside. And then they sent you to the factory. You had to do whatever they asked you to do.

To Jin Jiaman, the social entrepreneurs running NGOs in the United States seemed so autonomous and creative. She told me that just being around them gave her a sense of "release and openness." She had finally found a new approach to tackling the intransigent environmental problems that had frustrated her government institute for years.

The person who introduced me to Jin Jiaman repeatedly described her as "inspirational," and in person she exuded charisma, intelligence, passion, and ambition. She was born in Beijing in 1954, to a scientist mother and a cadre father, a privileged position in Maoist China. However, as with Gu Wei and Xu Yongguang, Jin Jiaman's early life was derailed by the Cultural Revolution. From the ages of 15 to 28, she was essentially exiled from Beijing: first she was sent to a rural village and then assigned to a job in a factory in Hebei Province. Eventually, her parents were able to use their connections (to "pull *guanxi*") to bring her back to Beijing through a job at an environmental research academy. Her new workplace sent her to college, where she was trained in atmospheric sciences. Her career took off. In the 1980s, Jin was one of the few people at the institute trained to use computers to analyze and alleviate air pollution, and she was promoted to a cadre position in the administration. Like her parents before her (and due in part to their position and connections), Jin had reached an elite position in China's status hierarchy. With her scientific credentials, she was well placed to succeed in a government bureaucracy that was increasingly invested in the ideology of *suzhi*.

Even though her career was flourishing, Jin Jiaman felt more and more constrained by the limitations of state environmental work. By the early 1990s, air pollution was already a serious problem in the PRC, and nothing her institute did seem to result in real improvements. She explained:

> We started to import some foreign technologies and facilities that we hoped would solve China's environmental problems.... But all of these purely technical methods didn't work because China was going through all this economic development. The environment is a very interdisciplinary thing. The people who study the environment can't control the environment because of the social issues involved. And all these social issues will always affect the environment.

Even more frustrating, if someone came up with an innovative idea, it was almost impossible to implement it. Not only was the Chinese party-state bureaucracy full of red tape, but government officials were inherently risk-averse, waiting for dictates from above before making any moves.

It was at this time, however, that Jin Jiaman began to discover the global environmental NGO sector. In the early 1990s, Jin learned about the world of international foundations when, through her position as a cadre, she was invited to participate in a Rockefeller Foundation training program about sustainable development. Beijing in 1995, the UN convened the Fourth World Conference on Women, and countless Chinese women encountered NGOs for the first time. That led to the trip that Jin took to the United States in 1996, which was specifically designed to train Chinese women to start NGOs.

After visiting many different American NGOs, Jin Jiaman found herself in Pennsylvania for two weeks, interning at Ecologia, an environmental NGO.[1] One of her fellow interns was Wang Yongchen, a journalist and environmentalist who worked for China National Radio. Jin Jiaman learned that Ecologia had small grants for educational environmental activities. She and Wang talked about becoming social entrepreneurs and establishing an environmental NGO (also known as an ENGO) in China. Their plan was to spread environmental awareness in the PRC by inviting people to participate in environmental activities, such as planting trees or cleaning up garbage. Wang could publicize the activities and solicit volunteers through her radio show. The grant from Ecologia "was maybe a little more than one thousand dollars," Jin recalled, and it would be enough to fund some activities. The result was Green Earth Volunteers, established in 1997 as one of the PRC's first environmental NGOs.[2] Although Jin worked for Green Earth Volunteers, she kept her day job at the state research academy, just as Wang kept her position at China National Radio.

Eight years later, in 2004, Jin Jiaman turned 50 and was able to retire from her state position. Armed with her pension, she was ready to launch into social entrepreneurship full-time. Joined by three of her friends from her research academy, she established her own ENGO. GEI (Global Environmental Institute) was dedicated to designing and implementing "market-based models for solving environmental problems in order to achieve development that is economically, ecologically, and socially sustainable."[3] Her supervisors wanted them to stay and establish the organization as an institute within the state research academy, but Jin Jiaman refused. "We wanted independence," Jin explained.

Guanxi was the key to GEI's success. By the time Jin founded GEI, she had a number of friends well placed to help her. She had excellent connections with important people in the government, thanks to her parents and her own work experience. Through her friendship with Wang Yongchen, she had access to the Chinese media, as well as good *guanxi* with well-established Chinese ENGOs. Just as important were her ties outside of China. Although GEI partnered with the Chinese government on many projects, it almost never received any funding from the state. Instead, the money came from overseas, and through her personal connections. One of her former colleagues, Zhang Jiqiang, moved to the US to work at the Rockefeller Foundation and then moved on to the Blue Moon Fund. These two organizations became GEI's major financial supporters, and also helped to open the doors to other wealthy Western funders. In 2008, GEI received about 75 percent of its funding from international foundations. Since Jin Jiaman had *guanxi* in the US, most of these foundations were American, including the Clinton Global Initiative. The other 25 percent of GEI's funding came from Western governments, including the European Union and the UK.

ENGOs in the sweet spot: foreign money and state allies

Jin Jiaman's story highlights an aspect of Chinese social entrepreneurship that this book has ignored until now – the importance of international influence, international connections, and international resources. Among the first generation of Chinese NGOs, no sector was more successful than environmental NGOs. ENGOs were more numerous than other types of Chinese NGOs.[4] They were more likely to be legally registered, less likely to suffer from political suppression, and more likely to benefit from political support.[5] Chinese ENGOs were also socially and politically influential. They were able to inspire moral panics among the population to pressure the government into action, for example elevating air pollution from a nonissue into one of the top concerns in the PRC.[6] When ENGOs and other environmental activists protested that a 2012 draft of China's new Environmental Protection Law was too weak, the government revised the law to be much stronger. The new law, which went into effect in 2015, permitted ENGOs to file environmental lawsuits against violators, including government organizations.[7]

Why were Chinese ENGOs so successful? In the 1990s and early 2000s, social entrepreneurs were able to capitalize upon the global environmental movement as a source of both influential ideas and extensive resources. They were able to build international connections with wealthy and powerful partners all over the world. Chinese environmental social entrepreneurs benefited from the fact that the global environmental movement's dominant discourse – the ecological framework – fit well with *suzhi* ideology, allowing environmental arguments to be easily accepted by both the ruling regime and the Chinese populace. It also helped that the global environmental sector at the turn of the century not only had a lot of money, but was very interested in investing that money in China's environmental issues.

Chinese ENGOs could also exploit conflicts between party-state actors about the importance of environmental protection, as well as the fact that government funds were perpetually inadequate for environmental work. Environmentally-minded government officials were always seeking allies, especially ones that could help them with their resource problems. They developed a strategy where most of the financial costs of Chinese environmental protection were outsourced to foreign funders. Chinese environmental social entrepreneurs, with their foreign connections, could act like cultural translators between the world of international foundations and Chinese government cadres. Chinese ENGOs also became unofficial state subcontractors, carrying out a great deal of environmental work that would be difficult for state environmental departments to do. Conveniently for the state, these ENGOs were also funded by foreign sources, relieving the government once again of shouldering environmental costs.

Yet not all aspiring Chinese social entrepreneurs had access to these opportunities. Those that were able to capitalize on this state of affairs were the ones with *guanxi*, like Jin Jiaman. Indeed, a significant number of China's most influential first-generation ENGOs can be traced back to a high-status group of friends, classmates, and colleagues in Beijing who enjoyed close ties to important state actors, as well as connections to international research institutes and foundations.

The global environmental movement: big ideas and big money

The ecological framework and the ideology of suzhi

One of the reasons why Chinese social entrepreneurs were able to build productive ties with global environmentalists is because their language and worldviews overlapped. Just like *suzhi* ideology, the ecological framework is concerned with "quality of life" and focuses on the ways that external conditions impede or foster human development. Just like *suzhi* ideology, this version of environmental discourse sees science as the ultimate authority and source of legitimacy. These overlaps were not a result of coincidence. Environmental discourse likely contributed to the development of *suzhi* ideology.

Most environmental historians trace the emergence of the current global environmental movement to the 1960s.[8] There were, of course, earlier movements that advocated for the protection of the natural environment against the depredations of civilization. Taoists, Druids, and European Romantics all found nature more holy, true, and pure than anything human society had to offer. Throughout history, people have rescued animals, whether they were Buddhists saving ducks from the cooking pot or wealthy hunters creating reserves for elite recreational activities. In more modern times, the Industrial Revolution led to an almost immediate backlash. Henry David Thoreau retreated to Walden Pond, while others in the US and Europe started movements decrying air pollution, promoting public sanitation, conserving wilderness, or fighting for consumer protection.[9] John Muir founded the Sierra Club in 1892. Yet each of these concerns was seen as a separate problem rather than multiple facets of a single issue called environmentalism.

What changed in the mid-twentieth century was the rise of an *ecological framework* that insisted that all of these disparate issues – urban sanitation, animal extinction, public health, industrial development, the destruction of wilderness – were all part of the same story. Perhaps the turning point was the atom bomb and the studies of its effects on not just human victims, but also on animals, plants, waterways, the atmosphere, and the soil.[10] Perhaps it was the postwar boom of consumerism, fueled by cheap oil, which substantially sped up the unsustainability of the economy and fed fears of a population explosion.[11] Perhaps it was the rising panic about cancer, reinforced by the Thalidomide scandal in the US and Europe, which fed fears that human "progress" was secretly destroying human health.[12]

In any case, by the time biologist Rachel Carson wrote *Silent Spring* in 1962, a book about the toxic chemicals of modern agriculture and their effects on nature could become a huge bestseller and a cultural phenomenon. It was excerpted in popular magazines and translated almost immediately into German and French. In it, Carson wrote,

> ...the central problem of our age has ... become the contamination of man's total environment with such substances of incredible potential for harm – substances that accumulate in the tissues of plants and animals and even penetrate the germ cells to shatter or alter the very material of heredity upon which the shape of the future depends.[13]

In Carson's quote, we can see the ecological framework – an understanding of the environment in which toxicology, medical pathology, geography, plant biology, genetics, ornithology, entomology, agricultural sciences, geography, and economics all come together to illuminate a complex of interrelated problems.

According to Jan Ivo Engels, this new framework has four central characteristics:

1 The "environment" encompasses an entire suite of natural and social issues, whose interconnections are revealed through a holistic view of "ecology." Environmental problems affect the *quality of life*, broadly speaking – not just of humans, but of all natural things.
2 Environmental issues are global issues, crossing national boundaries and endangering both humankind and the planet as a whole. This justifies the global spread of the ecological framework and environmental institutions.

3   Our understanding of environmental problems and solutions is based on science and legitimated by scientific experts, such as Rachel Carson. This was a shift from traditional nature conservation, which had often positioned itself as antagonistic to science and modernity. Despite the fact that the new environmentalism is critical of the techno-consumerism of industrial societies and suspicious of scientific meddling, it still relies on scientific authority for truth claims.
4   Environmental problems are a political issue that will not be solved simply through technical solutions, but instead require mass mobilization and political involvement.[14]

Of course, within this framework, there have always been disagreements and conflicting views. Mainstream environmental discourses focus on keeping nature in balance to protect human health and quality of life, and preserving biodiversity for moral and aesthetic reasons. Instead of criticizing capitalism, they argue that economic development is fine as long as it takes environmental factors into consideration along with economic, technological, political, and social ones.[15] In contrast, alternative environmental discourses such as ecofeminism, environmental justice, and deep ecology are much more critical of current economic and political institutions and demand radical transformation. Not surprisingly, the mainstream, development-compatible environmental discourses are more influential in China than other versions of environmentalism, just as they are in the West.

The impact of this new environmental perspective was widespread, rapid, and enduring. Only a few short years after *Silent Spring*, millions of people worldwide celebrated the first Earth Day on April 22, 1970. Environmental concerns became so prevalent in the United States that even a conservative president, Richard Nixon, felt he had no choice but to establish the Environmental Protection Agency (EPA) in 1970. Environmental ministries were also set up in Japan, East Germany, and France around this time.[16] Even capitalist corporations eventually jumped on the environmental bandwagon.[17]

Just as the global environmental movement was emerging, the People's Republic of China was taking its first steps to build ties with Western nations. China joined the United Nations in October of 1971. Just a few months later, in June of 1972, the UN Conference on the Human Environment was held in Stockholm, Sweden, with the PRC as one of its participants. One of the Chinese delegates, Qu Geping, described the Stockholm summit as a turning point in Chinese environmentalism.[18] Despite the fact that China was still in the midst of the Cultural Revolution, the summit inspired the Chinese government to hold its own national environmental conference the following year, as well as to establish the National Environmental Protection Office in 1974.[19] After Deng Xiaoping established his power in 1978, one of his first initiatives was to promulgate China's first Environmental Protection Law.[20]

It was at this moment that Western environmentalism inspired one of the CCP's most notorious policies: the 1980 Birth Planning Policy, known in the

West as the "One Child Policy."[21] China's new environmentalists were impressed by Paul Ehrlich's argument in *The Population Bomb*.[22] The ecological framework taught them that uncontrolled growth led to poverty and devastation, while reducing quantity led to a higher quality of life. Translating these arguments from English to Chinese, the CCP formulated a new term, "population quality" (*renkou suzhi*). This was the first usage of the term *suzhi* in its current definition. As discussed in Chapter 4, state propaganda for the Birth Planning Policy spread the mantra of "quality over quantity" throughout the nation (see Chapter 4, Figure 4.7).

By the time that party-state officials, political dissidents, and ordinary citizens assembled a new national ideology after the 1989 Tiananmen Protests, they had already been introduced to the concept of a holistic "quality" from the global environmental movement, both directly and refracted through state birth planning propaganda. The ecological framework taught that each person's "quality of life" was shaped by the "quality" of his or her total environment. With Maoist ideology looking increasingly irrelevant and bankrupt, Chinese people sought a new source of authority and legitimacy besides the Communist Party. Environmental discourse reinforced the message that educated people, especially scientists, held the key to truth in a modern society.

The overlap between the ecological framework and *suzhi* ideology was enormously beneficial to the first generation of environmental social entrepreneurs in the PRC. It allowed Chinese environmental activists to use the language of "quality" – a language that was both politically and popularly resonant in the PRC – to argue for environmental protection and intervention. Social entrepreneurs in other areas had to start from scratch to persuade the Chinese populace that certain social problems even existed. The first generation of environmental activists, by contrast, benefited from the fact that government officials and international organizations helped advertise the importance of environmental issues.

The global environmental sector: "best practices" backed up with targeted funding

Although the global environmental movement began as a set of influential ideas, it soon had to be structured into institutions and organizations – an organizational field with conferences, government departments, NGOs, foundations, mass media, and scientific and educational institutions. From that moment onward, the spread of the ecological framework ideology was accompanied by the spread of these organizational practices. As we just noted, soon after governments in Western industrialized nations established environmental protection agencies, countries like China set up their own versions. In addition to government agencies, one important way that the global environmental movement institutionalized from the beginning was through NGOs.

In the US and other Western countries, NGOs predated the new environmental movement. The numbers of ENGOs rose precipitously from the mid-1960s to 1990, clearly becoming one of the organizational models of choice for environmental activists.[23] Two hundred and fifty NGOs attended the 1972 UN Conference on the Human Environment in Stockholm.[24] Two decades later, at the 1992 UN Conference on Environment and Development in Rio de Janeiro, over 1400 NGOs participated. Ten years after that, 3200 NGOs joined in at the 2002 World Summit on Sustainable Development in Johannesburg.[25]

Western environmentalists not only proselytized their ideology to developing nations, they also brought the expectation that the movement had to be carried out, at least in part, through ENGOs. If the target nation did not have a tradition of NGOs, well, then it would just have to import one. When Longhofer and Schofer charted the global history of ENGOs, they found two patterns. The first wave of ENGOs started in the 1960s in industrialized Western countries. Domestic ENGOs outnumbered international environmental organizations in these countries for the rest of the twentieth century. By contrast, the rest of the world did not have an ENGO boom until about a decade later, and it came mostly in the form of North American and European organizations opening branches in foreign countries.[26] In these countries, domestic ENGOs did not emerge until about a decade after international ENGOs were established. In other words, outside of the industrial West, social entrepreneurs did not develop their own grassroots ENGOs until after they had years of experience with Western ENGOs, learning their organizational practices.

The PRC was an exception to this pattern. In China, government policies forbade international NGO activity in the country almost completely in the 1960s and 1970s, and these restrictions were barely lifted in the 1980s. As a result, the first generation of Chinese social entrepreneurs, such as Peter Xu and Xu Yongguang, had essentially no experience of foreign NGOs before they started their own organizations. However, as we can see in Jin Jiaman's story, as soon as international ENGOs were able to enter China, they began socializing environmental activists in their own image. They immediately began carrying out training programs, like the Rockefeller Foundation program in sustainable development that Jin attended. The 1996 trip she took to the US was explicitly designed to teach Chinese women about American NGOs. Ecologia, the ENGO Jin interned at in Pennsylvania, had a history of promoting "awareness of the critical role that nongovernmental organizations play in developing civil societies" in the Soviet Union and Central Europe, before it added China to its list.[27] After 2000, international "capacity-building" workshops began to proliferate in China, funded by foreign foundations and NGOs.[28]

Western environmentalists could spread their ideas and practices because they had access to money, and lots of it. The global environmental movement benefited greatly from the fact that it attracted elites with power over significant resources, both in government and in the private sector. Money began flowing into the environmental sector in the 1970s, but increased exponentially in the 1990s (see Figure 6.1).

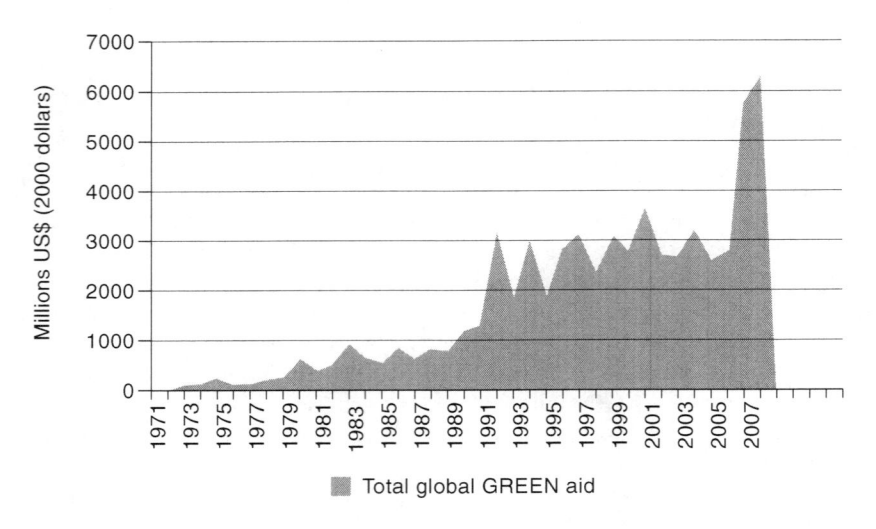

Figure 6.1 Total global GREEN aid 1971–2008, in fixed 2000 US$.

Source: AidData.org.

Note

"Green" Aid "designates projects that address global or regional environmental problems, and encompass projects that positively affect environmental outcomes outside the recipient country." This is a strict definition of environmental aid that does not include, for example, aid for sanitation work such as drinking water treatment or sewer projects. Robert L. Hicks and others, *Greening Aid?: Understanding the Environmental Impact of Development Assistance*. Oxford; New York: Oxford University Press, 2008, 31.

These funds could be available to Chinese social entrepreneurs, but only if they had *guanxi*. NGO founders with the right connections to international organizations could reap generous financial benefits if they followed approved practices. Jin Jiaman got her first ENGO grant from Ecologia, the same organization where she interned in 1996. When she founded GEI, the initial funds came from the Rockefeller Foundation and the Blue Moon Fund because her former colleague went to the US to work at those organizations. An Feng, who founded iCET (Innovation Center for Energy and Transportation) immigrated from China to the US in the 1980s to earn his doctorate.[29] He maintained enough important *guanxi* contacts in China to found a transnational ENGO, with offices in San Francisco and Beijing. Most of iCET's funding came from the Hewlitt Foundation, both directly and through its China Sustainable Energy Program. In 2008, an iCET employee admitted to me that this double dipping might violate foundation regulations, or at the very least be ethically questionable. An Feng was so good at raising funds, the employee said, "We almost have too much money."

The amounts of money that well-connected Chinese ENGOs could receive from foreign foundations could be generous, covering both administrative costs and staff compensation. Chinese NGOs in other sectors struggled to pay their employees almost anything at all, but environmental NGOs with foreign grants could afford to pay well enough to attract job applicants with high levels of *suzhi*. Both GEI and iCET were able to hire not just Chinese college graduates, but Western ones. Vance Wagner, whom I interviewed at iCET, had a mechanical engineering degree from Stanford University, while Lila Buckley, an employee at GEI, graduated from Middlebury College.

Learning to work with international environmentalists

In order to build international connections, and access all that lovely foreign money, Chinese ENGOs had to negotiate some cultural differences. Although global environmental discourses meshed well with China's *suzhi* ideology, Western organizational practices sometimes clashed with Chinese ones.

When we look at some of the capacity-building training programs run by foreigners for Chinese NGOs, we can see some of the differences between the two cultures. The ostensible purpose of these programs was to "professionalize" Chinese NGOs and teach them "best practices." In practice, "professionalization" meant operating more like Western organizations, and displaying characteristics deemed desirable by Western donors. At one capacity-building program, run by Americans, participants were immediately given a glossary of 60 terms to learn that included *mission statement, strategic plan, Board of Directors, executive committee, accountability, stakeholders, credibility, transparency,* and *risk management*.[30] As an American looking at this list, it is easy for me to see how the institutions and jargon of the US business world had influenced American NGO practices. Not surprisingly, the majority of the board members for the North American organizations running these programs had backgrounds in business or professional fields.[31]

Research in the United States reveals that foundations tend to give money to American environmental organizations that are mainstream and supportive of the status quo, rather than ones that are radical and demand significant social transformation.[32] Foundations also favored organizations that were run by a hierarchy of professional staff rather than through the participation of members, and ones that based their decision-making on professional scientific expertise rather than democratic consensus. Organizational sociologists call this "institutional isomorphism": organizations in a society copy characteristics and behaviors from successful firms, regardless of whether or not those characteristics and behaviors are truly ideal.[33] Because those practices feel more legitimate than any alternatives, it is easy for insiders to believe that they are genuinely the "best practices." One American consultant explained that the training program "didn't want it to be only an American model. But, honestly, we saw that, while some countries were doing great things with nonprofit issues, the US is really setting the benchmarks on most of these things."[34]

In China, because the first generation of social entrepreneurs almost all worked in the state sector before starting their non-profits, indigenous Chinese NGOs were more likely to mimic the structures and practices of party-state departments than capitalist corporations.[35] The Chinese trainees in these capacity-building programs felt both enlightened and frustrated. The programs revealed what foreign donors wanted, but the requirements seemed irrational. Chinese social entrepreneurs complained to me that business-oriented foreign foundations were so obsessed with clear expectations and accountability that grantees were supposed to be able to guarantee their "deliverables" in their proposals. How could anyone know what the results would be before they even started the project? One GEI employee grumbled that the only projects that received funding from Western foundations were the ones that promised to deliver reports and conferences – "because that's what they can promise. No matter what they actually do on the ground, no matter if they actually change anything in China, they know they can write a report!"[36]

Chinese social entrepreneurs not only believed that Western foundations cared about the wrong things, but also that they failed to pay attention to the factors that mattered for success in the PRC, like building *guanxi* relationships. Vance Wagner, an American citizen who worked for iCET for several years, explained:

> I can't tell you how many conferences I've sat in where you have these foreigners from foreign NGOs ... give a presentation with ... all this data, and the basic message is: China's environment is in terrible shape and you should do *this*.... This is very culturally Western. It's built on a platform of very orderly, logical, data-based brainstorming logic.... And in your implementation you have checks and measures to measure that there's compliance. It's on paper and it's very clear, but that's not at all how you work in China. You know, the slides and slides of data don't really mean anything in China. They don't mean nearly as much as a really strong relationship where they're going to trust you and trust your data is good and trust your ideas are solid, and they are going to work with you and implement what you have to say based on how much they trust you.

Jin Jiaman and other Chinese social entrepreneurs expressed exasperation and even amusement at the bumbling mistakes that foreign environmental organizations made in China. Jin described a project where GEI partnered with a local government agency in Yunnan Province to set up an eco-tourism site, only to find that an American-based environmental NGO had already been working on a similar project for two years, but without consulting the government. The predictable result was that the government ignored all of the Western NGO's work. "If there are two versions of the project, the government is *always* going use its own version," Jin exclaimed, throwing up her hands at the idiocy of foreigners. The Chinese government implemented the version that it designed in collaboration with GEI. Jin pointed out that if the American NGO had just collaborated with the government from the beginning, it could have prompted the state to invest in eco-tourism much sooner. But instead, "they used 400,000 [yuan] to do this, and it was a waste."

In some ways it was a privilege to have these problems. Most Chinese NGOs would never get invited to these training sessions in the first place. The ones that were there with the ones that were already successful and/or had *guanxi* connections to get them through the front door. The content of the training sessions might be frustrating, but they were an opportunity to make useful connections and access resources. Even if Chinese social entrepreneurs such as Jin Jiaman, An Feng (iCET), and Wang Yongchen (Green Earth Volunteers) were bemused by the cultural quirks of Western environmentalists, they understood them well enough to do what it took to access the funds. Through their own experiences in the West or through *guanxi* connections with friends who worked overseas, they had insight into the mindset and cultural expectations of foreign funding organizations. This knowledge allowed them to serve as valuable cultural translators between foreign environmentalists and Chinese state actors when the Chinese government sought foreign funding for China's environmental problems.

The Chinese state and the environment: outsourcing funding to foreigners and work to ENGOs

Does the Chinese government really care about the environment?

Turn-of-the-century Chinese environmental NGOs benefited from the fact that the Chinese party-state has publicly claimed to support environmental protection since the 1972 Stockholm summit. In contrast to, say, the United States, there was never a "debate" among Chinese political leaders about the validity of global warming or that human activity was contributing to climate change. Instead, there has been widespread agreement among Chinese party-state officials that the PRC must deal with environmental issues or risk serious consequences.[37] Beginning in the 1970s, the environmental sector of the government grew, more or less consistently, both in terms of size and power for the next four decades. In 1974, the National Environmental Protection Office was established, along with equivalent offices at the provincial level. In 1988, this office was upgraded to become the National Environmental Protection Agency. In 1998, the agency was elevated from subcabinet status to ministerial rank and renamed the State Environmental Protection Agency (SEPA). In 2008, SEPA was reorganized and promoted up to cabinet level, which is the one of the highest administrative levels in the Chinese state. At that point, it was renamed the Ministry of Environmental Protection (MEP).[38]

These moves up the party-state hierarchy were usually accompanied by an increase in personnel, even when the overall government bureaucracy was shrinking. In the early 1980s, when Jin Jiaman's parents were pulling strings to get her back to Beijing, they found her a job at an environmental research academy. Jin admitted to me that no one in her family knew anything about the environment at the time. However, in a time of government cutbacks, environmental departments were one of the few state sectors that were growing and hiring. Jin's timing was fortuitous. Her career ascended in tandem with the rise of the state environmental sector. Between 1995 and 2004, the number of state employees working in environmental protection increased from 88,000 to 160,000.[39]

Over the same time period, the Chinese state also increased the strictness and scope of environmental regulations and laws. The first pollution regulations were implemented in the early 1970s, and the first Environmental Protection Law was promulgated in 1979. Environmental protection was declared to be a "national basic policy" in 1984.[40] In the mid-1990s, a series of environmental regulations were passed, not only enforcing stricter controls, but also increasing the authority of those officials tasked with environmental oversight.[41] By the early 2000s, the government had implemented a partial logging ban, shut down tens of thousands of pollution-intensive enterprises, and set vehicle-fuel economy standards that were significantly stricter than ones in the US.[42] In January, 2015, China implemented a new comprehensive Environmental Protection Law that many environmentalists considered to be groundbreaking in scope and strength.[43]

During the same time period, however, China's actual environmental conditions deteriorated on almost every important measure: air pollution, water pollution, desertification, soil erosion, and energy consumption.[44] In 2007, China surpassed the US as the biggest source of carbon emissions in the world. According to the World Bank, environmental degradation cost the PRC 9 percent of its gross national income in 2008. Even the Chinese government admitted to significant problems. In 2011, a government ministry disclosed that there were more than 1700 water pollution incidents a year. In 2012, China's state newspaper, the *People's Daily* reported that 40 percent of China's rivers were "seriously polluted."[45]

It is easy to look at the disconnect between rhetoric and outcomes and assume that the Chinese party-state's "environmentalism" was hypocritical lip service, and that the ruling regime valued short-term economic development more than it valued environmental protection. Although this view has some merit, it obscures much of the complexity of the situation. It would be more accurate to say that when it came to the environment, the Chinese party-state suffered from a multiple personality disorder. As pointed out in Chapter 5, the Chinese "government" is not a monolithic entity, but instead is a conglomeration of bureaucratic organizations, each with its own interests. In any given situation involving environmental issues, multiple government agencies are involved. Depending on the circumstances, each state organization may be fighting for environmental protection or against it, depending on its particular set of interests.

We can see this in the controversy over damming the Nu River in Yunnan Province.[46] In 1999, the National Development and Reform Commission (NDRC), the central state organization for economic planning, approved a plan to build 13 dams on the Nu River in southwestern China. The plan was supported by a powerful state hydropower company and the provincial government, which in 2003 signed a letter of intent to proceed. However, the project was opposed on environmental grounds by the State Environmental Protection Agency (SEPA) and experts from Qinghua University, Yunnan University, and the Chinese Academy of Social Sciences, all of which are state institutes.[47] Some members of the state-controlled media acted as mouthpieces for the pro-dam provincial government, while other state journalists published exposés of the projects' potential downsides. Other environmental cases involved the Ministry of Forestry, the Ministry of Water Conservation, or the Ministry of Agriculture, as well as village and county governments and state agencies for cultural heritage, or tourism.

Unfortunately, in the early twenty-first century, pro-environmental actors in the Chinese party-state were handicapped on a number of levels. Despite the fact that the environmental protection sector of the government had garnered more authority and more resources over the years, it still did not have enough of either. At the national level, SEPA was outranked by the pro-development NDRC, arguably the most powerful organization in the government.[48] Local Environmental Protection Bureaus reported to SEPA, but received their funding from provincial- or local-level governments. Although there were exceptions, local government officials tended to prioritize economic growth over environmental protection, because their political careers depended on delivering higher standards of living and impressive "development" statistics to their higher-ups. Due to constraints, pro-environment state actors found themselves in a position where they needed to cultivate allies. Environmental social entrepreneurs were happy to help.

Outsourcing the environmental bill to foreign funders

Initially, ENGOs were not a factor in Chinese environmentalism. In the 1970s, 1980s, and the early 1990s, Chinese environmentalism was strictly state centered because ENGOs were all but nonexistent. This changed dramatically in the 1990s, when Chinese environmental state actors discovered the same thing that Jin Jiaman learned on her trip to the United States: the global environmental sector had a lot of money that could potentially be invested in China, and NGOs were a significant component of that sector.

In the 1980s, China was not a major recipient of environmental aid, taking in less money than Algeria.[49] In the 1990s, however, the Chinese government discovered a new tactic: the PRC would only comply with international environmental requests if foreigners would foot the bill. In 1990, China (along with India) refused to sign the Montréal Protocol on climate change until the international community promised to provide significant financial support and technological expertise for environmental protection. Wealthy nations capitulated.[50] In 1994, China promised to become the first country to develop its own national Agenda 21, following the global Agenda 21 sustainable development action plan. It immediately convened a meeting with representatives from foreign governments, international institutions, and corporations, and let them know that China's Agenda 21 would only succeed if the international community footed between 30 and 40 percent of the bill.[51] Once again, the developed nations of the world came through with the funding.

136 Environmental NGOs

In the 1990s, China received more environmental aid than any other country in the world. Fortuitously, it did so when the total amount of global environment aid was rising precipitously, so the amounts were enormous (see Figure 6.1). In 1996, China received US$565 million in green aid, about 20 percent of the world total (see Figure 6.2). Between 1990 and 1999, the World Bank alone gave China US$3.7 billion in environmental aid.[52] In the late 1990s, one source estimated that as much as 80 percent of China's environmental protection budget came from international sources.[53]

These funds allowed the Chinese state to implement environmental projects without spending its own money. For example, from 2006 to 2012, the World Bank and the European Commission funded a watershed rehabilitation/water management project in Sichuan that cost over US$115 million. The Chinese government, through the Ministry of Water Resources, provided only staff, offices, and "coordination," but it benefited from the fact that hundreds of thousands of rural households enjoyed a better standard of living and millions of tons of carbon were sequestered.[54]

State environmentalists and ENGOs in partnership

During the same years that Chinese state actors were perfecting their strategy of extracting foreign money from environmental donors, Chinese social entrepreneurs such as Jin Jiaman and her fellow Ecologia intern Wang Yongchen were discovering NGOs for themselves and starting their own organizations. Before long, environmentally-minded state actors and these new Chinese ENGOs

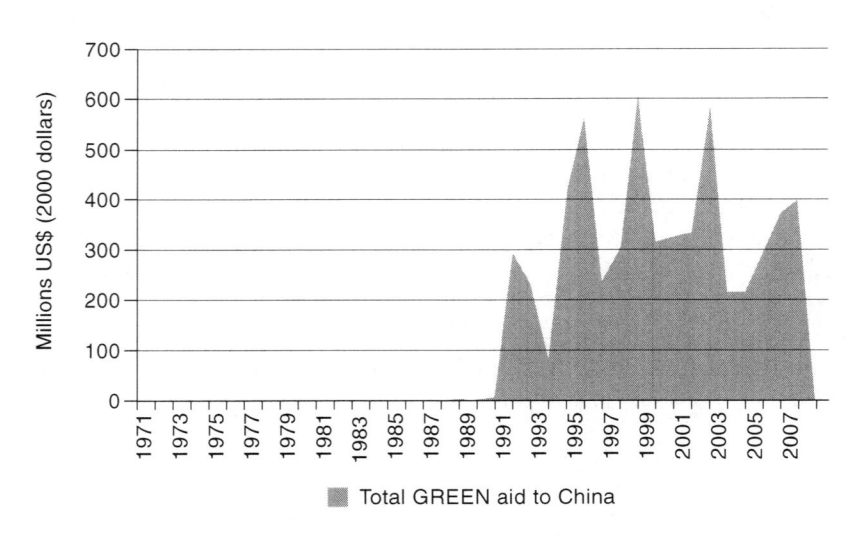

Figure 6.2 Total GREEN aid to the People's Republic of China 1971–2008, in fixed 2000 US$.

Source: AidData.org. See note in Figure 6.1.

became allies. By the turn of the century, the Chinese state was not only outsourcing its environmental funding to foreign funders, but also outsourcing a significant amount of environmental work to domestic ENGOs.

Chinese state officials found Chinese ENGOs attractive partners for a number of reasons. No doubt one of the most important ones was that Chinese ENGOs did not ask their party-state allies for any money. In 2008, Jin Jiaman told me that she had once dreamed of making GEI the first ENGO to receive substantial amounts of direct funding from the Chinese government, but eventually concluded that would be impossible. If an ENGO wanted to succeed in China, it had to be financially self-sufficient. Although ENGOs did a lot of work for Chinese state organizations, their services were almost never formalized in any sort of contract. Their connection with state officials was based on informal *guanxi* networks, and the relationships were between people, not the organizations.[55]

Instead, the most successful Chinese ENGOs received most if not all of their money from international organizations and foundations.[56] These international sources included the same sources that funded Chinese state governmental projects: the World Bank, the Asian Development Fund, and foreign governments. ENGOs also attracted money from organizations that fostered civil society or that had ideological or political reasons to avoid funding the Chinese party-state. For example, the US government phased out funding state environmental efforts in China in 2012 for political reasons, but still allowed some of its other funding to go to Chinese NGOs.[57] GEI and iCET obtained most of their funds from US foundations. Green Earth Volunteers, the ENGO Jin Jiaman founded with her friend Wang Yongchen, received money from the Global Environment Fund, the Ford Foundation, Conservation International, and the Dutch government.[58]

Chinese ENGOs could carry out certain types of work that Chinese state-employed environmentalists could not. In Chapter 5, I described how NGOs often acted as unofficial research and development offices for government departments, taking on risks to design innovative social solutions that could be "cut and pasted" by the state. Many ENGOs engage in these kinds of activities, including GEI. In this chapter, I will describe two more ways that ENGOs worked with state environmentalists. First, ENGOs helped environmentally-minded state actors by drawing public attention to the environment and teaching citizens to see environmental issues through a *suzhi* framework as serious, significant problems. Second, social entrepreneurs worked with state environmentalists directly, coordinating multifaceted campaigns that could involve the mass media, public protests, international exposure, and direct pressure on government officials.

Teaching people to see environmental quality

One of the most important ways that Chinese ENGOs helped state environmentalists was to educate the Chinese population to notice environmental problems, and interpret them as a significant component of the quality of life. As a self-described populist democracy promoting the ideology of *suzhi*, the ruling regime legitimated its authority by claiming that it could deliver the best standard of living for its citizens. As long as Chinese citizens ignored environmental conditions when assessing quality of life, the government could ignore them as well. If, however, an environmental problem caused a moral panic, the party-state would have to respond. In Chapter 4, I described how one social entrepreneur, Xu Yongguang, elevated rural education from an issue that most Chinese urbanites never considered into one that they believed was a central measure of good government. After two decades of Project Hope's powerful marketing campaign, the state reformed its educational policies and substantially increased investment in rural schools. China's environmentalists, whether they worked for the government or ENGOs, wanted the same thing to happen for environmental problems.

Unfortunately, even in the 1990s, Chinese citizens tended to pay very little attention to environmental issues and measured "quality of life" economically. Joy Zhang, a sociologist who grew up in Beijing, admitted that as a young person, it never occurred to her that the city's palpable air pollution was a problem, and no one else she knew seemed to notice it either. Sure, blue skies were rare, but the "economy was booming, life quality was improving, world culture and global fashion were filling the streets, and everyone seemed to be getting along happily."[59] State environmentalists could promote some level of environmental education, but they were constrained by the fact that it was not politically correct to draw attention to the party-state's failures instead of its successes. Chinese ENGOs were also somewhat limited in how much they could criticize the government, at least if they wanted to maintain good relationships with state allies, but they had more leeway to be creative and clever in their approaches.

For some ENGOs, the goal was simply to get Chinese citizens to take note of their natural surroundings by starting birdwatching clubs, providing photography lessons, or giving river tours. Some of these projects were grassroots while others were connected to international ENGOs such as the Waterkeeper Alliance. These organizations often kept their political agendas low-key and simply advertised their projects as recreational clubs or leisure activities. Fan Xiaoxi, an environmental volunteer in a Shanghai photography group, explained:

> The point of photography is not really how pretty these animals and sceneries are, but how [nature] connects to the local, how it connects to us, and how its destiny may be connected to our destiny as human beings.... The participants found it interesting, because when you are capturing things with lenses rather than bare eyes, you are no longer taking what you see for granted.[60]

When Wang Yongchen and Jin Jiaman used their small grant from Ecologia to start Green Earth Volunteers, they were well aware that their garbage cleanup projects would barely make a dent in China's pollution, and that their tree-planting sessions would not turn the tide on China's desertification. Instead, the real purpose was to teach young people to see the pollution, to pay attention to trees, and to believe that their actions could make a difference.

One area where Chinese ENGOs were very successful in transforming how Chinese people saw the environment was in regard to air pollution. Before 2008, only environmentalists and scientists in China had ever heard of PM2.5. This is a technical term referring to particulate matter in the air that is less than 2.5 μm in diameter. Because these tiny particulates have been linked to serious health issues, the PM2.5 level was used for monitoring air quality in many nations in Europe, North America, and Asia, including India and Thailand. The Chinese government, by contrast, continued to measure only larger particulate matter, presumably because that made its air quality measures look less terrible. Beginning in 2008, however, the US Embassy in Beijing began reporting PM2.5 levels from its monitor every day. The numbers were not good, to put it mildly, and on many days the embassy rated Beijing's air quality significantly worse than the official rating coming from the Chinese government. Chinese state scientists denounced the reports, claiming (correctly) that one data point could not be used to represent an entire city's air quality. They also hinted that the Americans might be publishing false data for the purpose of embarrassing China.[61]

In 2011, the Chinese ENGO Green Beagle came up with the brilliant idea of handing out free portable air pollution monitors to urban residents. With the pollution monitors, people could take random PM2.5 readings all over the city and then post their data on the ENGOs website.[62] Green Beagle swathed the project in patriotism, calling it the "I Monitor the Air for My Country" campaign. It claimed to be aiding the Chinese state by providing it with better data through the collective action of the masses. If the nefarious Americans dared to publish tainted data to blacken China's good name, they would be exposed by China's loyal citizens! An article on the campaign in *Southern Weekend*, a state publication known for its outspokenness, even came with a cartoon propaganda poster, complete with chiseled chins, raised fists and red flags.[63] The "heroes" in this faux propaganda poster were not peasants, workers, or soldiers, but dressed in the uniforms of high-*suzhi* urban professionals: suit jackets, ties, and intellectual spectacles. Copycat campaigns sprang up in other cities across China.

To no one's surprise, the "I Monitor the Air for My Country" campaign confirmed rather than undermined the US Embassy's claims. Although the data gathered through the citizen monitors did not meet the highest levels of scientific rigor, every new piece of information made the case against China's air quality more persuasive. Moreover, the cheeky campaign drew a great deal of public attention, with the result that ordinary Chinese people not only now knew what PM2.5 measures meant, but also began to grow increasingly worried about air pollution. According to the Pew Research Center, in 2008, 31 percent of respondents agreed that air pollution was "a very big problem" in China. By 2013, the number who agreed had risen significantly, to 47 percent – almost half of the people polled believed that air pollution was a major national problem.[64] In contrast to the unconcerned urban citizens of the 1990s, after 2010 middle-class Chinese were constantly worried about air pollution: they talked about it with their neighbors, monitored air quality data on the internet, and fretted for their children. They assumed that it was a significant component of quality of life.

The rise in popular anxiety about environmental issues gave state environmentalists ammunition to push for more government action. In conjunction with ENGOs, they were able to demand changes to drafts of China's 2015 Environmental Protection Law to make it stronger.[65] In March 2014, China's President Xi Jinping publicly "declared war" on pollution and condemned "inefficient and blind development."[66] In that year, China's coal consumption declined 3 percent, and carbon dioxide emission levels fell for the first time in 15 years. This was not enough to mute popular concerns about air pollution, and in March 2015, Premier Li Keqiang admitted "the progress we have made still falls short of the expectations of the people," and vowed that new, stricter environmental regulations would be fully enforced by the government.[67]

The battle over the Nu River

In addition to raising environmental awareness in general, Chinese ENGOs also partnered with state environmentalists in more direct ways. State environmentalists would call on ENGOs for expertise, to mobilize media attention, to lobby or pressure other state officials, or even to incite protests. We can see this by exploring the example of the Nu River controversy, which is described in fascinating detail in Andrew Mertha's book, *China's Water Warriors*.[68] As mentioned above, in the spring of 2003, a plan to build 13 dams on the Nu River was authorized. The plan was opposed by environmental researchers from top universities and institutes, as well as state environmentalists in SEPA (the State Environmental Protection Agency).[69] However, it was supported by other state actors, including the powerful National Development and Reform Commission (NDRC), a state hydropower company, and the Yunnan provincial government, who mobilized local media sources to propagate stories favorable to the project.[70] The resulting conflict reveals the importance of *guanxi* connections between state environmentalists and ENGO activists.

The river itself is located in a remote and rural corner of Yunnan Province and Tibet, and it flows into Myanmar – far from the view of China's educated urbanites. The plan to dam the Nu could have easily been implemented without ever crossing the consciousness of most of China's concerned citizens. To prevent this in August 2003, one of the state environmentalists contacted Wang Yongchen and asked her if she could provide "ammunition" for SEPA in its battle against the pro-dam officials in the state bureaucracy.[71] Wang, if you recall, had cofounded Green Earth Volunteers with Jin Jiaman, and she was also a journalist on Chinese National Radio. She was very well-connected with environmentalists all over China and around the world, and immediately put her *guanxi* to work. Wang called Professor He Deming, the head of the Asian International Rivers Center at Yunnan University, and an expert on the Nu River, and asked him to help. SEPA immediately organized a conference attended by 70 experts and ten journalists where Professor He carefully explained the problems with the plan and his opposition to the project.

Within a few weeks, Wang Yongchen had used her *guanxi* network to organize a petition with 62 signatures from Chinese scientists, artists, journalists, and environmental social entrepreneurs. A month later, Green Earth Volunteers and a number of other Chinese ENGOs participated in the World Rivers and People Opposing Dams meeting in Thailand. Over 80 international ENGOs signed a letter to the Chinese ambassador in Thailand protesting the Nu River Project. Through her contacts in the state media, Wang made sure the Nu River Project and the campaign against it were well-publicized. She held a monthly salon with journalists, government officials, and social entrepreneurs, and used it as a platform to educate influential people about the case. Wang also made multiple trips to the river site, often bringing a group of journalists with her. As a result of her efforts, and the efforts of other environmental activists, between August 2003 and September 2004, there were more than 100 domestic and international media stories about the Nu River Project.[72]

Behind the scenes, Wang and other ENGO leaders personally encouraged state environmentalists to "stand firm and never give up."[73] These officials managed to force the state hydropower company to undertake an environmental impact assessment. A delegate to the National People's Congress went on record demanding an "independent and authoritative investigation before any decision on [the Nu River Project's] future is made." As publicity and public opinion against the project mounted, it became less and less popular among Chinese officials. On February 18, 2004, less than a year after the letter of intent to implement the Nu River Project was signed, Premier Wen Jiabao, China's second-most powerful leader and a trained geologist, weighed in. He declared that, "such a large hydropower station project that draws high social attention, and has environmental controversy, should be cautiously studied, and scientifically decided."[74] This statement effectively suspended the project for a decade. In 2008, Wang Yongchen was named a "Hero of the Environment" by *Time* magazine in the US.[75]

Unfortunately, the story of the Nu River protests does not have a happy ending. After Wen Jiabao stepped down as premier in 2012, supporters of the dams successfully revived their efforts, although the number of proposed dams was reduced from 13 to five. It should be noted that part of the reason why plans for those five dams were revived is because there were environmental arguments supporting both sides of the conflict. Despite the environmental damage produced by dams, hydroelectric power is a cleaner and more renewable energy source than coal or oil. Given that the Chinese government was trying to cut down on the use of fossil fuels and reduce air pollution, building dams seemed like a reasonable strategy. The environmentalists at some local Environmental Protection Bureaus also supported the Nu River Project because they believed that if the project did not proceed, it would be replaced by a plethora of small, local hydropower projects. Such small projects were more likely to remain relatively unregulated in China and cause even more environmental damage than a large, nationally-publicized system of dams.[76]

The Nu River case reveals that the relevant divisions were not always between government officials and social entrepreneurs, or between Chinese and foreigners. Instead, the lines of conflict fell between those who insisted that the environmental costs of the project outweighed its economic benefits, and those who believed the opposite. Although Wang Yongchen was an ENGO leader and an advocate of citizen mobilization, she was also a government employee at Chinese National Radio. Chinese social entrepreneurs in the environmental sector benefited enormously from the fact that they could not only build useful relationships with government officials, but could also act as comrades-in-arms. ENGOs could also act as a bridge between state and international environmentalists. A cadre in SEPA could not call on foreigners to condemn the Nu River project, but Wong Yongchen and other ENGO activists could.

The elite circle: Chinese ENGOs and *guanxi*

In the first decade of the twenty-first century, successful Chinese ENGOs were the envy of the emerging NGO sector in the PRC. They enjoyed glamorous international connections and generous funding from well-heeled foreigners, as well as productive partnerships with powerful party-state officials that resulted in both political protection and political influence. However, these benefits were not available to every Chinese social entrepreneur who aspired to start an ENGO. Instead, it was a privileged position enjoyed by an elite circle of interconnected friends, classmates, colleagues, and protégés, centered in Beijing. Membership in this select club was limited to "high quality" people with impressive educational credentials and excellent *guanxi*, such as Jin Jiaman.

The first prerequisite of Chinese ENGO success was geographical. The Chinese environmental social entrepreneurs who were able to take advantage of both international resources and Chinese political connections almost all worked in Beijing. It was the site of China's first domestic ENGOs and continued to be the center of ENGO activity for the next two decades. Beijing was both China's political capital and a global city. It was the right place to build relationships with the PRC's most powerful political officials, and the right place to make connections with moneyed foreigners. To a great extent, the powerful political officials controlled access to the moneyed foreigners. International grant-makers, such as the Rockefeller Foundation, had to go through the Chinese government to establish programs in the PRC. The cadres involved in the process could informally introduce foundations to their favorite social entrepreneurs and ENGOs.

Research in other parts of China reveals that the conditions faced by environmental social entrepreneurs tended to be very region-specific, but none were as favorable as Beijing. Lei Xie found that party-state officials in Shanghai were much less friendly toward ENGOs than the ones in Beijing, and it was significantly more difficult for Shanghai ENGOs to register legally.[77] Wu Fengshi found that ENGOs in neither Guangdong nor Guangxi Province were able to access generous grants from international funders on the scale that the Beijing organizations did. Indeed, in Guangxi Province, most environmental work was done by branches of Beijing organizations.[78] Many ENGOs flourished in Yunnan Province, and it received a significant amount of foreign funding. But organizations there had much smaller budgets than their Beijing counterparts, and they received most of their money from government resources rather than international foundations.[79]

However, simply being located in Beijing was not enough to access the sweet spot of ENGO success. That privileged position was largely limited to a group of friends and acquaintances who helped each other through *guanxi* connections. Not surprisingly, most came from China's elite and had substantial levels of *suzhi*. We can see this in Jin Jiaman's biography. Jin was the daughter of two highly-placed government officials who were able to use their *guanxi* to get her a position in Beijing at a government research academy. Because she was a relatively high-ranking cadre in a national-level institute, Jin was invited to the Rockefeller Foundation training program about sustainable development, and to the trip to the US. By the time Jin founded GEI, she had excellent connections with important people in the government, both through her own work experience and through her parents. This put her ENGO in a prime position to conduct research and development for state organizations, as well as to influence policy. For instance, GEI worked with the State Environmental Protection Agency and other government departments to write up environmental policies for China's overseas investment projects.

This kind of state-controlled access to important foreigners not only meant that Jin built direct relationships with wealthy Westerners, but that she was more likely to have friends and acquaintances that had valuable connections. Several of her institute colleagues parlayed those international connections into jobs in the United States, including Zhang Jiqiang, who was employed at the Rockefeller Foundation before using his connections there to move onto the Blue Moon Fund. Jin waited until 2004 to start GEI in part because she wanted to secure her state retirement benefits, but also because she wanted to make sure she had friends established at US foundations before taking the plunge. Most aspiring social entrepreneurs, even if they were located in Beijing, were much less likely to have former co-workers at the Rockefeller Foundation.

But perhaps the most beneficial relationships that Jin enjoyed were the ones with other successful Beijing ENGO founders. Even if Jin did not have *guanxi* with powerful state officials or wealthy foreign foundations, a friend like Wang Yongchen could have helped her make those connections. By the time Jin founded GEI in 2004, Wang had been running Green Earth Volunteers for seven years, receiving grants from an array of international foundations. Through her high position at China National Radio, Wang was well connected with important cadres, especially those in the state-run media. The Chinese media, of course, was under government control. However, Wang understood that, in the early twenty-first century, even state media outlets needed to compete for market share, and journalists were always on the lookout for exciting and dramatic stories. Environmental social entrepreneurs with the right connections could build symbiotic relationships with state journalists, providing juicy leads in return for media coverage.

144 *Environmental NGOs*

When we look at the first generation of Beijing ENGOs, we see that *guanxi* with other environmental social entrepreneurs was one of the most important factors predicting success. Indeed, a network analysis of China's most successful ENGOs reveals that many of them were connected to each other through school ties, shared workplaces, or institutional partnerships. A significant number can be traced back to a single social entrepreneur: Liang Congjie, the founder of Friends of Nature (see Figure 6.3). Liang Congjie, who passed away in 2010, was the son of Liang Sicheng, a famous architect, and the grandson of Liang Qichao, a political reformer from the late Qing Dynasty that every Chinese schoolchild knows from history books. Liang Congjie attended Beijing University, one of China's top two colleges. Inspired by the example of Greenpeace, Liang decided that China needed a similar organization. In 1993, he founded Friends of Nature, China's first registered ENGO.[80] Although Friends of Nature fought deforestation, it arguably made a bigger impact on China's environment by fostering the first generation of Chinese ENGOs. According to one 2009 study of Chinese ENGOs, the founders of at least 17 organizations were once employees, members, volunteers, or supporters of Friends of Nature.[81] Wang Yongchen was an early member of the group, and she went on to start Green Earth Volunteers. Some of those ENGOs spawned their own progeny, such as Green Earth Volunteers leading to GEI (see Figure 6.3).

Although I described the Beijing environmental social entrepreneurs as an elite circle, it would be wrong to see it as an exclusive club rather than an expanding network. As depicted in Figure 3.2, the rules of *guanxi* in China make relationships

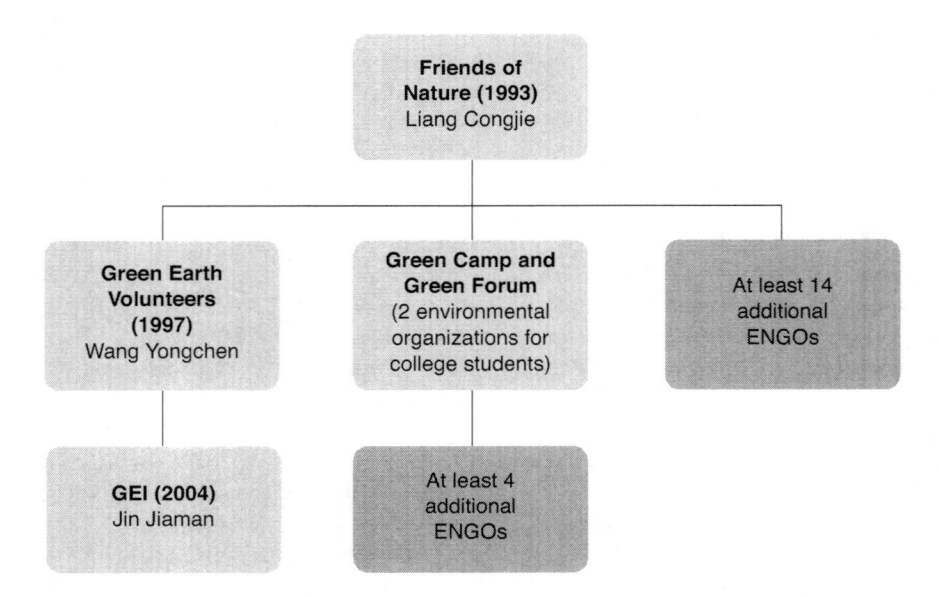

Figure 6.3 The influence of Friends of Nature on Chinese ENGOs, *c.*2004.

both extremely useful and extremely easy to develop. Because of the "chain of favors" rule, if your friend was unable to help fulfill your request, she would ask her friends who would ask their friends until someone was found who could do the deed. This meant that that if Jin Jiaman became your friend, for example, you not only gained access to all of her resources, but to the resources of her entire social network, including powerful cadres in the Ministry of Environmental Protection, all of Wang Yongchen's connections in the state media, and introductions to Jin's friends at American foundations. No wonder so many of Liang Congjie's employees and acquaintances ended up as successful ENGO founders; simply working at Friends of Nature would give anyone an enormously useful network of resources for environmental social entrepreneurship.

Theoretically, it would be possible to start an ENGO even without a well-connected family, a degree from a top university, or high-ranking cadre position, as long as you had *guanxi* connections with people who did have these benefits. In reality, however, the people who were able to take advantage of these *guanxi* connections tended to come from China's upper classes. By the time their ENGOs were successful, Jin Jiaman, Wang Yongchen, and Liang Congjie were more likely to meet people on airplanes than buses. Because Jin, Wang, and Liang came from well-placed families, attended elite colleges, and worked in the upper levels of government bureaucracy, they tended to meet people with similar backgrounds. One 2009 study of Chinese ENGOs found that 85 percent of the founders had a college degree, compared with less than 6 percent of the general population. Over 70 percent had a professional career prior to starting their organization.[82]

A recipe for ENGO success: suzhi, guanxi, *and foreign money*

Chinese environmental social entrepreneurs used the language of *suzhi* to teach their fellow citizens to see environmental conditions as a vital component of their quality of life. Like Xu Yongguang of Project Hope, these activists understood that creating a moral panic was an effective tactic in a state that claim to be a populist democracy. Chinese environmental social entrepreneurs also exploited the similarity between *suzhi* ideology and the views of wealthy foreign environmentalists. By drawing attention to the overlap between the desires of the global environmental movement and their own interests, they were able to access enormous amounts of funding from foreigners. This strategy was adopted by activists in the area of AIDS/HIV prevention when international groups (the Global Fund, USAID, the Gates Foundation, and others) became interested in funding that issue in the PRC.[83] Through these methods, environmental social entrepreneurs founded the most successful NGO sector in turn-of-the-century China. However, these methods were only available to a specific network of people who had high levels of *suzhi* themselves. Furthermore, like Xu Yongguang and Peter Xu, these environmental activists were often willing to let the state take credit for their work, as long as environmental conditions improved. From the perspective of a populist democracy, they were very effective citizens, but their strategies did not necessarily raise the profile of social entrepreneurship, NGOs, or activism in China.

Notes

1 According to the mission statement,

> Ecologia's programs bring international perspectives and resources to local sustainable development projects, and bring locally-based "on the ground" experience back to the world of international decision-making.... Ecologia works by creating direct people-to-people connections. By linking individuals to one another, we foster the emergence of a global civil society – a worldwide network of individuals and organizations sharing common interests, information and resources.

China is one of its main regions of interest. See www.ecologia.org/index.html.
2 Green Earth Volunteers was still going strong in 2015. http://eng.greensos.cn/default.aspx. For more on the organization's early history, see Lei Xie, *Environmental Activism in China*, Vol. 9 (London; New York: Routledge, 2009), 213, Chapter 4.
3 GEI website: www.geichina.org/index.php?controller=Default&action=Index.
4 Shawn Shieh et al., *Chinese NGO Directory (251 NGO Profiles and Special Report): China's Civil Society in the Making* (Beijing: China Development Brief, 2013), xvi.
5 Timothy Hildebrandt, *Social Organizations and the Authoritarian State in China* (Cambridge; New York: Cambridge University Press, 2013); Jiang Ru and Leonard Ortolano, "Development of citizen-organized environmental NGOs in China," *Voluntas: International Journal of Voluntary & Nonprofit Organizations* 20, no. 2 (2009): 141–168.
6 www.pewglobal.org/2013/09/19/environmental-concerns-on-the-rise-in-china/.
7 Mingyuan Wang and Jin Feng, "Some thoughts on the amendments to the Environmental Protection Law of China," *Asia Pacific Journal of Environmental Law* 17 (2014): 191.
8 Donald Worster, *Nature's Economy: A History of Ecological Ideas* (2nd ed.) (Cambridge: Cambridge University Press, 1994); Ramachandra Guha, *Environmentalism: A Global History* (New Delhi; New York: Oxford University Press, 2000), 161; Frank Uekoetter (Ed.), *The Turning Points of Environmental History* (Pittsburgh, PA: University of Pittsburgh Press, 2010); Joachim Radkau and Patrick Camiller, *The Age of Ecology: A Global History* (Cambridge: Polity, 2014), 546.
9 Radkau and Camiller, *The Age of Ecology: A Global History*, Chapter 1, especially Section 2.
10 Worster, *Nature's Economy: A History of Ecological Ideas*, see Chapter 16.
11 Christian Pfister, "The '1950s syndrome' and the transition from a slow-going to a rapid loss of global sustainability," in F. Uekoetter (Ed.), *The Turning Points of Environmental History* (Pittsburgh: University of Pittsburgh Press, 2010), 90–118.
12 Radkau and Camiller, *The Age of Ecology: A Global History*, 77, 103.
13 Rachel Carson, *Silent Spring* (25th anniversary ed.) (Boston: Houghton Mifflin, 1987), 8.
14 Jens Ivo Engels, "Modern environmentalism," in *The Turning Points of Environmental History* (Pittsburgh: University of Pittsburgh Press, 2010), 124–125.
15 For a topology of different environmental discourses, see Robert J. Brulle and J. Craig Jenkins, "Foundations and the environmental movement: Priorities, strategies, and impact," in *Foundations for Social Change: Critical Perspectives on Philanthropy and Popular Movements* (New York: Rowman & Littlefield, 2005), 151–173. For a discussion of ecological modernization, see Michael Mayerfeld Bell, *An Invitation to Environmental Sociology* (Thousand Oaks: Sage Publications, 2012), 191–194.
16 Radkau and Camiller, *The Age of Ecology: A Global History*, 79–89.
17 Andrew J. Hoffman, *From Heresy to Dogma: An Institutional History of Corporate Environmentalism* (Stanford, CA: Stanford Business Books, 2001), 3–4.

18 Radkau and Camiller, *The Age of Ecology: A Global History*, 92.
19 Arthur P.J. Mol and Neil T. Carter, "China's environmental governance in transition," *Environmental Politics* 15, no. 2 (2006): 152.
20 Abigail R. Jahiel, "The organization of environmental protection in China," *The China Quarterly*, no. 156, Special Issue: China's Environment (1998): 767.
21 Radkau and Camiller, *The Age of Ecology: A Global History*.
22 Paul R. Ehrlich, *The Population Bomb* (New York: Ballantine Books, 1976).
23 Jason T. Carmichael, J. Craig Jenkins, and Robert J. Brulle, "Building environmentalism: The founding of environmental movement organizations in the United States, 1900–2000," *The Sociological Quarterly* 53, no. 3 (2012): 433.
24 Michele M. Betsill and Elisabeth Corell, "Introduction to NGO diplomacy," in *NGO Diplomacy: The Influence of Nongovernmental Organizations and International Environmental Negotiations* (Cambridge, MA: MIT Press, 2008), 1.
25 Ibid.
26 Wesley Longhofer and Evan Schofer, "National and global origins of environmental association," *American Sociological Review* 75, no. 4 (2010): 517.
27 www.ecologia.org/about/programs/past.html.
28 Anthony J. Spires, "Lessons from abroad: Foreign influences on China's emerging civil society," *China Journal*, no. 68 (2012): 125–146.
29 An Feng's surname is An. In the US, he goes by Feng An.
30 Spires, *Lessons from Abroad: Foreign Influences on China's Emerging Civil Society*, 129.
31 Ibid., 130.
32 Brulle and Jenkins, *Foundations and the Environmental Movement: Priorities, Strategies, and Impact*, 151–173.
33 Paul J. DiMaggio and Walter W. Powell, "The iron cage revisited: Institutional isomorphism and collective rationality," in W. Powell and P. DiMaggio (Eds.), *The New Institutionalism in Organizational Analysis* (Chicago: University of Chicago Press, 1991), 63–82.
34 Spires, *Lessons from Abroad: Foreign Influences on China's Emerging Civil Society*, 133.
35 Carolyn L. Hsu and Yuzhou Jiang, "An institutional approach to Chinese NGOs: State alliance versus state avoidance resource strategies," *The China Quarterly* 221 (2015): 100–122; Carolyn L. Hsu, "Market ventures, moral logics, and ambiguity: Crafting a new organizational form in post-Socialist China," *The Sociological Quarterly* 47, no. 1 (2006): 62–92.
36 Interview with Lila Buckley, an American citizen who had worked for GEI for three years: April 14, 2008.
37 Elizabeth Economy, *The River Runs Black* (2nd ed.) (Ithaca: Cornell University Press, 2010), 194.
38 Ibid., 111.
39 Mol and Carter, *China's Environmental Governance in Transition*, 152.
40 Ibid.
41 Jahiel, *The Organization of Environmental Protection in China*.
42 Hicks *et al.*, *Greening Aid?: Understanding the Environmental Impact of Development Assistance* (Oxford; New York: Oxford University Press), 64.
43 Wang and Feng, *Some Thoughts on the Amendments to the Environmental Protection Law of China*, 191.
44 E. Economy *The River Runs Black* (2nd ed.) (Ithaca: Cornell University Press), 364.
45 Xin Miao *et al.*, "The latent causal chain of industrial water pollution in China," *Environmental Pollution* 196 (2015): 473.
46 Andrew Mertha, *China's Water Warriors: Citizen Action and Policy Change* (Paperback ed.) (Ithaca: Cornell University Press, 2010).
47 Ibid., 117.

48 Even after SEPA was upgraded to the Ministry of Environmental Protection in 2008, it was still outranked by the NDRC.
49 Hicks *et al.*, *Greening Aid?: Understanding the Environmental Impact of Development Assistance*, 61.
50 Economy, *The River Runs Black*, 188.
51 Ibid, 198.
52 Hicks *et al.*, *Greening Aid?: Understanding the Environmental Impact of Development Assistance*, 61.
53 Economy, *The River Runs Black*, 199.
54 www.worldbank.org/en/results/2013/07/11/china-protecting-environment-and-improving-livelihoods-of-farmers.
55 Hildebrandt, *Social Organizations and the Authoritarian State in China*, 150.
56 Xie, *Environmental Activism in China*, 91.
57 Thomas Lum, *US Assistance Programs in China* (Congressional Research Service, 2013).
58 Xie, *Environmental Activism in China*, 93.
59 Joy Yueyue Zhang and Michael Barr, *Green Politics in China: Environmental Governance and State-Society Relations* (London: Pluto Press, 2013), 35.
60 Ibid., 43.
61 Ibid., 68–69.
62 Ibid., 70–71.
63 *Southern Weekend*, "I monitor the air for my country." October 28, 2011. www.infzm.com/content/64281.
64 www.pewglobal.org/2013/09/19/environmental-concerns-on-the-rise-in-china/.
65 www.chinadialogue.net/article/show/single/en/6938-The-three-year-battle-for-China-s-new-environmental-law.
66 www.theguardian.com/environment/chinas-choice/2014/apr/25/china-environment-law-fines-for-pollution.
67 www.nytimes.com/2015/03/16/world/asia/chinese-premier-li-keqiang-vows-tougher-regulation-on-air-pollution.html.
68 Mertha, *China's Water Warriors: Citizen Action and Policy Change*.
69 In 2008, SEPA became the Ministry of Environmental Protection (MEP).
70 Mertha, *China's Water Warriors: Citizen Action and Policy Change*, 117.
71 Ibid., 119.
72 Ibid., 145.
73 Ibid., 121.
74 Ibid., 122.
75 http://content.time.com/time/specials/packages/article/0,28804,1841778_1841781_1841806,00.html.
76 Mertha, *China's Water Warriors: Citizen Action and Policy Change*, 124.
77 Xie, *Environmental Activism in China*, 213, Chapter 6.
78 Fengshi Wu, "Environmental activism in provincial China," *Journal of Environmental Policy & Planning* 15, no. 1 (2013): 89–108.
79 Jennifer Y.J. Hsu, Carolyn L. Hsu, and Reza Hasmath, "NGO strategies in an authoritarian context, and their implications for citizenship: The case of the People's Republic of China", *Voluntas* (2016): DOI 10.1007/s11266-9806-0.
80 Xie, *Environmental Activism in China*, 89.
81 Ru and Ortolano, *Development of Citizen-Organized Environmental NGOs in China*, 151.
82 Ibid., 153.
83 Hildebrandt, *Social Organizations and the Authoritarian State in China*.

Bibliography

Bell, M.M. 2012. *An Invitation to Environmental Sociology.* Thousand Oaks: Sage Publications.

Betsill, M.M. and Corell, E. 2008. Introduction to NGO diplomacy. *NGO Diplomacy: The Influence of Nongovernmental Organizations and International Environmental Negotiations.* Cambridge: MIT Press, pp. 1–18.

Brulle, R.J. and Jenkins, J.C. 2005. Foundations and the environmental movement: Priorities, strategies, and impact. *Foundations for Social Change: Critical Perspectives on Philanthropy and Popular Movements.* New York; Rowman & Littlefield, pp. 151–173.

Carmichael, J.T., Jenkins, J.C., and Brulle, R.J. 2012. Building environmentalism: The founding of environmental movement organizations in the United States, 1900–2000. *The Sociological Quarterly*, 53(3), pp. 422–453.

Carson, R. 1987. *Silent Spring* (25th anniversary ed.) Boston: Houghton Mifflin.

DiMaggio, P.J. and Powell, W.W. 1991. The iron cage revisited: Institutional isomorphism and collective rationality. In: W.W. Powell and P.J. DiMaggio (Eds.), *The New Institutionalism in Organizational Analysis.* Chicago: University of Chicago Press, pp. 63–82.

Economy, E. 2010. *The River Runs Black* (2nd ed.). Ithaca: Cornell University Press.

Ehrlich, P.R. 1976. *The Population Bomb.* New York: Ballantine Books.

Engels, J.I. 2010. Modern environmentalism. *The Turning Points of Environmental History.* Pittsburgh: University of Pittsburgh Press, pp. 119–131.

Guha, R. 2000. *Environmentalism: A Global History.* New Delhi; New York: Oxford University Press.

Hicks, R.L., Parks, B.C., Roberts, J.T., and Tierney, M.J. 2008. *Greening Aid?: Understanding the Environmental Impact of Development Assistance.* Oxford; New York: Oxford University Press.

Hildebrandt, T. 2013. *Social Organizations and the Authoritarian State in China.* Cambridge; New York: Cambridge University Press.

Hoffman, A.J. 2001. *From Heresy to Dogma: An Institutional History of Corporate Environmentalism.* Stanford, CA: Stanford Business Books.

Hsu, C.L. 2006. Market ventures, moral logics, and ambiguity: Crafting a new organizational form in post-socialist China. *The Sociological Quarterly*, 47(1), pp. 62–92.

Hsu, C.L. and Jiang, Y. 2015. An institutional approach to Chinese NGOs: State alliance versus state avoidance resource strategies. *The China Quarterly*, 221, pp. 100–122.

Hsu, C.L., Hasmath, R., and Hsu, J.Y.J. 2015. NGO strategies in an authoritarian context, and their implications for citizenship: The case of the People's Republic of China, *Voluntas* (2016): DOI 10.1007/s11266-9806-0.

Jahiel, A.R. 1998. The organization of environmental protection in China. *The China Quarterly*, (156, Special Issue: China's Environment), pp. 757–787.

Longhofer, W. and Schofer, E. 2010. National and global origins of environmental association. *American Sociological Review*, 75(4), pp. 505–533.

Lum, Thomas. 2013. *US Assistance Programs in China* (Congressional Research Service).

Mertha, A. 2010. *China's Water Warriors: Citizen Action and Policy Change* (paperback ed.). Ithaca: Cornell University Press.

Miao, X., Tang, Y., Wong, C.W.Y., and Zang, H. 2015. The latent causal chain of industrial water pollution in China. *Environmental Pollution*, 196, pp. 473–477.

Mol, A.P.J. and Carter, N.T. 2006. China's environmental governance in transition. *Environmental Politics*, 15(2), pp. 149–170.

Pfister, C. 2010. The "1950s syndrome" and the transition from a slow-going to a rapid loss of global sustainability. In: F. Uekoetter (Ed.), *The Turning Points of Environmental History*. Pittsburgh: University of Pittsburgh Press, pp. 90–118.

Radkau, J. and Camiller, P. 2014. *The Age of Ecology: A Global History.* Cambridge, UK: Polity.

Ru, J. and Ortolano, L. 2009. Development of citizen-organized environmental NGOs in China. *Voluntas: International Journal of Voluntary & Nonprofit Organizations*, 20(2), pp. 141–168.

Shieh, S., Liu, H., Zhang, G., Brown-Inz, A., and Gong, Y. 2013. *Chinese NGO Directory (251 NGO Profiles and Special Report): China's Civil Society in the Making.* Beijing: China Development Brief.

Spires, A.J. 2012. Lessons from abroad: Foreign influences on China's emerging civil society. *China Journal*, (68), pp. 125–146.

Uekoetter, F. (Ed.). 2010. *The Turning Points of Environmental History.* Pittsburgh, PA: University of Pittsburgh Press.

Wang, M. and Feng, J. 2014. Some thoughts on the amendments to the Environmental Protection Law of China. *Asia Pacific Journal of Environmental Law*, 17, p. 191.

Worster, D. 1994. *Nature's Economy: A History of Ecological Ideas* (2nd ed.). Cambridge, UK: Cambridge University Press.

Wu, F. 2013. Environmental activism in provincial China. *Journal of Environmental Policy & Planning* 15, no. 1, pp. 89–108.

Xie, L. 2009. *Environmental Activism in China.* London; New York: Routledge.

Zhang, J.Y. and Barr, M. 2013. *Green Politics in China: Environmental Governance and State-Society Relations.* London: Pluto Press.

7 Conclusion
After the earthquake

Jiang Quan's parents were peasants in Heilongjiang Province, farming potatoes, corn, and soybeans. An excellent student, he tested into Jiangxi Normal University. He knew that his family did not have the money to send him to college, but he had heard that there were programs to help students like him. After a rather mysterious selection process, he was chosen by Project Hope to receive his entire tuition, ¥6000 per year. After graduation, all the prizes of a high *suzhi* life were now within his reach: a white-collar career and a middle-class life in the city.

But first, Jiang took a detour back to rural poverty. In 2007, he became a volunteer teacher for Project Hope. It was a new program, not unlike Teach for America in the United States. Corporations donated funding to bring 60 of the best and brightest college graduates to poor rural schools all over the PRC for year-long stints in the classroom. Students from China's top universities flocked to apply, and only those who scored the highest on a set of rigorous examinations were chosen. When I asked Jiang why he chose to delay his career for a year, he told me that it just seemed like the right thing to do:

> I didn't even have to think about it when I applied. There was a call for volunteers, and I just applied for it. After all, I was helped by other kindhearted people, and it was time to do something in return. It was quite natural. I had suffered a lot when I was in school, and I do understand how those school dropouts feel. Now that I've graduated, it's time that I should do something meaningful.

Jiang explained that the people in his generation were not like the children of the 1980s and 1990s, who had been primarily concerned with making more money:

> Sometimes when I call my friends, I tell them that I'm a volunteer for Project Hope, and they are envious of me doing something that they would never have a chance to do.... In my opinion, if my friends would have the chance, they would have tried to become volunteers as well.

One month before I interviewed Jiang Quan in Heilongjiang, the 2008 Wenchuan Earthquake struck in Sichuan, inspiring a flood of volunteers and

NGOs. The young people of Jiang's generation drew on their volunteer spirit, mobilized their middle-class resources, and utilized their organizational experience to serve their fellow citizens in crisis. The geological earthquake had revealed a transformation caused by a different kind of earthquake in China's civil society: the rise of social entrepreneurship in the PRC. The first wave of Chinese NGOs had not only helped a generation of young people gain *suzhi*, but had also taught this new generation a new ethic of giving through social entrepreneurship, activism, and volunteerism. In this chapter, we will explore some of the ways they in turn changed social entrepreneurship in China.

Suzhi, guanxi, and citizenship in a populist democracy

As we have seen in this book, the rise of *suzhi* ideology in China in the 1980s and 1990s created conditions that social entrepreneurs exploited in order to develop a new form of activist citizenship. As I explained in Chapter 1, in a populist democracy, good citizenship is not defined as successfully limiting state power, but instead as enabling the state to understand and meet the needs of the people, and provide them with a good quality of life. Because *suzhi* ideology transformed the definition of "quality of life," it also opened the door to a way of practicing good populist democratic citizenship. The central argument of *suzhi* ideology is that individual lives, communities, and the nation itself will become healthier, wealthier, and stronger if educational, environmental, and economic conditions are improved. For ambitious citizens blessed with high levels of *suzhi*, this ideology provided a formula for social change. By bringing public attention to social problems, they could create moral panics and inspire middle-class citizens into collective action. Public attention could also compel the party-state to increase its investment in social welfare, or risk the loss of political legitimacy. The fact that *suzhi* ideology also led to downsizing in the party-state bureaucracy made Chinese cadres all the more eager to build alliances with social entrepreneurs and NGOs.

The result of the rise of social entrepreneurship in turn-of-the-century China was impressive, not just because of the sheer number of NGOs, but also in terms of real results. Although it is possible that the Chinese government would have eventually helped the blind and visually impaired, improved access to rural education, and addressed environmental problems, there is every reason to believe that the work of social entrepreneurs forced the state to confront these issues sooner, and to invest more in alleviating the social problems, than it would have otherwise. As good populist democratic citizens, social entrepreneurs enabled their government to serve the people better.

By the second decade of the twenty-first century, there were signs that the party-state was willing to acknowledge the benefit of social entrepreneurs and NGOs in the PRC, although within limits. Regulations were revised in 2013 so domestic NGOs no longer necessarily needed to have supervising agencies.[1] In 2015, a new environmental law went into effect that empowered NGOs, giving them the right to bring lawsuits against environmental violators.[2] In March 2016, the government promulgated the Charity Law, the first systematic set of legal regulations covering social welfare organization since 1999. This new law not only made it much easier for NGOs to operate without violating obscure and irrational regulations, but it also facilitated NGO fundraising and provided generous tax incentives for donors.[3] Even the laws that seemed to suppress civil society may have been designed to benefit Chinese NGOs. When the Overseas NGO Management Law was announced in April 2016, the Western media decried the new regulations for foreign NGOs as a "clampdown on civil society," and "a severe blow to nonprofit groups."[4] However, it is possible that the purpose of restricting foreign organizations was to benefit Chinese NGOs by protecting them from competition.[5] This would be in line with Xi Jinping's policies in other areas of Chinese society and explain the pro-NGO policies in the domestic sphere. In June 2016, the Ministry of Civil Affairs issued drafts for new policies on Chinese NGOs that, if passed as written, would be beneficial for these organizations.[6]

Despite these positive developments, it is important to note the constraints limiting the model of social entrepreneurship described so far in this book. First, we cannot ignore the real restraints of class position. Those who succeeded in starting influential NGOs in the 1990s and early 2000s were disproportionately those with high levels of *suzhi*: college degrees, urban residency, and prior professional careers. Moreover, high levels of *suzhi* go hand-in-hand with high levels of *guanxi*. As the case studies examined in this book make clear, China's most powerful social entrepreneurs were very likely to start off with enviable social networks of connections with important people, both inside the party-state bureaucracy and outside the borders of the country. People from lower class backgrounds with less *guanxi* did attempt to start NGOs, but their organizations were much less likely to succeed or to have significant social influence.[7]

Second, although social entrepreneurs found a way to build alliances with state actors and shape government policy, the strategy they developed called for much of the work of NGOs to remain hidden from the populace. Because these activists were willing to allow government departments to "cut and paste" their ideas, even the direct beneficiaries of their work often assumed that the state deserved all the credit. Because NGOs were willing to take such a low profile, China's citizens were less likely to learn about this form of social organization and active citizenship. By its nature, this type of populist democratic citizenship increases the power of the state.

Yet the first generation of Chinese social entrepreneurs also designed strategies that utilized *suzhi* ideology to inform middle-class urbanites of social problems, and organized people to participate in voluntary collective action. They taught citizens to notice the problems of rural education and environmental pollution, and to see them through the lens of *suzhi*. They also taught them to act upon these problems by participating in an action that would bring better quality conditions to people less fortunate than themselves, for example by sponsoring a student or carrying around an air-pollution monitor. Chinese NGOs taught people to *volunteer*. Moreover, they taught them to volunteer with non-state organizations.

The next generation: volunteerism and new forms of social entrepreneurship

The rise of social entrepreneurship and NGOs in China taught people a new mode of citizenship, one where it was normal to engage with social problems through volunteerism. When Peter Xu, Xu Yongguang, Gu Wei, and Jin Jiaman were young, they also wanted to "serve the people." Growing up in Maoist China, they assumed that the only way to do so was through a position in the government bureaucracy, following directives from above. By contrast, Jiang Quan's generation grew up volunteering through student clubs and NGOs. They assumed that it was normal to serve society outside of the state. They also assumed that it was normal for citizens to organize themselves and to come up with their own innovations to address social problems. By the first decade of the twenty-first century, volunteering with NGOs became especially popular among middle-class young people. This is true whether they were born into the urban middle-class, or achieved middle-class status through educational success. In either case, they spread the ideology of *suzhi* wherever they went.

For some of these young people, like Jiang Quan, the motivation for service came from a desire to serve poor children who reminded them of themselves and to hopefully pass on the social mobility that they experienced through *suzhi*. Another Project Hope volunteer, Qi Shushan, said that he hoped the students would see him as an example of a rural peasant child who became a success. Ideally, when the children grew up, they would give back just as he was giving back:

> If these young kids have a younger teacher, maybe they can connect with us more and study harder. I can be a model for the students and tell them about my life. I want to pass on the spirit of volunteering. When we hang out with them or are in class, we ask them if they want to be volunteers when they grow up. If everyone in China has a spirit of contribution – but if they're not taught from a young age to think big, they won't.

Sabrina Wang came from a peasant family in Shandong Province. Neither her parents nor her brothers graduated from high school, but Sabrina attended China Women's University in Beijing. After graduation, she turned down a better-paying job as a manager at a four-star hotel in order to work for Golden Key, Peter Xu's NGO for blind and visually impaired children. Sabrina joked that in her family, she had the highest level of education but the lowest salary. However, there were more important things than money, she explained: "If you work in a real NGO or charity, it is meaningful because you can do something to help others. I think that's what's most important for me." Her job at Golden Key was to organize projects all over the country, identifying blind and visually-impaired children and setting up teacher training programs.

Other young people came from more privileged backgrounds, but wanted to serve nonetheless. Li Na came from a middle-class family, but he put off starting his master's degree in finance for a year in order to volunteer for Project Hope in Gansu Province. When I asked him why his generation was so invested in service, his perspective was very different from that of the young people who had grown up as peasants:

> Let me think. It probably has to do with the fact that nobody has to be incredibly worried about getting a job anymore. You know you can get a decent one. So that means people can think about other things. They can think about what interests them, and not just what brings in a paycheck.... Another factor is that we are all the only child in our families. We've had pretty narrow lives because we've been held close to our parents' side. We feel like we need to see more of the world. That's why I volunteered for this for the year.

Li was enjoying his work, especially the chance to transform lives. "It's been really satisfying. Even though we don't receive much compensation in terms of money, there's a spiritual compensation." He described all the opportunities he had to talk to rural middle and high school students about what college was like, about economics and finance, and about life in the Northeast city where he grew up. "As I talk to them, I can to see their eyes opening up to a bigger world. It's really moving. It makes me feel almost like a missionary." Li was indeed a missionary, preaching the gospel of *suzhi* and the wonderful life of college, finance, and urban cosmopolitanism to peasant children.

China's new generation of young people were not just interested in working for NGOs, but in starting their own organizations as social entrepreneurs themselves. Although this new wave began before the 2008 earthquake, the disaster and its aftermath inspired a huge upsurge in interest in social entrepreneurship. It is too soon to analyze the characteristics of the second wave of Chinese NGOs, but also there are reasons to think that this generation will do things differently than their forebears. The social entrepreneurs in the first generation were mostly state bureaucrats before they founded their organizations. Peter Xu was an architect in a state institute, Xu Yongguang and Gu Wei were cadres in the Youth League, and Jin Jiaman was a researcher for the government. It is not surprising that they built organizations that worked well with party-state departments, even to the point of acting like outsourced offices of the government. The young people who came of age in the twenty-first century grew up in market socialist China, not Maoist China. They also drew upon their own areas of expertise when creating their NGOs. However, their skills and experiences did not come from working in the government, but from organizing school clubs and surfing the World Wide Web.

We can see this in the story of Wang Chen, the co-founder of VJoin. Unlike Jiang Quan, Wang enjoyed a high-*suzhi* upbringing with access to excellent *guanxi* connections. Although his parents were born peasants, his mother earned a college degree and became an accountant, while his father had a Master's degree and managed a factory. Wang grew up in one of China's wealthiest cities, Guangzhou, and attended one of China's top high schools, Zhixin High School. There, he served as the president of the Student Union for two years. In his interview, he emphasized the fact that the Zhixin High School Student Union was totally independent from the school administration:

> There are 11 departments in the Student Union. We emphasize democratic ideology and internal management. Therefore, even the school administrators have no authority to interfere with the Student Union. Most importantly, we are financially independent from the school administration. We raise funds for the Student Union programs, and we are completely responsible for the financing.... I am pretty sure it is one of the most mature, professional student unions in a Chinese high school.

By working through the Student Union's Volunteering Department, Wang learned the importance of helping the needy and gained experience in coordinating projects with several NGOs. He also expanded his *guanxi* network. Many of the volunteers we interviewed had also belonged to student organizations that conducted charitable activities and worked with NGOs.

After graduating from high school, Wang's level of *suzhi* was so high that he earned one of its most covetable rewards: admission into a top US college – the University of California, Berkeley. However, leaving China was no obstacle to starting a Chinese NGO for Wang and his friends. If former bureaucrats like Jin Jiaman and Peter Xu spent decades learning the ins and outs of the Chinese party-state bureaucracy, these younger NGO leaders had spent their lives on the internet, gaining skills and competencies in using and exploiting the World Wide Web. They were fluent in the language of blogs and social networking. The three founders of VJoin and their 35 early members were scattered at universities around China and North America, so they held their meetings virtually using Skype, MSN Messenger, and QQ.

In fact, Wang Chen and his partners designed VJoin to exist mainly on the internet.[8] They started with their own personal experience of the Common Application, the online platform they had just used to apply to American colleges and universities. Wang and his friends felt that Chinese NGOs were not taking sufficient advantage of internet technologies to scale up their organizations. They decided to adapt the Common App and create a similar platform to help NGOs recruit qualified members in a more rationalized manner. It would also be a site for NGOs to market themselves and raise awareness of the volunteer sector. Their goal was to create a social networking site where people would want to hang out, virtually. There would be space for discussion, people would be able to post videos and pictures, and participants could even become "fans" of NGO initiatives. Their vision was impressive enough to earn them a grant from Google Philanthropy.

Another second-generation Chinese NGO was 1KG, founded in 2004 by An Zhu. In Chinese cities, online backpacking clubs had become popular: web-based communities where young people could find hiking partners.[9] 1KG was a backpacker community with a twist: each hiker heading to a poverty-stricken area pledged to bring one kilogram of supplies to give to local residents, such as school supplies, books, clothing, or food.[10] The 1KG website allowed participants to search the villages near their hiking routes and look at lists of the items needed by those communities. Returning backpackers would update the website with new needs. By exploiting the characteristics of the internet, 1KG was able to access enormous amounts of labor at almost no cost. Five years after its inception, the organization still only had five paid staff members, but was able to boast of thousands of volunteers.

By the early twenty-first century, most NGOs used the internet. But for a more traditional organization, such as Golden Key or GEI, that meant a website so that people could learn about the NGO and its initiatives. For younger social entrepreneurs, by contrast, the internet was not just another marketing outlet, but the center of the organization's strategies. Their NGOs existed primarily in cyberspace, not in a physical set of offices. One of the benefits of this approach was that these social entrepreneurs could claim that their NGOs were not formal organizations at all, but rather just informal social networks – and therefore did not come under the jurisdiction of state regulations for NGOs. Web-based strategies also allowed next-generation NGOs to scale up their impact without having to raise a lot of money or hire a lot of people. Older NGOs, such as Project Hope and GEI, essentially increased their effectiveness by allowing state officials to "steal" their models and apply them as government policies. Organizations such as 1KG outsourced their work by breaking it down into tiny components and parceling it out among large populations of volunteers accessed through web-based social networking.

It is too early to state definitively that the new generation will create Chinese NGOs that are different from the ones that arose earlier. As these new organizations mature, there are some signs that new social entrepreneurs will rediscover that older strategies, such as building good *guanxi* relationships with state officials, are necessary in China. We interviewed one young social entrepreneur, Wang Xuan of Shelter China, who received a grant from Google Philanthropy, only to have the Chinese government prevent the project from being implemented. To avoid these kinds of setbacks, 1KG participated in a "Non-Profit Incubator" run by the Communist Party, allowing the organization to become a government-approved national-level provider.[11] In 2014, a young social entrepreneur named Zhao Liang, the founder of Tianjin Future Green Leaders Association, wrote an article arguing that it was counterproductive for NGOs to antagonize the government. Instead, NGOs should consider the "difficulties" that government departments faced, and "then try to establish communication and help solve them." NGOs, he explained should act "as a buffer, connecting public and government, filtering out antagonism and assisting rational communication."[12] His argument had circled back around to a strategy that would have looked familiar to Peter Xu or Jin Jiaman.

Regardless of whether their strategies focused on scaling up through social media or building *guanxi* relationships with state officials, there was one tactic that young educated activists in China rarely adopted: street protests. This is notable because public demonstrations are a common tactic for idealistic middle-class youth elsewhere in the world, from Egypt's Tahrir Square to Hong Kong's Umbrella Movement to Black Lives Matter demonstrations on US college campuses. There is also a powerful history of student demonstrations in China, including the 1919 May 4th Movement and the 1989 Tiananmen Protest.[13] Furthermore, street protests have been common in the PRC since the 1990s.[14] Workers have taken to the streets over layoffs, villagers have protested environmental pollution, and retirees have marched in anger over lost pensions, but college students and graduates generally stayed home. If they went out into the streets, it was as volunteers, not protesters. Perhaps public demonstrations felt like a low-*suzhi* form of activism because they were associated with peasant and working-class protests, or perhaps they felt passé because it was what their parents did in Tiananmen Square. In any case, China's young people were attracted to forms of activism that felt more innovative and elite, and required technological skills and insider knowledge.

More importantly, whether old or new, social entrepreneurship in China has been rooted in the ideology of *suzhi*. Both middle-aged and young social entrepreneurs tended to be people of "high quality": middle-class, cosmopolitan, well-educated. Even those who had been raised in peasant families in the countryside were now in the elite thanks to the golden ticket of college admissions. The purpose of their social entrepreneurship was to help those unfortunate citizens lower down on the *suzhi* hierarchy to rise up to become more like themselves. The way to accomplish this was by providing those "low-quality" people with better external conditions: cleaner environments, more effective healthcare, and better educational resources.

China's social entrepreneurs used the ideology of *suzhi* to wedge open a space in Chinese society for nongovernmental organizations, helping government officials and ordinary citizens to raise the quality of Chinese society. They applied enormous creativity and innovation in designing strategies to help impart *suzhi* to people and places of low quality, from Peter Xu's low-cost learning aids for the visually impaired to An Zhu's backpackers, carrying their 1 kg of school supplies to rural villages. To a great extent, they never questioned whether their views were condescending or insulting to their beneficiaries, or whether the ideology of *suzhi* itself led to prejudice, discrimination, and exploitation because it claimed that some people were intrinsically more valuable than others. Given how widespread the *suzhi* worldview was in China, why would they? Even the peasants they encountered would agree that nothing would be better than if their children could become less like their parents and more like the cosmopolitan, college-educated, professional social entrepreneurs. Everyone agreed that raising the *suzhi* of China's low-quality people and places would raise the quality of China itself.

Notes

1 Karla W. Simon, "Meaningful changes in the legal environment for civil society organizations: Their relationship to larger trends in China's 'new' governance" (University of Alberta, Edmonton, CA, August 16, 2013), https://docs.google.com/a/colgate.edu/file/d/0BxzGT6Btpa-kTnN1UzdNMVNkVE0/edit.a.
2 Mingyuan Wang and Jin Feng, "Some thoughts on the amendments to the Environmental Protection Law of China," *Asia Pacific Journal of Environmental Law* 17 (2014): 191.
3 Shawn Shieh, "Charity law FAQs," *NGOs in China*, March 29, 2016. http://ngochina.blogspot.com/2016/03/charity-law-faqs.html.
4 For example: Tom Phillips, "China passes law imposing security controls and foreign NGOs," *Guardian*, April 28, 2016. www.theguardian.com/world/2016/apr/28/china-passes-law-imposing-security-controls-on-foreign-ngos. Edward Wong, "Clampdown in China restricts 7000 foreign organizations," *New York Times*, April 28, 2016. www.nytimes.com/2016/04/29/world/asia/china-foreign-ngo-law.html.
5 It is also important to note that prior to the Overseas NGO Management Law, there were no legal policies regulating foreign NGOs operating in China at all. With no recourse to law, international organizations were vulnerable to government suppression at any time for any reason. One could argue that the creation of the law was beneficial to foreign NGOs, even if the content of it was rather restrictive. See Carolyn L. Hsu and Jessica C. Teets. "Is China's new overseas NGO management law sounding the death knell for civil society? Maybe not." *Asia-Pacific Journal* 14, no. 4 (2016): 3.
6 Shawn Shieh, "2016: The year of regulation in the new future for civil society?" *NGOs in China*, June 11, 2016. http://ngochina.blogspot.com/2016/06/2016-year-of-regulation-and-new-future.html.
7 Anthony Jerome Spires, *China's Un-Official Society: The Development of Grassroots NGOs in an Authoritarian State*. Yale University.
8 http://baike.baidu.com/item/VJoin.
9 Ning Zhang, "'Donkey friend' communities: Harmonious networks and harmonious tourism," *China Media Research* 4, no. 4 (2008): 76–84.
10 Ning Zhang, "The emerging civil society in travelers' communities in post-reform China," *Annual Meeting of the American Anthropological Association*, November 28 – December 2, 2007, Washington, DC.
11 Patricia M. Thornton, "The advance of the party: transformation or takeover of urban grassroots society?" *The China Quarterly* 213 (2013): 11.
12 Zhao Liang, "NGO criticism in China is 'making things worse'," *Chinadialogue*, May 11, 2014. https://www.chinadialogue.net/article/show/single/en/7424-NGO-criticism-in-China-is-making-things-worse-.
13 Jeffrey N. Wasserstrom, *Student Protests in Twentieth-Century China* (Stanford, CA: Stanford University Press, 1991).
14 Xi Chen, *Social Protest and Contentious Authoritarianism in China* (New York: Cambridge University Press, 2012), 241; Yanhua Deng and Guobin Yang, "Pollution and protest in China: Environmental mobilization in context," *The China Quarterly* 214 (2013): 321–336.

Bibliography

Chen, X. 2012. *Social Protest and Contentious Authoritarianism in China*. New York: Cambridge University Press.

Deng, Y. and Yang, G. 2013. Pollution and protest in China: Environmental mobilization in context. *The China Quarterly*, 214, pp. 321–336.

Hsu, C.L. and Teets, J.C. 2016. Is China's new overseas NGO management law sounding the death knell for civil society? Maybe not. *Asia-Pacific Journal*, 14(4), p. 3.

Philips, T. 2016. China passes law imposing security controls on foreign NGOs. *Guardian*, April 28, 2016.

Shieh, S. 2016. "Charily law FAQs." *NGOs in China*, March 29, 2016. http://ngochina.blogspot.com/2016/03/charity-law-faqs.html.

Shieh, S. 2016. "2016: The year of regulation in the new future for civil society?" *NGOs in China*, June 11, 2016. http://ngochina.blogspot.com/2016/06/2016-year-of-regulation-and-new-future.html.

Simon, K.W. 2013. Meaningful changes in the legal environment for civil society organizations: Their relationship to larger trends in China's "new" governance, *Forum on NGO Governance and Management in China*, August 16, 2013.

Spires, A.J. 2007. *China's Un-Official Society: The Development of Grassroots NGOs in an Authoritarian State*. PhD Thesis, Yale University.

Thornton, P.M. 2013. The advance of the party: Transformation or takeover of urban grassroots society? *The China Quarterly*, 213, pp. 1–18.

Wang, M. and Feng, J. 2014. Some thoughts on the amendments to the environmental protection law of China. *Asia Pacific Journal of Environmental Law*, 17, p. 191.

Wasserstrom, J.N. 1991. *Student Protests in Twentieth-Century China*. Stanford, CA: Stanford University Press.

Wong, E. 2016. Clampdown in China restricts 7000 foreign organizations. *New York Times*, April 28, 2016.

Zhao, L. 2014. "NGO criticism in China is 'making things worse'," *Chinadialogue*, May 11, 2014. https://www.chinadialogue.net/article/show/single/en/7424-NGO-criticism-in-China-is-making-things-worse-.

Zhang, N. 2007. "The emerging civil society in travelers' communities in post-reform China," *Annual Meeting of the American Anthropological Association*, November 28 – December 2, Washington, DC.

Zhang, N. 2008. "Donkey friend" communities: Harmonious networks and harmonious tourism. *China Media Research*, 4(4), pp. 76–84.

Index

Page numbers in **bold** denote figures.

1KG 157

acupressure massage therapy 56
administrative method of fundraising 119n40
affection, relationships of 28–9; *see also guanxi*
Africa, sub-Saharan 39n21
Agenda 21 135
air pollution 109, 139
altruism versus reciprocity 28–30
An Feng 130, 133
An Zhu 157, 158
animals, liberation of 34, 40n43
art propaganda *see* propaganda art and posters
Asian Development Fund 137

backpacking clubs 157
Bao Shuming 3
Beijing as center of ENGO activity 142–3
benevolent societies 34–5, 59
Birth Planning Policy 19n54, 79, 92n26, 103, 118n20, 127–8
blind and visually-impaired children 43–4, 54–6
Buckley, Lila 131

cadres: Deng's reforms and declining status of 58–9; difficulty attracting qualified staff 100; engineered inequality and 48–9; social entrepreneurs as former cadres 100–1; Tiananmen Square Protests and corruption among 83–4; *see also* Communist Party, Chinese (CCP)
capitalism 57, 59

Carson, Rachel 126–7
"chain of favors" rule **50**, 52, 62n17, 101, 145
Chang Kai-shek 44, 74
charity and donations: Christian missionaries associated with 43; *cishan* (charity) 43; Sichuan earthquake and 2; in sub-Saharan Africa and Muslim societies 39n21; Taoist and Buddhist influences on 38n15; as traditional in China 4; Western versus Chinese view of 24–9; *see also* imperial China, charity in
Charity Law (2016) 99, 153
Chen Zilong 30–1, 32–3
China, People's Republic of (PRC): birth of, declared by Mao 37; map **1**; as strong government nation 99; *see also* Communist Party, Chinese (CCP)
China Youth Development Foundation (CYDF): government policies undermining need for 89–90; Hua-Dan compared to 88–9; origins of 70–1; risks of government partnership 116; Xu Yongguang as social entrepreneur 68–71; Youth League and 108–14; *see also* Project Hope (CYDF)
Chinese Disabled Persons Federation (CDPF) 61
Christianity 54–5; *see also* missionaries
citizenship 11, 152–4
civil service examinations 32–3, 38n4
civil society: corporatism and 8–9; definition of 6; democratization and 6–8; state autonomy and 7–8; Tocquevillian theory of 6–9; *see also* NGOs in China; social entrepreneurship

Index

civil war, Chinese 44–5
clans 23–4, 50
class stratification: as constraint on social entrepreneurship 153; Maoist art propaganda and 72; Mao's new system of 47–9; Project Hope's critique of Maoist theories 75–6; *suzhi* and 12
Common Application 156
Communist Party, Chinese (CCP): civil war 44–5; corporatism and 8; legitimacy and 45, 84; membership criteria 58, 81; Non-Profit Incubator 157; rise of 37; socialist propaganda posters 71–3, **72, 73**; Soviet Union and 63n26; Tiananmen Square Protests and 83–4; *see also* cadres
Communist Youth League (CYL): CYDF, Project Hope, and 68–9, 108–14; defined 68; Heilongjiang Provincial Youth League 96–8, 100, 102; history of 108; loss of status 96, 100
Confucian philosophy: decline of Confucian system 35–7; Five Cardinal Relationships 29, 31, 36–7; learned–unlearned dichotomy in 33; love, particularized versus universal 26–8; reciprocity versus altruism 28–30; ruler–subject relationships 31–2, 37; Western, Judeo-Christian ideology of charity vs. 24–30
Confucius 33, 38n15, 39n22
corporatism, state-led 8–9, 47
corruption: cadres associated with 100; *guanxi* and 52; low-educated cadres and 83–4; Mao's campaigns against 53; market socialism and 59, 85; post-Tiananmen anticorruption campaigns 84; Tiananmen protests against 64n34, 83, 109
Cultural Revolution (1966–76) 53, 68, 78, 122

democracy, Chinese populist conception of 11
democratization and civil society 6–8
Deng Xiaoping: Environmental Protection Law and 127; market socialism reforms 56–9, 63n27, 68–9, 100, 108; son of 61; *suzhi* education and 78–83
donations *see* charity and donations

earthquakes: 1290 Jili 17n16; 1556 Shaanxi 17n16; 1920 Haiyuan 17n16; 1976 Tangshan 4–5; 2008 Sichuan 1–5, 9, 151–2

Ecologia 123, 129–30, 138, 146n1
ecological framework 126–8
economics: Deng and 56–7; Deng's comparison to Western capitalists 57; Mao's focus on 45, **46**; redistributive economy 46–7, 51, 69; rural areas left behind under Deng 69
education: blind children and 43–4; corruption and 83; Cultural Revolution and 78; declining enrollment in rural schools 102–4, **103**; Deng's reforms and 58, 78–83; environmental 109, 137–40; Mao's campaigns and 76–8; political versus academic 77; "Resolution on *Suzhi* Education" (1999) 89; rural–urban and rich–poor gaps 69, 89; social entrepreneurship, role of 104–7; state-funded 89, 93n56; *suzhi* education (*suzhi jiaoyu*) 79; value place on, by ordinary people 85–6; vocational colleges 63n28; *see also* Golden Key; Project Hope
Ehrlich, Paul 128
Engels, Jan Ivo 126–7
environmental NGOs (ENGOs): air pollution 109, 139; cultural differences, international 131–3; education and public attention 109, 137–40; foreign funding 124–5, 135–6, **136**, 145; global organizational practices and aid 128–31, **130**; *guanxi* and 124, 125, 130, 132–3, 140–1, 142–5, **144**; Nu River controversy 134–5, 140–2; state agencies and policies 133–5; state alliances 124–5, 136–7; success of 124–5; *suzhi* ideology and 125–8, 137–8, 145
Environmental Protection Law 124, 127, 134, 140

familiar people (*shuren*) 27, 50–1
Fan Clan charitable trust 25
Fan Lizhi 81
Fan Xiaoxi 138
Fan Zhongyan 23–5, 27–8, 30
federal state form 117n13
feudalism 45, 61n3
Five Cardinal Relationships 29, 31, 36–7
food shortages (Ming Dynasty) 30–1, 32
foreign funding *see* international investment
Four Modernizations 58
Friends of Nature **144**, 144–5

Gates, Bill 59, 84

GEI (Global Environmental Institute) 114–15, 124, 130, 131, 132, 137, 143
GENGOs (government-exploiting NGOs) 114
gentry class in Ming Dynasty 32–5
gift exchange as moral system 29–30
Global Environmental Institute 101–2
Golden Key 43–4, 55–6, 59–61, 105, 109, 154–5
GONGOs (government-organized nongovernmental organizations) 111–14; China Youth Development Foundation (CYDF) 68, 70–1, 73–4, 76, 88–90; corporatism and 8; Maoist China and 47
Google Philanthropy 157
government *see* cadres; Communist Party, Chinese (CCP); state
Green Beagle 109, 139
Green Earth Volunteers 123, 137, 138, 141, 146n2
Grove, Andy 59
Gu Wei 96–8, 100, 102, 112, 154, 155
guanxi (social connections or networks): "chain of favors" rule **50**, 52, 62n17, 101, 145; Christianity and 54–5; class constraints on social entrepreneurship and 153; corruption and 52; CYDF and 112–14; defined 30; ENGOs and 124, 125, 130, 132–3, 140–1, 142–5, **144**; expansion of **50**; government-NGO connections 101, 109; in late imperial china 27, **27**; Maoist socialism and "going through the back door," 49–52; next-generation volunteerism and 156; Project Hope child sponsorship and 70; reciprocity and 51; rural schools and 107
Guo Hong 3

Hao Lin 2
He Deming 140
Heilongjiang Provincial Youth League 96–8, 100, 102
Heilongjiang Youth Development Foundation (HYDF) 97–8
Hewlitt Foundation 130
How the Steel was Tempered (Ostrovsky) 49, 59
Hu Jintao 108
Hua-Dan 88, 90
Hua Guofeng 4

"I Monitor Air for My Country" campaign (Green Beagle) 109, 139

Iacocca, Lee 59, 84
iCET (Innovation Center for Energy and Transportation) 130–1, 132, 137
imperial China, charity in: benevolent societies 34–5; Confucian philosophy of charity 25–30; decline of Confucian system and story of Ning Taitai 35–7; Ming Dynasty food shortages and gentry charity 30–4; Song Dynasty and charitable trust of the Fan Clan 23–5
inflation 58, 63n33, 82
innovation: constraints on 51, 53, 123; failure rates and 97, 102; Fan clan trust and 24, 28; government protection as freedom for 111; government takeover and 61; new generation and 154; social entrepreneurship and 9–10
institutional isomorphism 131
intellectuals (*zhishi fenzi*) 76–7, 81–2, 91n17
international investment: Deng and 57; in ENGOs 124–5, 135–6, **136**, 145
international relations 57
"iron rice bowl" compensation 48

Ji, Ruth 55, 61
Jiang Quan 151–2, 154
Jiang, Yuzhou 10
jiaren (kin) 27
Jin Jiaman 101–2, 114–15, 122–5, 129–34, 136–8, 142–5, 154, 155

Lei Feng Hope School, Yunnan Province 106, 107
Li Keqiang 108, 140
Li Na 155
Liang Congjie 144–5
Locke, John 26
love, particularized versus universal 26–8

mandarins 23, 38n3
Mao Zedong: art propaganda and 71; campaigns against corruption, nepotism, and elitism 53; civil war and 44–5; Cultural Revolution (1966–76) 53, 68, 78, 122; Deng's criticism of bureaucracy of 80; international isolationism of 57; PRC declared by 37; reforms of 45–9; social welfare reforms 8, 45; on steel output 62n5
market relationships compared to charity and affection 28–9
market socialism: Christianity and 54; Deng Xiaoping and 56–9, 63n27, 68–9, 100, 108; *suzhi* and 79, 85

market ventures 96, 116n1
Mei Hu Primary School, Hunan Province 104, **105**, 107
Mencius 26, 31–2, 33, 40n43
Mertha, Andrew 140
migrant children 88, 104
migration, rural-to-urban 104
Ming Dynasty 30–5
Ministry of Civil Affairs 98, 153
Ministry of Environmental Protection (MEP) 133, 145, 148n48
missionaries 37, 43
money fever 81–2
moral panics 89, 108–9, 138, 145
Muslim societies, charity in 39n21

names in Imperial China 40n62
National Development and Reform Commission (NDRC) 134–5, 140, 148n48
National Environmental Protection Office/Agency 133
Nationalist Party 44, 74
networks, social *see guanxi*
NGOs in China: Chinese terminology and definitions 17n24; credit for initiatives 111, 115; failure rate 102; GENGOs (government-exploiting NGOs) 114; number of 5; PONGOs (party-organized NGOs) 119n34; price of state alliances 114–16; registration and supervisory agencies 98; regulatory environment for 98–9, 152–3; small number of, before 2008 earthquake 2; unregistered 5, 98; *see also* environmental NGOs; GONGOs; social entrepreneurship; *specific organizations and persons*
Ning Taitai 35–7
Nixon, Richard 127
Not One Less (film) 89
Nu River dam controversy 134–5, 140–2

"One Child Policy" *see* Birth Planning Policy
Opium Wars (1839–1860) 35–6
Ostrovsky, Nikolai 49, 59
Overseas NGO Management Law (2016) 153, 159n5

paternalism, socialist 44–9
patriarchal clans 23–4
Perry, Elizabeth 11
poetry clubs 34
PONGOs (party-organized NGOs) 119n34

posters *see* propaganda art and posters
Project Hope (CYDF): advertisements **66**, **67**, 73–6; Communist Youth League and 97–8; Hua-Dan compared to 88–90; risks of government partnership 116; schools improved by 105–6; schools ineligible for 107; Su Mingjuan as poster girl for **67**, 67–8; volunteer teacher program 151, 154, 155; Xu Yongguang as entrepreneur 68–71; Youth League and 108–14
propaganda art and posters: "After the guard in charge of the grain has gone (victory)" (woodcut) **75**; "Carry out family planning, implement the basic national policy," **80**; "Hold high the great red banner of Mao Zedong thought," **77**; "Lead the people to victory," **72**; Maoist era art 71–3; "Mutual help in plowing has brought more food," **46**; Project Hope advertisements **66**, **67**, 73–6; "A rock as a desk," **66**; "Studying for the mother country," **73**; Su Mingjuan: "I want to study, too," **67**; *suzhi* education and 79
Pruitt, Ida 41n75
Public Security Bureau 99

Qi Shushan 154
Qing Dynasty 35–7
Qu Geping 127

reciprocity: gift exchange as moral system 29–30; *guanxi* and 51; late imperial China and altruism vs. 28–30; Maoist socialism and 51; Project Hope child sponsorship and 70; ruler–subject relationship and 31; *see also guanxi*
redistributive economy 46–7, 51, 69
"Reform and Opening Up" policy (1978) 56
ren (benevolence or humaneness) 26, 34
renkou suzhi (human population quality) 79, 128
"Resolution on *Suzhi* Education" (1999) 89
Rockefeller Foundation 124, 129, 130, 142, 143
Rousseau, Jean-Jacques 11, 26
rural education *see* education

Salisbury, Harrison 24, 25
savings rate 5, 17n19

Index   165

schools: Lei Feng Hope School, Yunnan Province 106, 107; Mei Hu Primary School, Hunan Province 104, **105**, 107; Shaoshan Key School, Hunan Province **106**, 106–7; *see also* education
Schumpeter, Joseph 11
Shaoshan Key School, Hunan Province **106**, 106–7
Shelter China 157
shengren (strangers) 27, 51–2
shuren (familiar people) 27, 50–1
Silent Spring (Carson) 126
silver 35, 41n66
Smith, Arthur 24
Smith, Joanna Handlin 25
social entrepreneurship: benevolent societies 34–5, 59; civil society, theories of 6–9; class constraints on 153; concept and definition of 9; former cadres in 100–1; Maoist China and 47; new generation and 155–8; new missions for old organizations through moral panics 108–9; Sichuan earthquake and 5; *suzhi* ideology as weapon for 88–9; *see also specific organizations and persons*
social networks *see guanxi*
social welfare: "going through the back door" and 52; *guanxi* and 50; in imperial versus Communist China 37; Mao's reforms and 8, 45; public attention and 152; redistributive economy and 46; as state obligation 14, 31–2, 45, 60; *see also* imperial China, charity in
socialism: Mao and socialist paternalism 44–9; Maoist socialism, fall of 52–3; Xu's Golden Key and 60; *see also* Mao Zedong; market socialism
Song Dynasty 23–5
soup kitchens 31
Soviet Union 7, 49, 63n26–63n27, 129
state: agencies and policies related to ENGOs 133–5; bureaucratic agencies, vulnerability of 99–100; civil society and state autonomy 7–8; corporatism, state-led 8–9, 47; credit for NGO initiatives taken by 111, 115; education, state-funded 89, 93n56; *guanxi* and government-NGO connections 101, 109; legitimacy of 31–2, 33, 45, 84; paternalistic, in imperial China 31–2; *see also* cadres; Communist Party, Chinese (CCP); GONGOs
State Environmental Protection Agency (SEPA) 133, 134–5, 140, 143

Stockholm Summit 1972 (UN Conference on the Human Environment) 127, 129, 133
strangers (*shengren*) 27, 51–2
street protests as tactic 158; *see also* Tiananmen Square Protests (1989)
Su Mingjuan **67**, 67–8, 87, 89
Su Teh 37
suzhi education (*suzhi jiaoyu*) 79
suzhi ideology (quality ideology): birth control and 103; class and 12, 153; Deng's reforms and 58, 78–83; discrimination based on 86–7; ENGOs and 125–8, 137–8, 145; environmental versus economic quality 138; Maoist philosophy and public beliefs 76–8; new activist citizenship and 152; next-generation volunteerism and 156; old and new social entrepreneurship rooted in 158; ordinary people and value placed on education 85–6; Project Hope's Su Mingjuan as *suzhi* fairy tale 68, 87; *renkou suzhi* (human population quality) 79, 128; rise of discourse of 11–12; rural education and 75–6; school reputation and 105; self-esteem vs. 88–9

Taiping Rebelling (1850) 36
Thoreau, Henry David 126
Tiananmen Square Protests (1989) 7, 56, 64n34, 81, 83–4
Tianjin Future Green Leaders Association 157
Tocqueville, Alexis de 6–9
traditional Chinese medicine (TCM) 56

UN Conference on the Human Environment (Stockholm Summit 1972) 127, 129, 133

VJoin 156
vocational colleges 63n28
voluntary organizations in Tocquevillian theory of civil society 6–7
volunteerism 2–3, 151–2, 154–8

Wagner, Vance 131, 132
Wang Cheng 156
Wang, Sabrina 154–5
Wang Xuan 157
Wang Yongchen 123, 124, 133, 136–8, 140–5
Watson, Caroline 88, 90
wealth, strategies for 82

Web-based strategies 155, 157
Welch, Jack 59, 84
Wen Guowei 87
Wen Jiabao 89, 141
woodcuts, revolutionary 74, **75**
"wooden rice bowl" compensation 48
World Bank 136, 137
World Conference on Women, Fourth (1995) 57, 123
World Rivers and People Opposing Dams 141
Wu Fengshi 142

Xi Jinping 8, 84, 140, 153
Xia Yan 49, 52
Xie, Lei 142
Xu, Peter 43–4, 49, 51–61, 101, 105, 129, 145, 154, 155, 158
Xu Yongguang 68–73, 88–90, 97, 101, 108–16, 129, 138, 145, 154, 155

Yang Dongming 34, 59
Yang Zhengsheng 2
Youth League *see* Communist Youth League
Yuanyou, Kang 115

Zhang Jiqiang 124, 143
Zhang, Joy 138
Zhang Yimou 89
Zhao Liang 157–8
Zhixin High School Student Union, Guangzhou 156
Zhou Yongkang 84, 93n46
Zhu Yue *see* Fan Zhongyan
zou houmen ("going through the back door") 51